I0818829

Made possible by the support of

ZEIT
STIFTUNG
BUCERIUS

ארטיס أرتيس
artis

OSSIP KLARWEIN

An Architect's Journey from Berlin to Jerusalem

For Anat, Yigal, Eléonore, Sérafine,
Balthazar, Salvador and our children

Contents

6 Foreword

8 Ossip Klarwein – Life and Destiny
Jacqueline Hénard

22 Berlin: Designs for a Monumental Church
Johannes Cramer

32 Haifa: First Commissions in Context of the City's History
Dafna Berger Shperling

42 Memorial Architecture and Sanctified Space
Doron Bar

50 Nahariya: A Yekke Seaside Resort
Sigal Davidi

62 The Dagon Silos – Landmark of Haifa
Dafna Berger Shperling

74 Givat Ram: The Hebrew University Campus in Jerusalem
Diana Dolev

82 Contested Modernism: Plans for East Jerusalem 1947–1965
Noah Hysler Rubin

94 The Knesset: Balancing Space and Democracy
Talia Margalit

102 Annotated Catalog of Works
Johannes Cramer
104 Germany until 1933
118 Mandate Territory 1934 to 1948
130 Israel 1948 to 1970

154 List of Abbreviations

155 Joseph Klarwein's files at the Central Zionist Archives
Guy Jamo

156 Bibliography
157 Acknowledgements
159 Contributors
160 Colophon, Image Credits

OSSIP, JOSEF OR JOSEPH?

This is the first monographic exploration of the significant architect Ossip Klarwein. His life is both unique and exemplary for an entire generation from Eastern Europe.

Born in 1893 in Russian Poland, Klarwein grew up as an involuntary traveler between worlds. His family fled from Warsaw to escape the pogroms in the crumbling Tsarist empire, moving to Offenbach and Mainz. From a Polish- and Russian-speaking environment, Klarwein came to German-speaking Hesse, where he completed his education. His journey continued with studies and work in Bremen, Königsberg, Munich, Frankfurt, Berlin, Danzig and Hamburg. In 1933, he was forced to emigrate a second time, from Hamburg to Haifa, moving from well-off Charlottenburg in Berlin and the bourgeois suburbs of Hamburg along the Elbe river to the unstable British Mandate territory of Palestine. Throughout his life, Klarwein preferred to speak German, though he corresponded with his son in English. His notes were written in a mix of two or three languages.

Given such external turmoil, it is no surprise that Klarwein frequently altered his own first name, sometimes calling himself Ossip, other times Joseph; occasionally spelling it with "ph" and sometimes with "f." Within the family, he was always known as Ossip.

Life demanded a degree of adaptability from Klarwein not everyone could muster. Family and friends remember him primarily for his "good mood", his "lively and cheerful" disposition. A colleague wrote a poem for his 70th birthday: "What's always appealed to me is your friendliness to all." Klarwein was widely loved for his humor, the author adds, which helped him overcome many difficulties. However, he approached his work with the utmost seriousness, as evidenced by the extent of his output.

Although Klarwein significantly shaped the architectural landscape of the newly founded State of Israel, his oeuvre has received little recognition to date. His personal records are widely dispersed, both in archives and with family: 2.5 shelf meters of documents in the Central Zionist Archive in Jerusalem, records from archives in Germany, Poland, the United States, and a dozen removal boxes containing letters, photo albums, drawings, business documents and personal items with his descendants in Israel, Spain and France have been evaluated for the first time for this project. This has not answered all of our questions, but we hope our work will inspire further research.

The idea for this project originated in the late summer of 2022 in the a monumental church building located on Berlin's Hohenzollernplatz Square. The landmark building, locally known as "Powerhouse of God", is the venue for a renowned concert series, "NoonSong," which attracts music lovers from across the city every Saturday. Besides the music, the architecture is always impressive. The church is considered a masterpiece of German Brick Expressionism. A display board in the side aisle notes that Ossip Klarwein played a central role in its creation. This is how it all began.

With a bit of curiosity and thanks to fortunate coincidences, the foundation for a promising German-Israeli exhibition project was quickly established. The first financial backers had already been found when the events of 7 October 2023 and their aftermath threatened to derail the project. Most flight connections were suspended. Israeli society, and thus Israeli contacts, were deeply shaken. Why, under such circumstances, should they concern themselves with Ossip Klarwein, a name almost forgotten in their own country? In fact, against the backdrop of existential threats, a wonderful collaboration developed, with reciprocal visits as soon as the security situation allowed.

The Klarwein Project has no external impetus, no birthday and no anniversary. It is a collective endeavor, backed by no institution and driven by no commercial interests. It has been pursued by a passion for the subject and a great deal of personal commitment – with no one counting their hours. I am deeply grateful to all members of the team. Working together was a fantastic experience.

At this point, I would like to thank our supporters for their trust in our venture. Seed funding from the Alfred Toepfer Stiftung F.V.S. allowed us to launch the project. Shortly thereafter, the Ursula Lachnit-Fixson Stiftung made the necessary research trips possible. The Hermann Reemtsma Stiftung has consistently supported us with generous funding and valuable advice. A grant from the Ernst von Siemens Kunststiftung made this catalog possible. After a public grant fell through at short notice, they, along with the ZEIT STIFTUNG BUCERIUS, helped us out of difficult situation. To all of you, I extend my thanks not only for the financial support but also for unbureaucratic decisions and the human quality of our collaboration.

Jacqueline Hénard

LIFE AND DESTINY

OSSIP KLARWEIN 1893–1970

Jacqueline Hénard

"My entire existence was and is built on competitions. They are my hobby and my delight."

Ossip Klarwein with his stepsister Bronislawa, his father Mendel Menachem, his older sister Else, and his stepmother Leonore Sand. Around 1905

Family background

Ossip Klarwein grew up in a middle-class milieu. A prim family photo taken around 1905 shows his sisters and stepmother all buttoned up to the neck in long puffy sleeves, piping and pleats. His father is wearing a modern suit and has an open book in his hands. Nothing points to his humble origins or Jewish heritage. His son, dressed in a starched white collar, looks like a seminary student. Ossip Klarwein, a later atheist, went on to study architecture and convert to Catholicism, build Protestant churches in Germany and design the Knesset in Israel.

Ossip Klarwein was born on 6 February 1893 in Warsaw, when it was part of the Russian Empire. His father, Mendel Menachem Klarwein, was a carriage driver's son from the little town of Zawichost in East Poland. He had some success in business, running a trading company with a Polish partner[1] for a time, and later opening the Wiktoria macaroni factory in Dluga 48. This was clearly a modern company, as it already had a telephone connection back in 1898[2] and promoted its wares in Zionist newspapers[3]. Polish rather than Yiddish was spoken at home and the family could read Russian[4].

Ossip Klarwein's mother Rachel Century came from a rabbinical family[5]. Little is known about her other children. Her son Maksymilian chose to be baptised in 1898[6], presumably as a Catholic, in the spirit of the time[7]. Of a daughter Frania, only her name is known. Another daughter, Else, was born in 1891, but died in 1918 in the Jewish hospital in Mainz at the height of the Spanish Flu epidemic[8]. Rachel Century must have died shortly after Ossip was born, as it was not long before his father married Leonore Sand. His second wife gave birth to a daughter Bronislawa in 1898, with whom Ossip Klarwein formed a very close bond.

Presumably prompted by pogroms in the crumbling Zarist empire, the family moved to the west in 1905, making their new home in the Grand Duchy of Hesse[9]. Menachem Klarwein handed over the reins of the macaroni factory to a managing director and set himself up in Mainz as a mineral water trader[10].

Training and traveling years

Another land, another language to learn. Ossip Klarwein was 12 years old when he had to start all over again for the first time. At some point he had acquired sufficient German to attend the Großherzoglich-Hessische Kunstgewerbeschule (School of Applied Arts of the Grand Duchy of Hesse)[11]. He passed the so-called Kunstexamen (applied arts exam) in 1912 after completing his studies with distinction, twice winning first prize cum laude complemented by a special certificate of honour in the annual competitions of the architectural faculty[12].
His success led to his being hired by Heinz Stoffregen to work in his studio. The Bremen architect had been a member of the Deutscher Werkbund[13] since 1910, making him a sought-after mentor.

When the First World War broke out, Klarwein was 21 years old – and still a Russian citizen. He tried in vain to register for military service with the Ministry of Internal Affairs on two occasions[14], which would have opened up the pathway to citizenship. As a Russian, Klarwein was viewed with suspicion and even imprisoned for a time, but with the aid of a guarantee from his employer, he was released[15].
He found work behind the frontline, working on rebuilding the town of Gerdauen (today's Zheleznodorozhny) near Königsberg (today's Kaliningrad) which was badly damaged in 1914. Under the auspices of the "Ostpreußenhilfe"[16], he initially worked in the office of architect Paul Engler, then with the Koenigliches Bauberatungsamt (Royal Building Advisory Authority). The young Klarwein often represented Engler in talks with private developers forced to rebuild their livelihoods from scratch – an experience which stood him in good stead in Palestine after 1933.

Legitimation
für den
immatriculirten Meisterschüler der Akademie der Künste

Gültig bis ... ten ... 192
Prolong. bis ... ten ... 190
Berlin, den ... ten ... 19
~~Königliche~~ Akademie der Künste.
Der Präsident.

Beginning in 1921, 'Herr Architekt Ossip Klarwein' was enrolled in Berlin as one of just five master students studying under the renowned architect Hans Poelzig

Klarwein resumed his studies before the First World War ended. In October 1917, he moved from the Koenigliches Bauberatungsamt to the Technische Hochschule (University of Technology) in Munich. He was 23 years old when he submitted an impressive array of 17 certificates in his application for admission to study with Theodor Fischer[17], where he stayed for four semesters. In choosing his teachers, Klarwein was typical of German Jewish architects of his generation. Munich-based Fischer was popular with them, but the favourite was Hans Poelzig in Berlin, under whom about half of the 450 German Jewish architects had studied by 1933[18]. Klarwein, too, applied and was accepted into Poelzig's master class in 1921 as one of five students. His influence is unmistakable in many of Klarwein's later designs.

Where did Klarwein live from 1921 to 1926 and how did he earn a living? The evidence is very sketchy. In an affidavit in 1954[19] he wrote: "After completing my studies, I worked with a number of Berlin architects", but their names are not recorded. Apart from photographs of a "gentleman's room" he designed in the Berlin suburb of Hohenschönhausen, his estate contains only the signed and 1924-dated drawing of an apartment building "Haustyp B"[20].

A design drawing by Hans Poelzig, whose monumental, block-like architecture had a profound influence on Klarwein

Berlin

Klarwein formed a close bond with Berlin, which survived the move to subsequent employment with architecture firms in Hamburg. While at some point he gave up his first rooms at the Charlottenburg address of Schillerstrasse 108, he retained an apartment in Joachim-Friedrich-Strasse 47 in Wilmersdorf[21] from 1926 to 1934. Overall Ossip Klarwein spent a total of 12 years living in Berlin.

And he was not the only Klarwein in Berlin. The public Berlin address book includes an opera singer Franz Klarwein (no relation). His younger sister Bronislawa also lived not far from his first Charlottenburg lodgings, in Pestalozzistrasse 102. In the 1905 family photo, she was still a young girl closely resembling her brother, but by 1924 she had become an actress. At least that is what is listed as her occupation on the form completed when she left the Jewish congregation on 15 April 1924, which also records her conversion to Catholicism. Two weeks later, on 28 April, Ossip Klarwein also left Judaism behind[22].

Three months after his conversion, he married Berlin opera singer and labourer's daughter Martha Elsa Kumme. He was 31, his wife 30 – and a Protestant like most people in Berlin at that time[23]. They remained childless for a long time. Finally, after eight years, their son Matthias was born, who was to remain their only child.

Klarr, Alfred, Kfm. SW 61, Teltower Str 34 III
— Laura, Ww., SW 61, Teltower Str. 34 III
Klarwein, Ossip, Architekt, Wilmersdf., Joachim Friedrich-Str. 47 V. T. Uhld. 1086.
Klarzynski, Wladislaus, Fahrstuhlführ., SO 33, Falckensteinstr. 37 H. III.

Since 1922, the architect Ossip Klarwein had an apartment in Berlin – shown here is an excerpt from the 1924 address book

In July 1924, Klarwein married the Protestant opera singer Martha Elsa Kumme in Berlin-Charlottenburg

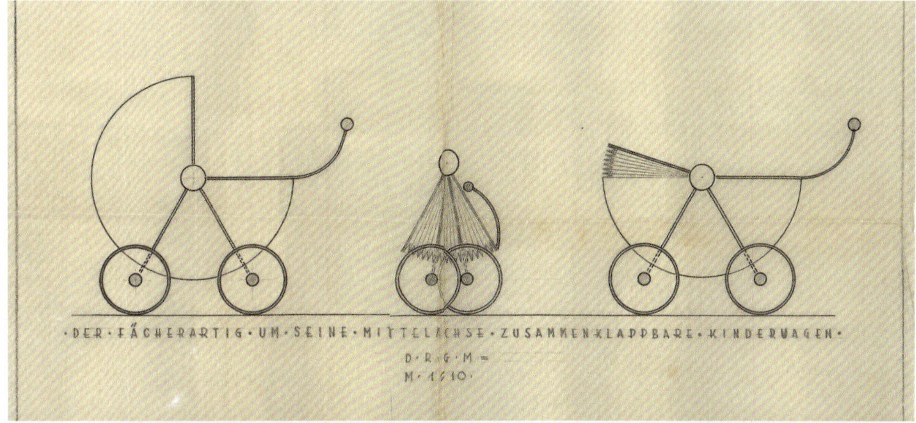

Undated sketch of a baby carriage that folds fan-like around its central axis – the only known design Klarwein ever created for an everyday object./ Pictured with him is his son Matthias, born in 1932

The Höger office around 1930. Head architect Klarwein is seated in the center, with Fritz Höger (wearing glasses) on the right

With Fritz Höger in Hamburg

In the mid-twenties, Ossip Klarwein was on the brink of his first career breakthrough. There was a brief interlude for a year in the practice of Distel and Grubitz in Hamburg, where he oversaw the renovation of the Stadttheater (city theatre) auditorium and worked on "a range of final plans for small villas and the headquarters of the Federation of German Trade Unions". Klarwein left Distel and Grubitz in late 1926 at his own request, according to the friendly, but not effusive letter of reference provided by Hermann Distel[24].

Klarwein (right) at the Höger office. The inscription on the back of the photo says: "Work? No, chess!"/ After work outing with colleagues. Klarwein (third from the left) was very popular for his sense of humour and his good mood

The next chapter in his career was marked by an entirely different duration, intellectual dimension and existential drama. Ossip Klarwein, now 33 years old, joined the practice of Fritz Höger – some 16 years his senior – and soon rose to the role of head architect[25]. Klarwein's net salary was 1,000 Reichsmark, a considerable sum in those days. Höger was keen to make him a partner "due to our successful and harmonious working relationship". Klarwein notes that: "Together we completed the following buildings (among others): Wilhelmshaven-Rüstringen Town Hall, the Lutheran Church on Hohenzollernplatz in Berlin, the Sprinkenhof building in Hamburg, the Neuerburg cigarette factory in Hamburg-Wandsbek, Hannoverscher Anzeiger editorial offices with planetarium in Hanover, etc"[26] – buildings which – as the epitome of German Expressionism – defined the cityscape.

The Chilehaus, completed in 1924 with its projecting prow, instantly made the Hamburg architect Fritz Höger world-famous. Poster by Willy Dzubas for the Reichsbahn Center for German Tourism

The "Master", as Höger was referred to by his employees, was already world-famous for building the iconic Chilehaus in Hamburg, with its protruding front reminiscent of a ship's prow. He was renowned for the revival of North German brick architecture with Gothic references. Höger was a trained carpenter who wrote poetry in the local Low German dialect. He was an impulsive man full of contradictions and defined by his rural background, the Reform movement and the spirit of the time. In October 1932 he became a member of the NSDAP, since 1933 he was President and "Führer" of the National Socialist-leaning "Wirtschaftliche Vereinigung deutscher Architekten" (Commercial Union of German Architects). But his hope of a career as State Architect of the Third Reich was not fulfilled. Höger's main body of work ended when the Protestant Church on Hohenzollernplatz was consecrated in March 1933. For reasons that have been thoroughly explored[27], Höger won no further major contracts. The church building on Hohenzollernplatz, however, is regarded internationally as a masterpiece of German brick expressionism. The plans, as per normal practice, were signed by the owner of the architectural firm, Höger, but numerous drawings bear Klarwein's signature[28].

The relationship between Fritz Höger and Ossip Klarwein was closer and lasted longer than could be expected, given the prevailing political climate. Many accounts of that period even today state that Höger dismissed Klarwein out of pure opportunism at the turn of the year 1932/33. In reality, the desperate economic position of his employer prompted Klarwein to hand in his notice himself: "In the wake of NS legislation and measures taken by the Reichskulturkammer (Reich Chamber of Culture) ...it was impossible for me to continue working for Prof. Höger. Prof. Höger was boycotted and attacked to such an extent in the press and by the Association of German Architects for continuing to employ me that I had no choice but to discontinue my employment with Prof. Höger[29]." Officially, the separation was effective from 1 January 1933.

However, Klarwein did continue working for Höger. A hand-written agreement dated 24 February 1933 was signed by him with the word "Agreed!". The document, qualified as "secret" in Höger's handwriting, specifies tasks and remuneration for Klarwein in detail. It expressly mentions the competition for the design of the Reichsbank (German Central Bank) extension. Klarwein remained Höger's head architect until November 1933. Meanwhile, the Reichskulturkammer received anonymous letters denouncing the actions of Höger. One submission dated 18 June 1933 complains that Höger had "drawings for Protestant churches completed by Ossip Klarwein, a Jew converted to Catholicism", describing this as "particularly grave"[30].

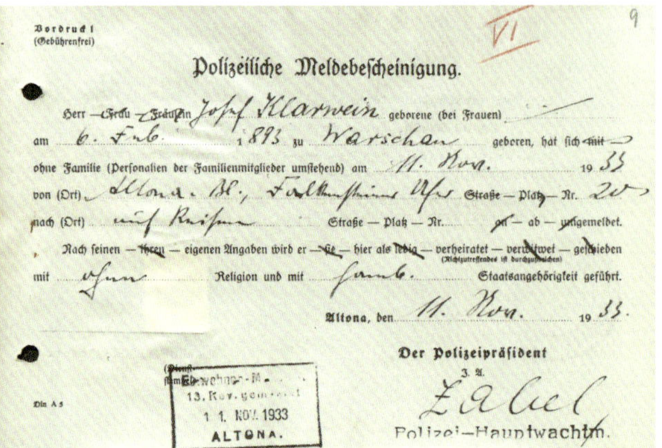

Vordruck I
(Gebührenfrei)

VI 9

Polizeiliche Meldebescheinigung.

Herr — ~~Frau~~ — ~~Fräulein~~ Josef Klarwein geborene (bei Frauen) —

am 6. Feb. 1893 zu Warschau geboren, hat sich ~~mit~~ — ohne Familie (Personalien der Familienmitglieder umstehend) am 11. Nov. 1933

von (Ort) Altona-Bl., Falkensteiner Ufer Straße — ~~Platz~~ — Nr. 20

nach (Ort) auf Reisen Straße — Platz — Nr. ~~an~~ — ab — ~~umgemeldet~~.

Nach seinen — ~~ihren~~ — eigenen Angaben wird er — ~~sie~~ — hier als ~~ledig~~ — verheiratet — ~~verwitwet~~ — ~~geschieden~~ (Nichtzutreffendes ist durchzustreichen)

mit ohne Religion und mit Hamb. Staatsangehörigkeit geführt.

Altona, den 11. Nov. 1933.

Der Polizeipräsident
J. A.

Polizei-Hauptwachtm.

13. Rev. 11. NOV. 1933 ALTONA.

Din A 5

Ossip Klarwein in a casually elegant pose on the beach promenade, 1932 / On 11 November 1933 Klarwein deregistered from his elegant Hamburg address "without family… traveling"

In this increasingly anti-semitic climate, Ossip Klarwein began preparing to flee to Palestine. Fritz Höger helped him acquire a tourist visa[31]. On 11 November 1933, Klarwein officially cancelled his residence status at his elegant Hamburg address on Falkensteiner Ufer 20 in Altona-Blankenese and recorded his departure "without family….for travel purposes". At that point, he declared himself to have "no religious affiliation" and to be a "Hamburg citizen"[32].

Höger bade him farewell on the same day with a two-page, closely-written, reference letter of almost overbearing enthusiasm. As well as praising their "wonderful shared understanding" on artistic and aesthetic questions, he wrote that during their seven-year working relationship, Klarwein had become a dear friend with whom he hoped to continue working in the future[33]. He had sent off other departing employers to uncertain futures with more matter-of-fact words of acknowledgment[34].

Palestine

At the age of 40 then, Klarwein had to start again for the second time in his life – another foreign country and another foreign language. He traveled to Haifa to assess conditions there. He could speak neither English nor Hebrew. His wife and child moved temporarily to his sister's in Berlin. They also needed entry visas. On 19 April 1934 the waiting was over: Klarwein's wife Else, their son Matthias and his now 82-year-old father Menachem set off for Palestine. The money for their relocation came from cashing in a life insurance policy[35]. The move included furniture and all kinds of personal belongings, which have remained in the family to this day: Klarwein's mandolin, his tennis racquet, his library, a lyre-shaped tube radio and a cloth-covered photo album with many photos of happier times in Germany.

A conscious effort was made to maintain the link to Germany by writing regular letters. Immediately after arriving in November 1933, Klarwein wrote to his office colleagues in Hamburg. One responded to "My dear Klarwein" in late December with friendly banter, as if Klarwein had moved to Haifa for no particular reason, mentioning in the same breath the ice and snowfall in Hamburg along with his own

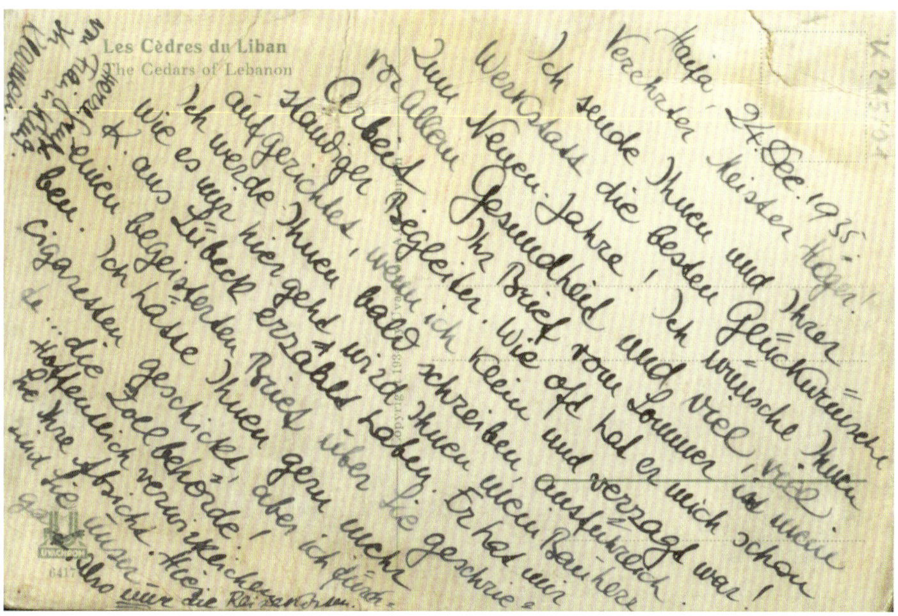

Haifa, 24. Dec. 1935.
Verehrter Meister Höger!
Ich sende Ihnen und Ihrer Werkstatt die besten Glückwünsche zum Neuen Jahre! Ich wünsche Ihnen vor Allem Gesundheit und viel, viel Arbeit! Ihr Brief vom Sommer ist mein ständiger Begleiter. Wie oft hat er mich schon aufgerichtet, wenn ich klein und verzagt war! Ich werde Ihnen bald schreiben, wie es mir hier geht und wird Ihnen mein Bauherr H. aus Lübeck ausführlich erzählt haben. Er hat mir einen begeisterten Brief über Sie geschrieben. Ich hätte Ihnen gern mehr Cigaretten geschickt, aber ich fürchte die Zollbehörde! [illegible]

In December 1935, Klarwein invited his former employer Fritz Höger to Haifa

happy plans for New Year and an architecture lecture Höger had given where he was criticised for his style. He wished the friend who had fled to Palestine a "good New Year", closing with the Nazi salutation: "Heil Deutschland, Heil Hitler!"

Klarwein received a brief note from Höger's secretary in June 1935, which was clearly part of a sporadic but continuous correspondence. "We talk about you very often – the Master and I – and reflect on the happy hours we were able to spend together ..., now there are only 2 architects, 3 students and the Master working in our large office."[36] Höger also corresponded with Klarwein over this period. "Your summer letter is my constant companion", replied Klarwein on a colour postcard of a cedar landscape, "how often it has cheered me up when I felt small and despondent!" Reading between the lines, it seems the former Hamburg star architect was considerably worse off financially than the new arrival in Palestine. Klarwein regretted not being able to send more cigarettes to his "revered Master Höger" due to customs duties. And he very much hoped Höger would make good on his intention to visit him in Haifa: "You will be our guest here. So just travel costs". [37]

Just a few months after his arrival, Klarwein secured some prestigious projects. He designed the monument for prominent Zionist Chaim Arlosoroff and won first prize in the competition to design the Architects' and Engineers' Association building, both in Tel Aviv. But initially the main focus of his work was in Haifa where Klarwein built villas and apartment buildings for German emigrants. He taught at the Technical College and set new standards for urban development with projects such as the first business centre, Beit HaKranot. Not every new immigrant architect was as well employed as he was[38], although the shortage of rental accommodation in the cities was already huge, and growing with the arrival of every additional ship. Shortly before the outbreak of war, rents in Haifa, Tel Aviv and Jerusalem were twice as high as in London or Paris[39].

Three generations of the Klarwein family shortly after arriving in Palestine

A photo from that early period shows a carefree Klarwein laughing behind his father and son, a young boy aged three or four[40]. Just how happy can that new start have been, given the growing number of people for whom Palestine was "not their chosen but an emergency home"[41]? The outbreak of the Second World War brought material hardship to the Klarwein family. The war disrupted the already fragile economy of Mandatory Palestine, along with the livelihood of freelance architect Klarwein. By the end of October 1939, he had no choice but to sell his wife's grand piano[42]. Klarwein had no further commissions. At the end of the year, he sent one job proposal after another to potential building developers[43]. But he never lost his self-confidence. In one of those letters, he wrote: "I assume you have already heard of me, so I can dispense with the need to beat my own drum."

His attempts to find work were a complete failure, leaving Klarwein unemployed. In March 1940 he entered the service of the Public Works Department[44] of the British Mandatory Authority as a Temporary Assistant Architect – a role well beneath his professional status. He was employed along with eleven other architects on a major building programme for 55 police stations – veritable fortresses erected as part of the British response to the Arab uprising of 1936. In particular, Klarwein was responsible for the construction of police stations in Nablus, Lajun, Jitflik and Jenin[45]. He was no model employee, as a reprimand by his immediate superior for unexplained absences reveals[46]. After five years, Klarwein resigned from that post and moved to the City Planning Department of Jerusalem on 1 April 1945.

First portrait photo of Klarwein at his new workplace in Haifa, December 1934

Employment contract as assistant architect with the British Mandate Administration's Public Works Department, dated March 1940 / Klarwein (center) in the early 1940s with colleagues at the Public Works Department

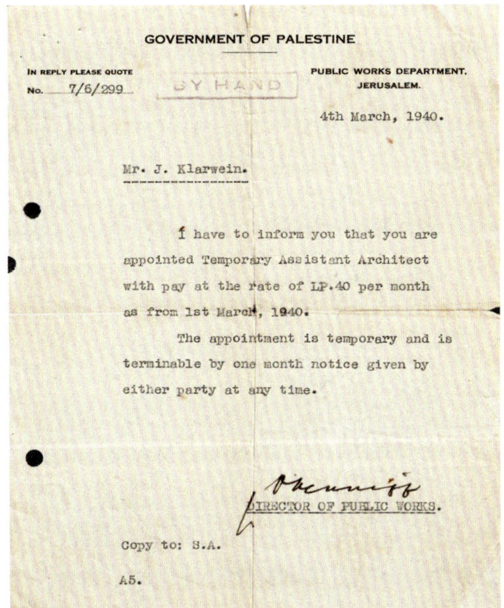

GOVERNMENT OF PALESTINE

IN REPLY PLEASE QUOTE No. 7/6/299 BY HAND

PUBLIC WORKS DEPARTMENT, JERUSALEM.

4th March, 1940.

Mr. J. Klarwein.

I have to inform you that you are appointed Temporary Assistant Architect with pay at the rate of LP.40 per month as from 1st March, 1940.

The appointment is temporary and is terminable by one month notice given by either party at any time.

DIRECTOR OF PUBLIC WORKS.

Copy to: S.A.

A5.

Trials and tribulations

In the meantime, his marriage had fallen apart. His first wife and the son whom both of them worshipped moved for a time to Nahariya[47]. His later second wife, who confusingly was also called Else, unintentionally landed in Palestine in 1939; her ship was supposed to have sailed from Trieste to New York[48]. With his new wife at his side, Ossip Klarwein established himself in Jerusalem[49]. The details of his private life following the divorce are not easy to ascertain – what became of his first wife, which parent their son lived with and Klar-

Klarwein's son Matthias as a student at the renowned Paris art school, Académie Julian

wein's exact whereabouts. These were turbulent times. Their son, the child of a Protestant German mother, grew up as an outsider. Shortly after the state of Israel was founded in 1948, they left for Paris together.

"I was 16; the British left Palestine", the son remembered[50]. "The state of Israel was proclaimed and Arab armies held Jerusalem under siege, mortar shells were exploding everywhere on roofs, in gardens, on water lines, on buses, there was no food or water, Jews and Arabs were fighting each other back and forth between one room and the next, with knives, bare hands, teeth and kebab skewers. We survived on several recipes of grass that I learned about from my previous Arab friends. I tiptoed over mine fields to bring home fresh figs. We were allowed one liter [sic] of water per person to drink and wash, and WHAMMO! KRACH! more bombs and mortars. ... As soon as the UN managed to enforce a cease-fire my mother decided we had enough gun smoke and got us a French visa."

Ossip Klarwein sorely missed his son and visited him often, in Paris, Saint-Tropez and later Mallorca. Unbeknownst to him, he had already lost his younger sister Bronislawa by then. She had remained in Berlin after 1933 and tried to get a visa for England in 1939. Klarwein wanted to help her. A connection in England gave them cause for hope[51], but their attempts were in vain. After the war was over, Klarwein filed repeated missing-person reports and kept searching for her. It was only in 1954 that he found out that Bronislawa had been killed ten years earlier. In 1944 she was deported to Theresienstadt and later Auschwitz[52]. His elder siblings, Maksymilian and Frania, also died during the Holocaust[53]. No one ever spoke of them in the family.

The construction of Israel

Klarwein greeting Ruth Stafford, the wife of James Grover McDonald (center), the first American ambassador to Israel

When the state of Israel was declared, Klarwein was 55 years old and the long-sought recognition finally arrived. In November 1948 he was appointed City Architect of Jerusalem[54]. Klarwein advised on plans for the seat of government. As a judge in prestigious architectural competitions, he helped to define the look of the new state. In addition, he ran his own practice for more than twenty years. No longer as an employee, but in his own right as an architect, he made submissions for projects all over the country – and often won first prize: for Theodor Herzl's monument, for buildings of the new Hebrew University and for the Police Headquarters in Tel Aviv.[55]. For various reasons, not every award won was ultimately implemented as a building project. But the list of buildings that were completed is impressive enough. His directory of works reads like a summary of an economic and social history of early Israel. For fifteen years, Klarwein worked on building and extending the Dagon silo for visionary entrepreneur Reuben Hecht in Haifa. He built the first cinema in Nahariya, the central railway station in Tel Aviv, the central bus station in Jerusalem, and in Ramat Gan, the country's first drama school.

Recognition, however, was not synonymous with prosperity. Initially Klarwein's living conditions were extremely modest. He declined the three-room apartment he was assigned in Jerusalem

Good times: Klarwein with his second wife in Venice

due to a lack of furniture. In 1952 he applied for allocation of an additional room to accommodate his employees. The application went through the office of the Prime Minister, who was more than happy to help “our Klarwein”. He received the requested third room and his everyday life gradually became more comfortable. Klarwein and his second wife dined in restaurants on a regular basis but, apart from that luxury, their habitual frugality prevailed. For instance, they took longer than all their neighbors did to replace the old icebox with an electric refrigerator.

The Knesset

The greatest success and biggest disappointment of Klarwein’s life were identical. When the fledgling state of Israel sought to erect a suitable parliament building, the jury in 1957 unanimously awarded first prize in the competition to Ossip Klarwein’s design. The ensuing dispute over the architectural expression of Israeli democracy, however, unfolded in the wake of a major donation from the estate of James de Rothschild. With his death occurring nine days before the deadline for submissions, the building project gained significant financial scope.

“My honorable colleagues, the leading architects of Israel and there [sic] adherence...to the so-called Progressive Architecture... have risen in protest to denouncing my winning design as inconsistent, classicist, eclectic”, wrote Klarwein in 1966 in an angry reflection on those times. His rivals had tried in vain to have the outcome of the competition overturned in their favour as “un-Israeli”, he stated. “I was pressed to make compromises. But there is nothing more destructive in Architecture than making compromises”[56]. Construction was delayed by this long-lasting dispute, which has been analysed many times[57]. In retrospect, the polemics can also be seen as part of the search by a fledgling state for its aesthetic self-portrayal. Where so many different cultures newly merge, democratically-derived agreement on a representative design can only be the product of a struggle.

This was no consolation to Klarwein. His exasperation at the ongoing harassment occasionally led him to seek refuge with his son, then living in Mallorca. "I cannot concentrate with this bitterness in my heart"[58], he noted. Eleven years after the initial call for submissions, the Knesset was finally completed on the basis of an architectural compromise. Thousands of Israeli citizens, foreign heads of state, parliamentary presidents and other dignitaries took part in the ceremonial inauguration on 30 August 1966.

By then, Klarwein had not set foot on the building site for two weeks. He found the interior design of Dora Gad simply "repellent"[59]. Ongoing criticism of his design – or what was left of it – infuriated him: "Everyone says the building is neo-classicist and fascist. But that is so wrong. Laughable. The last building I created in Berlin was a Protestant Church in 1933 and I was unable to attend the opening ceremony because Göring was there. In those days, I was vilified by the Germans for the mosaics, which were considered "racially impure". Yet here the accusation hurled at me is that the Knesset is fascist!"

Winning the contract for his design of the Knesset in 1957 made Klarwein world-famous. The French Académie d'architecture made him an honorary member and his name featured in major European and North and South American newspapers. He was also highly sought after by Israeli property owners who yearned for a "genuine Klarwein".

Klarwein with his second wife touring the UNESCO building in Paris, around 1959 / Klarwein on the beach in the bay of Deia on Mallorca. There, he built a house for his son Mati, who had become internationally successful as a painter

Klarwein traveling with his second wife, around 1966

Credo

The dispute had worn Ossip Klarwein down. Autobiographical notes in a mixture of German and English fill an entire folder[60]. "For the first time in my life, I find myself writing about architecture", he wrote. Ever since 1912 he had only worked, designed and built, he added, stating that theories, trends and fluctuating fads had never interested him. Only exceptional people like Le Corbusier or Frank Lloyd Wright could invent new things; the rest merely modified existing styles, he said. This was a side swipe at critics of his "out-of-date" Knesset concept. "Of course, [it] is reminiscent of Athens, the cradle of democracy", he wrote. "But there is nothing eclectic about that – it is timeless."

The notes also include his reflections on the path his life had taken. "My entire existence in Israel was and is built on the basis of competitions. They are my hobby and my delight". Back-room politics and all the wheeling and dealing were abhorrent to him. "I like working alone, from the first design to the last detail." Klarwein emphasises that he does not belong to any party or union. He repeatedly returns to the Knesset in his reflections. His view of democratic statehood did not include Zionist symbols such as a portrait of Herzl hanging in the Knesset chamber. "We should not see ourselves here as 'Zionists'; we are Israelis"[61].

The time for major projects was over. Klarwein was 73 years old and unwell. But he did take part in one more competition. It concerned a monument to commemorate the old Central Synagogue in Munich, which had been demolished on Adolf Hitler's personal orders in June 1938. Why did he participate? Klarwein had no personal connection to Munich, nor was he a practising Jew. West-German commemorative culture was still in its cranky beginnings. Initially, the city wanted only Bavarian artists to take part in the competition, but then placed adverts in Israeli daily newspapers[62]. In the summer of 1968, when Klarwein was 75 years old, he was informed that he had not made it onto the shortlist.

In a collection of small notes, Klarwein tried to arrange his thoughts about God and the world into a kind of personal creed[63]. Religions he had experienced first-hand – Judaism, Catholicism, Protestantism, Islam – do not feature. He did not believe in God, as he regretfully told his son: "I wished I could believe!" "God" to him was "a concept only humans could invent". In other contexts he spoke of "die Natur [nature] which is God". He distinguished between the "dumb" body and the immortal soul, which is liberated from "that apparatus" in death. "The soul of a person cannot die; it must live on". He had a clear-eyed view of his own death. "I am slowly, slowly taking leave of life, of every hour of the day, every hour of happiness, my own creativity, every hour of rest, every hour of contentedness, quite consciously, as clear as crystal, it is the hour to bid farewell to this life -..."[64]

Ossip Klarwein died in Jerusalem on 9 September 1970.

Klarwein's gravestone at Har HaMenuchot cemetery in Jerusalem, designed by his step-son-in-law Dan Hoffner

1 Information provided by POLIN, Museum of the History of Polish Jews, Warsaw **2** Echo Muzyczne, 4 June 1898 **3** Hazfira 25 July and 11 September 1898 **4** Macabee, 1966 **5** Information provided by Jane Century, Philadelphia **6** Neofici Polscy 1904 **7** Information provided by Prof Dr Ruth Leiserowitz, German Historical Institute, Warsaw **8** Mainz City Archive.Else Ester Klarwein was unmarried and worked as a housekeeper, as notd in the civil registry entry dated 22 October 1918 **9** Offenbach City Archive, resident card index **10** Mainz City Archive, death register of Leonore Sand **11** CZA A455/1 **12** CZA A455/1 and private archive **13** German Craft Guild – an influential association of artists, architects, designers and industrialists **14** CZA A455/1 **15** CZA A455/1 **16** Private organisation dedicated to the reconstruction of East Prussian towns damaged during the Russian campaign **17** All documents from private archive **18** Warhaftig, 2005, Foreword, p.5 **19** StaHH, restitution file Joseph Klarwein **20** CZA A455/61 **21** Berlin address books https://digital.zlb.de/viewer/berliner-adressbuecher/ **22** Exit card, Centrum Judaicum (Jewish Centre) Berlin **23** https://www.ancestry.de/imageviewer/collections/2957/images/48458_prep551^000117-00542?pId=279563212 **24** CZA A455/1 **25** Confirmed by multiple sources, such as StaHH, reparations file **26** Affidavit 1954 **27** Bucciarelli, 1992; Quiring (formerly Turtenwald), 2003; Höhns, 2013 **28** CZA A455/61 **29** Underlined by Klarwein. StaHH, reparations file **30** StaHH, NL FH **31** StaHH, reparations file **32** StaHH, reparations file **33** CZA A455/1, original; StaHH, restitution file, carbon copy **34** KuBi, NL FH, reference for Berckenhagen **35** StaHH, reparations file **36** CZA A455/3 **37** Postcard dated 24 December 1935. StaHH NL FH **38** Myra Warhaftig, They laid the first stone **39** Mitteilungsblatt (MB) July 1939 **40** CZA A455/47 **41** MB 1938 **42** Palestine Post on 25 and 27 October 1940 **43** CZA A455/3 and private archive **44** Work contract dated 5 March 1940, private archive **45** Information provided by Gad Kroizer, Bar-Ilan University **46** CZA A455/3 **47** Mati Klarwein, Collected Works 1959-1975, Raymond Martin Press, Markt Erlbach, 1988 **48** Information provided by the family **49** StaHH, reparations file **50** Mati Klarwein, Collected Works 1959-1975, Raymond Martin Press, Markt Erlbach, 1988 **51** CZA A455/3 **52** Tracing documentation for Bronislawa Klarwein, Arolsen Archives **53** Macabee, 1966 **54** Palestine Post, 11 November 1948 **55** CZA A455/7 **56** To his great annoyance, his designs were sometimes adopted by other architects and built under their name: "Some Shikumin [simple apartment blocks for new immigrants] in Tel Aviv...were built by other architects because I was still unknown, and still connected with the Histraduth." Source: private archive and confirmed in Klarwein's 1952/53 accounts. **57** Sheila Hattis Rolef 2000, contribution Talia Margalit in this publication **58** Private archive **59** Haaretz, 26 August 1966 **60** Private Archive **61** Underlined by Klarwein **62** Private archive **63** CZA A455/2 **64** Private archive

BERLIN
DESIGNS FOR A MONUMENTAL CHURCH

Johannes Cramer

Architectural models with a tall neogothic portal, the cross in the middle of the tower, and of the entire complex, still with flat roofs, presented to the parish council by Höger on 31 May 1928

Early situational studies, signed by Klarwein

Preparations to build a “Northern Church” (the official working title of the project)[1], began in the early 1920s. In 1926 the parish was finally able to purchase the Hohenzollernplatz site which was originally earmarked for an office building. The parish council was not satisfied with the outcome of a 1927 architecture competition for a church, parish hall, community centre with meeting rooms and a minister’s residence, with participation by the architectural firms of Otto Bartning, Helmuth Grisebach, Otto Kuhlmann, Leo Lottermoser and Hans Rottmayer. Grisebach, Kuhlmann and Rottmayer were asked to rework their designs but their revisions were also deemed unacceptable. Quite by chance Ernst-Erik Pfannschmidt, who was working for the Höger studio, brought a Höger lecture at the Charlottenburg Technical University in 1928 to the attention of his father, church artist Ernst-Christian Pfannschmidt, who then made contact with the parish. This led to Höger presenting his credentials and some initial designs for the “Northern Church” to the parish on 31 May 1928, who were sufficiently convinced of their merit.

On 17 September 1929, the parish council[2] chose “Option II, pointed arches, no gallery” out of three detailed drawings of the interior provided by the Höger firm. On 30 October 1929, Höger received the contract to begin work and, after further discussion of numerous variations, submitted his final plans on 11 February 1930. The quote, which amounted to 1,600,000 Reichsmark, was discussed on 29 April 1930[3]. The cornerstone ceremony took place on 30 September 1930 and the church was consecrated on 19 March 1933.

The basic structure of the church consists of 13 reinforced concrete arches of a type commonly used at that time, in commercial construction in particular. The facades of the building complex, on the other hand, consist entirely of hard-fired clinker with different decorative shapes and surface textures. Adjoining the church, which is raised above the parish hall, are the parish offices and the minister’s residence. The individual buildings were initially conceived as clean, flat-roofed cubes in a loose assembly dictated by the irregular outline of the site. Inclined roofs were only added in the course of further planning.

The church is dominated by the 60-meter-high bell tower in front of the facade with its towering cross, and by the monumental box-like nave with a flat-pitched copper roof, originally designed to be hidden by a parapet[4]. In line with the contours of the cast-concrete arches of the underlying structure, the volume tapers as the building extends

The entire complex in the 21st century

upwards. The transition to the side walls is formed by a series of closely spaced, almost overstretched pilaster strips behind which the windows of the church interior are all but concealed. The strips continue to the main facade where they embrace the semi-circular stairs extending out of the facade. Thus, the elaborately decorated, arched entrance crowned by a tall golden cross within the masonry, is both integrated and enhanced. The monumental, semicircular stairway leading up to the main entrance also points to the significance of the building. Low, windowless side aisles accompany the formidable cube. Because the parish hall had to be accommodated below the church, the nave interior is raised about three metres above street level.

The parish offices with their simple grid facade, originally comprising only four floors with an additional drying loft below a flat roof, form a subordinate link to the minister's residence in Nassauische Strasse. This is emphasised by extended balconies. The five-storey minister's residence, initially designed with flat roof and drying loft, also appears in the early sketches and models as a simple cube with evenly spaced windows, with a small semi-circular balcony on the 5th floor being the only element to slightly soften the overall severity. During construction, Höger did try to defend the idea of a flat roof (green roof, space for drying washing) but was obviously overruled, as he had been with the design of the church roof. The drying loft was replaced by a high-pitched, hipped roof and the front ordered by a regular series of bay windows. The gradual adaptation of the design unmistakably reflects the preferences of the rising new political class.

The interior is defined by 13 arches of reinforced concrete. In the development phase, suggestions were made for the arches to have either parabolic or pointed crests, while retaining the same concept of construction. One sketch with parabolic crests was labelled by Klarwein, while another with pointed arches was signed by Höger. The surface of the arches was left in fair-faced concrete, decorated with indented chisel work until a redecoration completed in 1991. The horizontal joints of the shuttering work, in beton brut[5] style, were deliberately left unfilled and remain clearly visible as a structural element to this day. During construction, Reverend Ulich tried to persuade Höger to have the arches painted, but Höger refused – more than likely in consultation with Klarwein.

Visitors make their way from the pointed-arch door, elaborately decorated in gold and glass mosaics, through a brick-walled triumphal arch to the raised altar in an apse lined with turquoise tiles. The vertically arranged rectangular plates have a remarkably lively surface.

Construction site around 1931

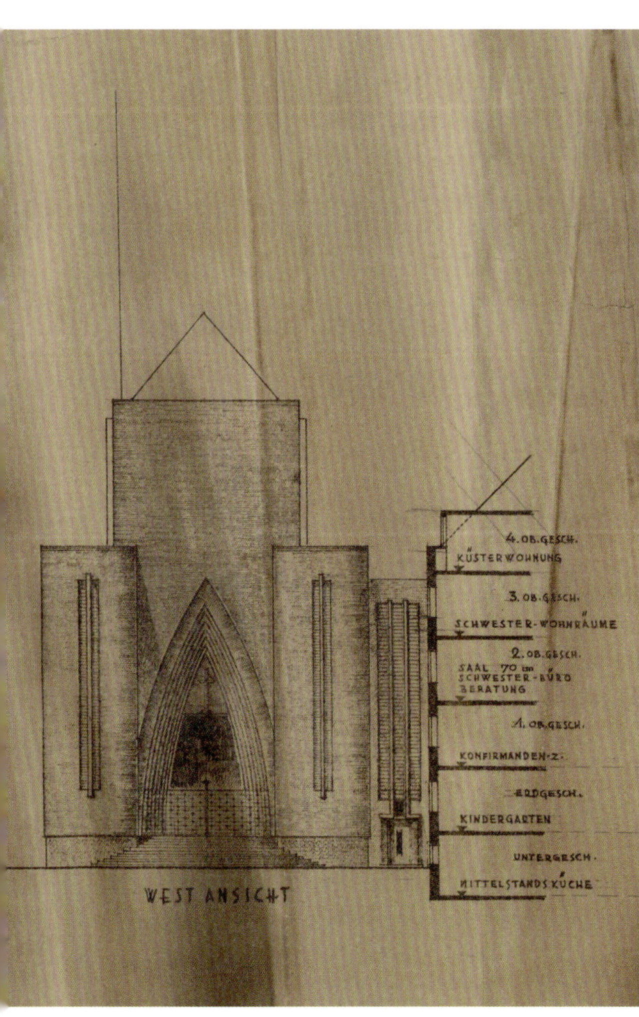

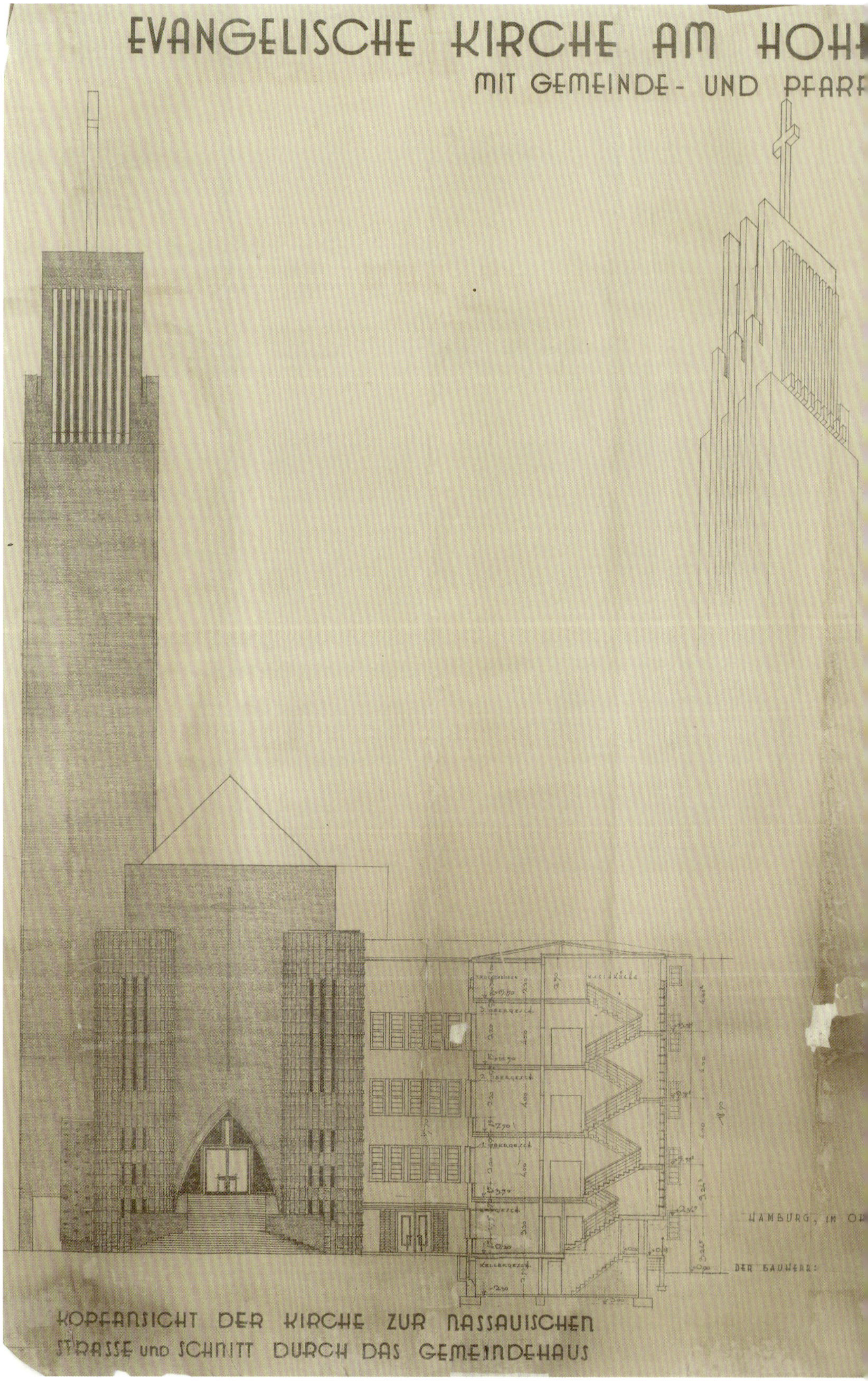

EVANGELISCHE KIRCHE AM HOH

MIT GEMEINDE- UND PFARR

KOPFANSICHT DER KIRCHE ZUR NASSAUISCHEN
STRASSE UND SCHNITT DURCH DAS GEMEINDEHAUS

Various designs for the western facade with the main portal. First with tall pointed arch, later reduced. Different proposals for the bell tower

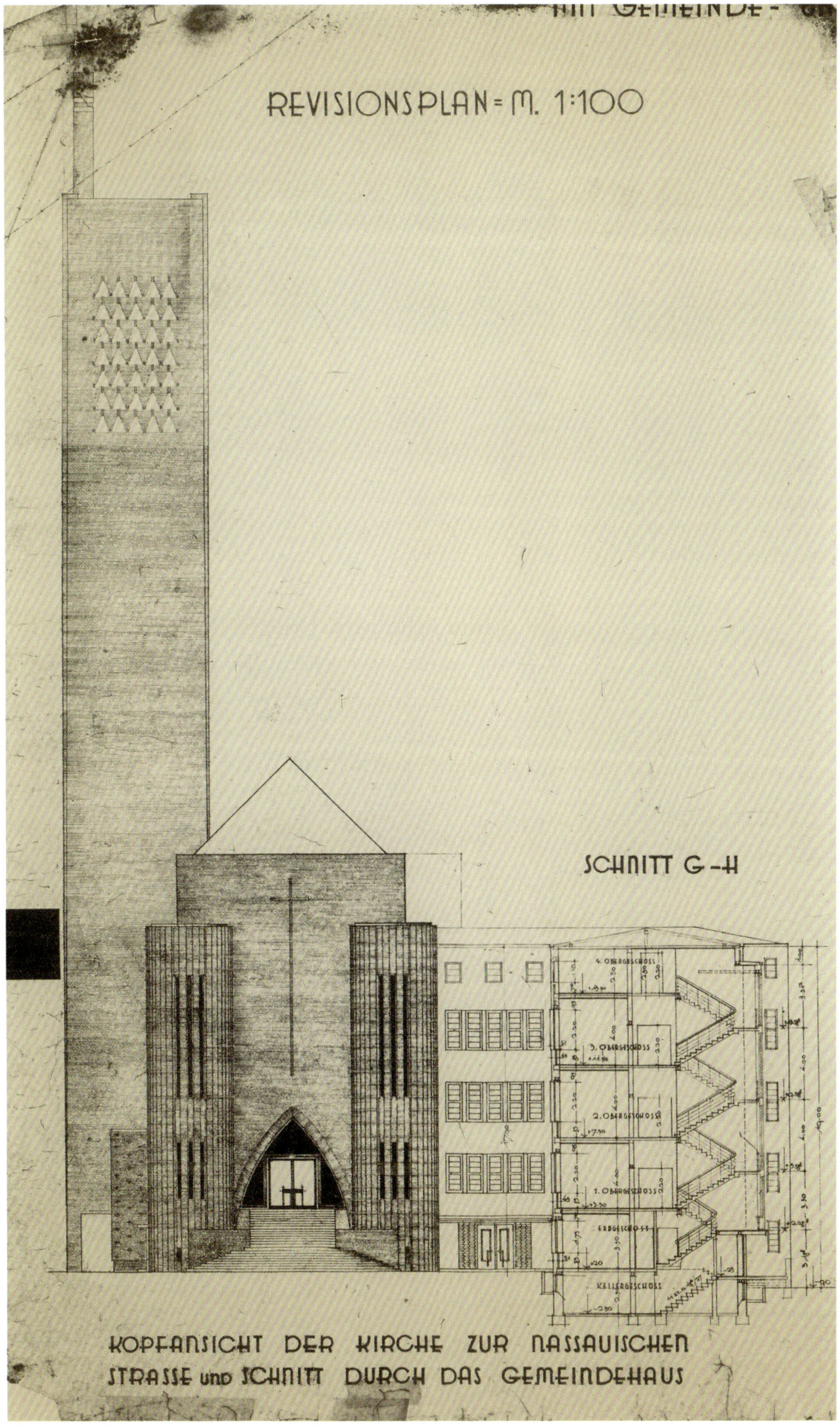

REVISIONSPLAN = M. 1:100
SCHNITT G-H
KOPFANSICHT DER KIRCHE ZUR NASSAUISCHEN
STRASSE und SCHNITT DURCH DAS GEMEINDEHAUS

SCHNITT A-B

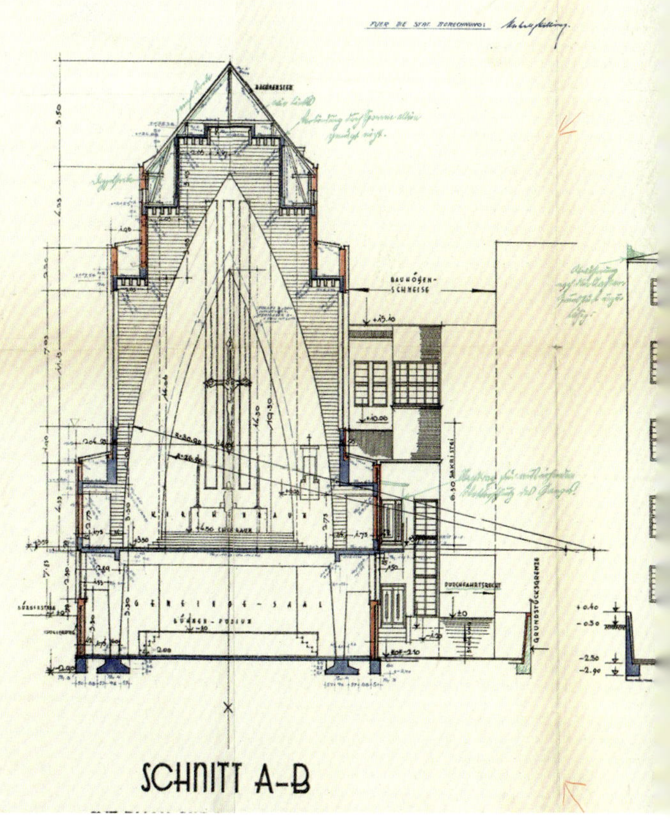

Section from the official building submission with a view of the chancel. Notable are the tall pointed arches and the highly complicated construction of the roof section

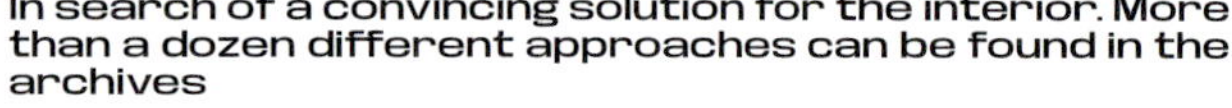

In search of a convincing solution for the interior. More than a dozen different approaches can be found in the archives

Proposals by Klarwein top left and Höger top right. Drawing of the final project and the end result in 1933

Klarwein's share

Based on comprehensive material in numerous archives[6] the hotly debated authorship of the Hohenzollernplatz Church can be summarized as follows:

Höger was undoubtedly responsible for initiating the contract and corresponding with Reverend Ulich. Initial sketches relating to city planning and the massing of the buidings are unequivocally annotated and signed by Klarwein. The design of the surfaces, including various masonry patterns as well as the use of gold-glazed bricks is evident in early mass models and also appears in the official submission plans. They could well be attributable to Klarwein. The geometry of the principal portal has the hallmarks of a Klarwein design, too. The first (?) mass model comprises a very tall neogothic portal with tympanum, similar to one executed a year earlier by Höger in Delmenhorst[7]. Höger later presented a different model option with a horizontal lintel. What finally emerged was a compromise between Höger and Klarwein with an abstracted, pointed-arch form. There is clear evidence that the round windows and relieving arches designed to structure the roof section of the nave were designed by Höger[8].

The early perspective drawings for the interior are partly annotated by Klarwein and all characteristic of his style, so that this part of the design can safely be attributed to him. Later refinements and the pointed-arch option were then added by Höger. According to the available sources, the official submission drawings were largely produced by their colleague Seeger[9]. The selection of and discussions with artists contributing to the interior and the colour scheme for the walls were handled by Höger himself[10]. According to the correspondence[11], construction management was the responsibility of Höger's colleagues Lorenzen and Brandt.

When all this information is considered, in conjunction with progress reports on the work within the Höger firm, one can conclude that the initial massing as well as construction (?) and overall effect of the interior are mainly the work of Klarwein. The design of the exterior of the building was a combined effort, while the interior decoration was undertaken by Höger alone.

Design drawing by Puhl&Wagner company for the triple window in the chancel

1 The official name originally; the name "Kirche am Hohenzollernplatz" (Church on Hohenzollern Square) was not approved by the parish council until 15 March 1933. **2** All information sourced from the parish archives "Church Construction" section 1929-33. **3** Plus a further 250,000 RM (Reichsmark) for bells, fittings and furnishings and architect's fee. **4** This roof was barely visible in the original draft sketches. It was only as the design developed that the roof pitch became steeper and the eave over the front porch, which was initially set back about three meters, was brought forward so the roof became clearly visible. **5** "Beton brut" first appeared in the early 20th century and was subsequently utilized by Auguste Perret as well as, above all, by Le Corbusier. **6** The building plans, including revised versions of this project, are held in the building-file archives of the Charlottenburg-Wilmersdorf District Council. Sketches and preliminary drawings are held in the Hamburg State Archives, the Berlin Art Library, the church's own archives and in the Central Zionist Archives in Jerusalem. Most of the correspondence on this building project remains in the church's own archives. **7** ... "by turning the sketches over and drawing a revised version on the underside of the paper. That was how the square main entrance became the pseudo-Gothic arch he often favoured in his designs." Berlin, Kunstbibliothek; From Fritz Höger's estate: Letter from Ernst-Erik Pfannschmidt to Eckhardt Berckenhagen, 29 June 1977 **8** Berlin, Kunstbibliothek; from Fritz Höger's estate: Letter from Ernst-Erik Pfannschmidt to Eckhardt Berckenhagen, 29 June 1977 **9** Berlin, Kunstbibliothek; From Fritz Höger's estate: Letter from Ernst-Erik Pfannschmidt to

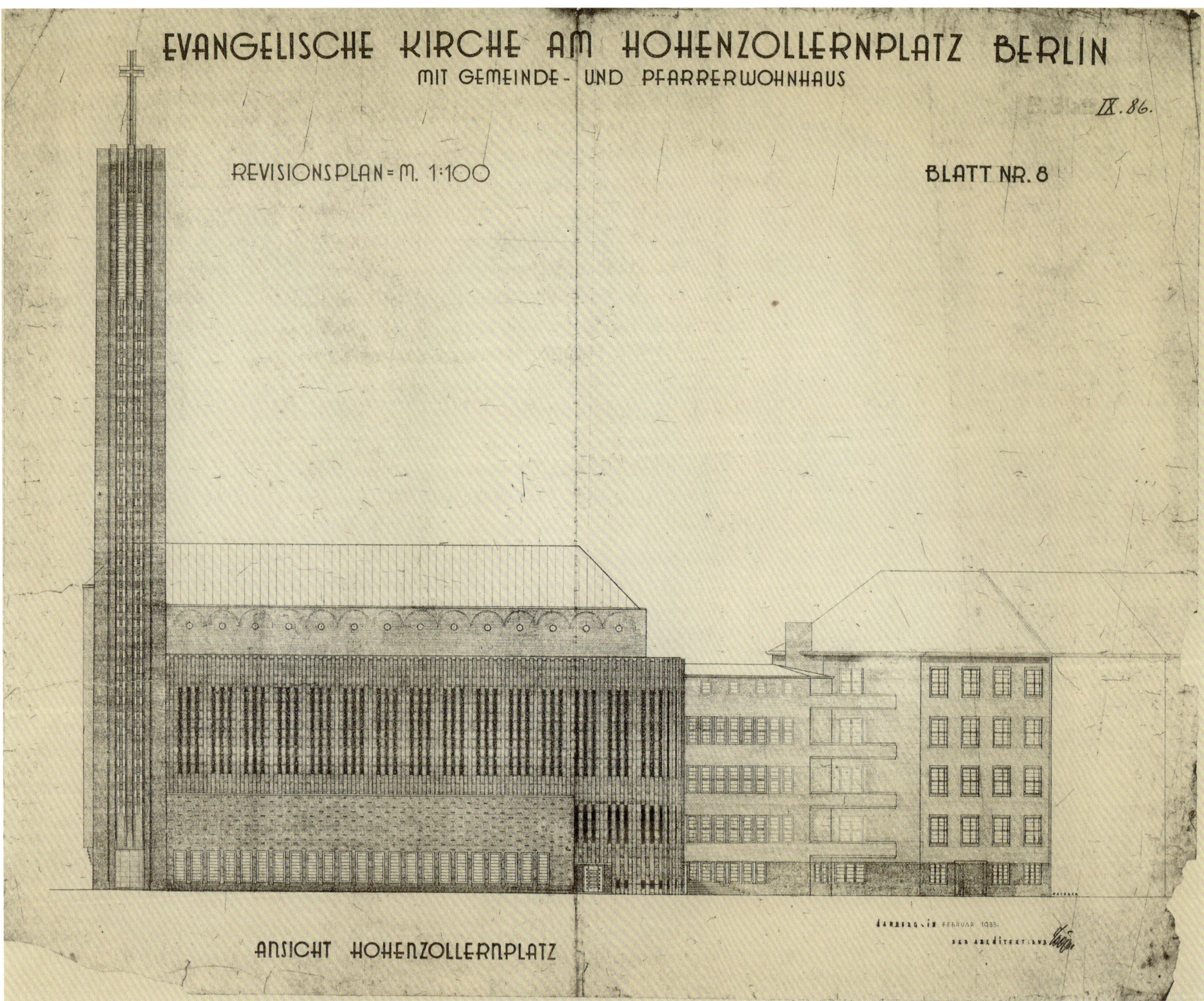

View from the north, revised plan, with detailed treatment of the facades, already with slanted roofs

Eckhardt Berckenhagen, 29 June 1977 "The primary design architect was Ossip Klarwein ... The detailed implementation plans were drawn up by Seeger." **10** Puhl&Wagner: Altar window; Constantin Starck (1866-1939): cross above altar; Erich Waske (1889-1978): Sgraffiti triumphal arch; Prof. Hermann Sandkuhl (1872-1936): Sgraffiti side walls; Ernst-Christian Pfannschmidt (1868-1949): mural in the parish hall **11** Parish archives, Church Construction section, 1931-33. Klarwein does not appear there, despite having a – presumably small – apartment nearby at Joachim-Friedrich-Strasse 47, according to the 1932 Berlin address book.

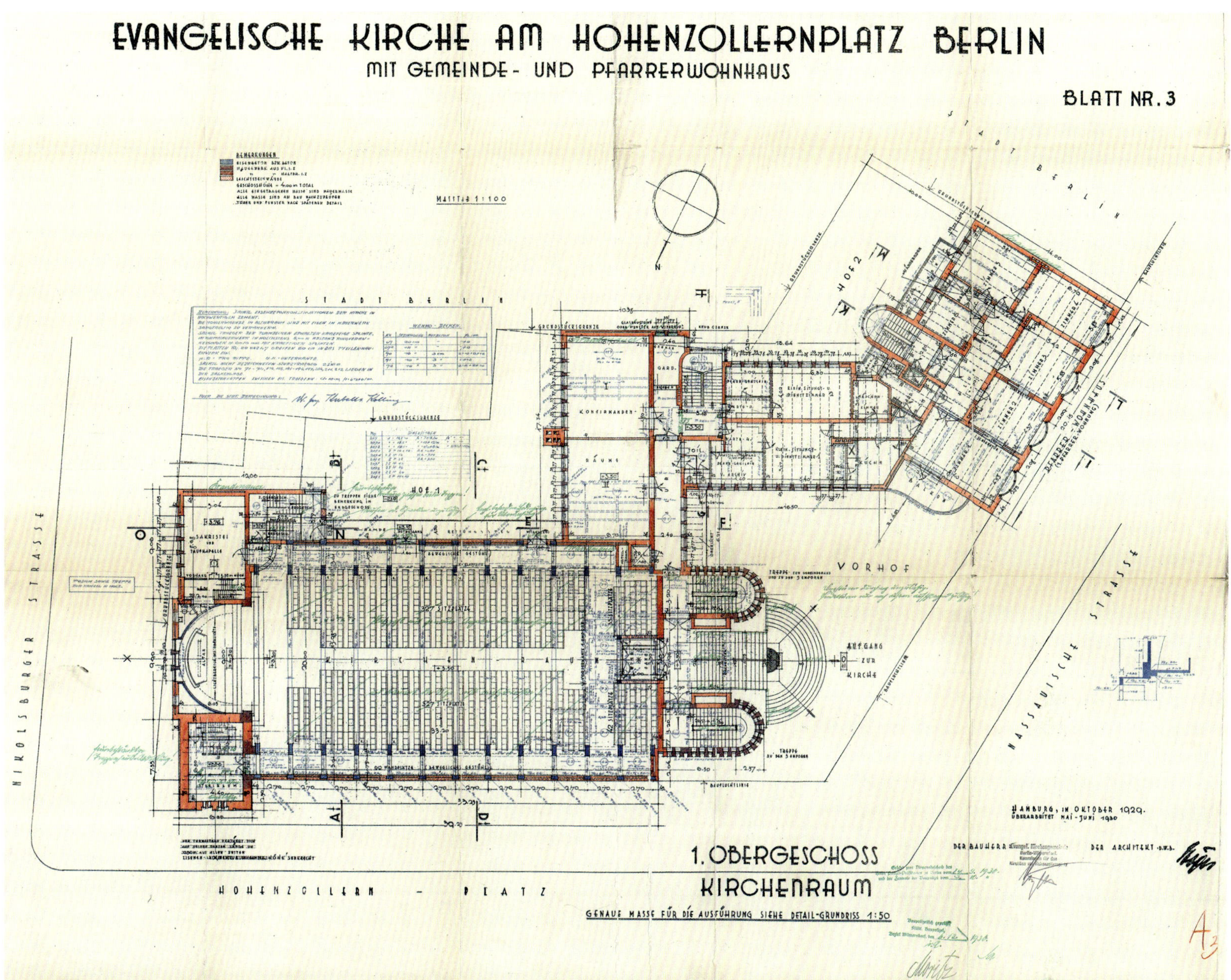

Floor plan of the church from the official building submission

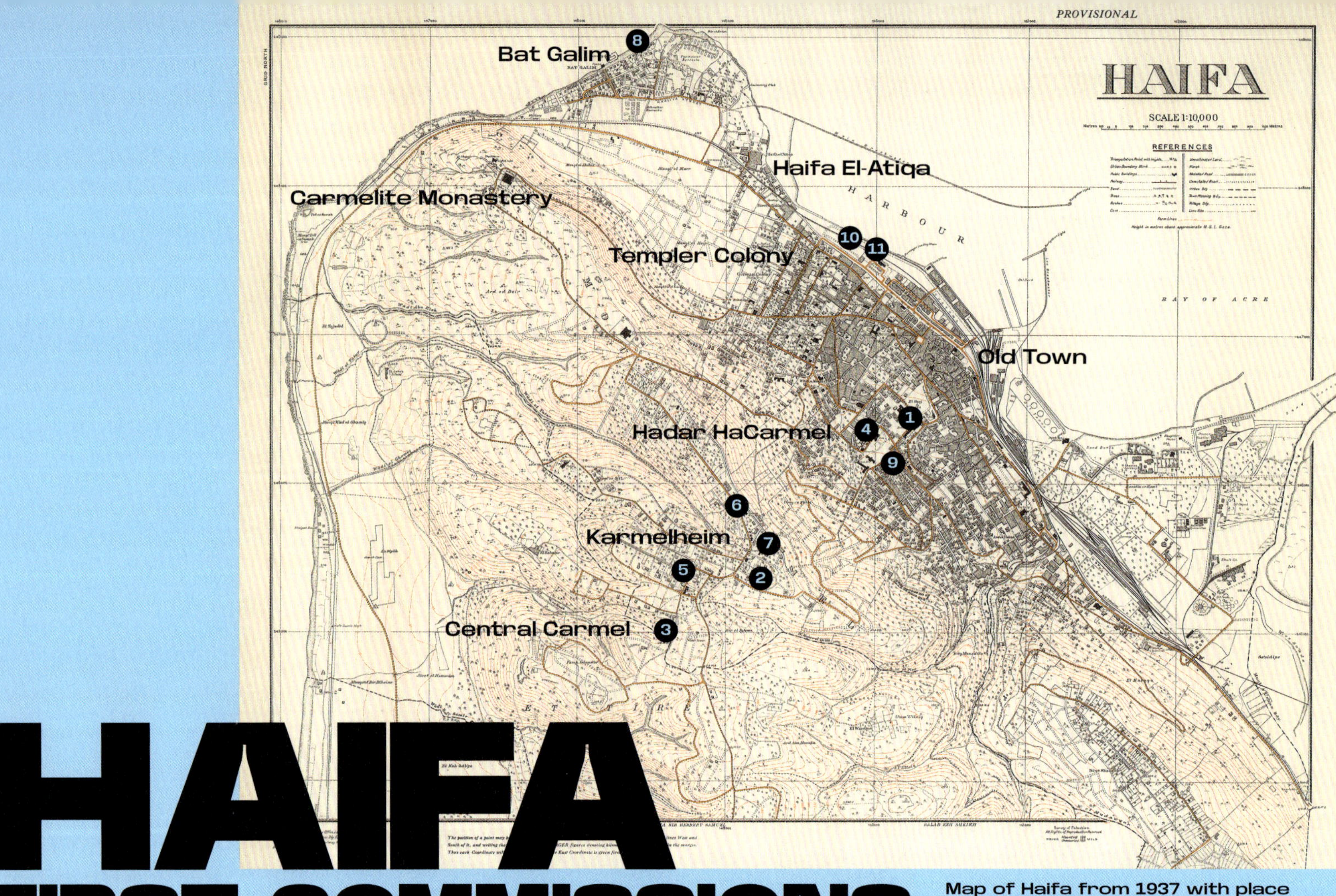

HAIFA

FIRST COMMISSIONS IN CONTEXT OF THE CITY'S HISTORY[1]

Dafna Berger Shperling

Map of Haifa from 1937 with place names mentioned and mapping the Klarwein projects

1. Beit Zang (1935)
2. Beit Karseboom (1935-37)
3. Beit Aschner (1937)
4. Beit HaKranot (1937/40/56)
5. Beit Rachel (1938)
6. Beit Abraham (1939)
7. Beit Bernstein (1939)
8. Beit Kodesh (1939)
9. Beit Gottesmann (1940)
10. Dagon Silo (1952-55/1960/1962/1971)
11. Dagon Administration (1965)

1 Carmel 1969; Stern 1974; Yazbak 1998; Aharonowitz 1958; Herbert 1993; Ben-Artzy 2004

Joseph Klarwein immigrated to Haifa in 1933 and set up his business there. He planned four apartment buildings on Mount Carmel, all of them in many ways characteristic of the 1930s in the area. Beit Karseboom (Elhanan St. 8 – 1937) shows a typical solution on the Carmel for planning in long and narrow plots. Klarwein created two buildings with a shared wall and shifted them relative to each other, ensuring that both have uninterrupted views. The buildings initially had wide balconies with rounded corner but were eventually built with rectangular ones. Just like Beit Aschner (Lotus St. 13 – 1937), they have an uninterrupted view to the west and the Mediterranean Sea.

Beit Bernstein (Megiddo St. 8 – 1939) has subtle geometric decoration in plaster and finely designed entrance and architectural details in the stairwell. The footpath and stairs leading from the street to the building are made of roughly cut stones that apparently resonate with both local and German landscaping trends of the time.

Beit Wolfgang Abraham (HaTishbi St. 113 – 1939) is exceptional among the residential buildings Klarwein planned in Haifa. It was first built in 1934 in traditional style with a pitched roof, incorporating local and European architectural features. It was planned by architect Karl Ludwig Wehlau of Berlin, who was the owner's brother in-law. Just five years later Klarwein converted it into an apartment building. Extensive changes included another floor replacing the pitched roof, adding balconies, changing the location of the interior and exterior

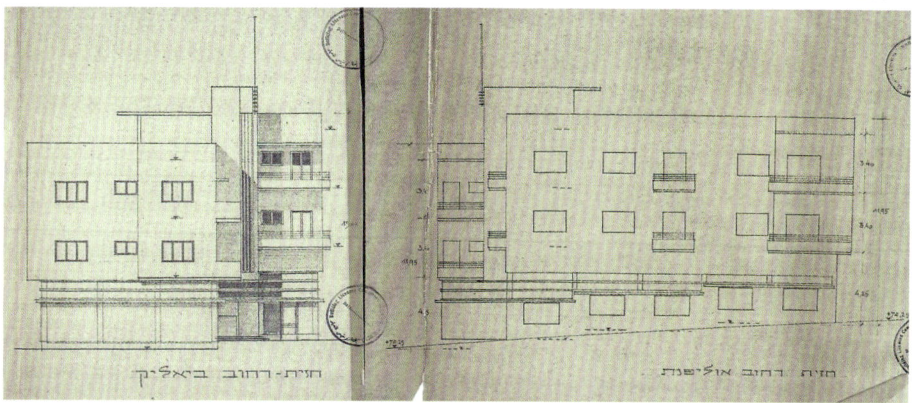

1 Beit (=building) Zang (1935): Klarwein's first commission in Haifa. His name appears on the construction signboard

❷ Beit Karseboom (1935-37): the multi-family house composed of cubes of different sizes was constructed in phases

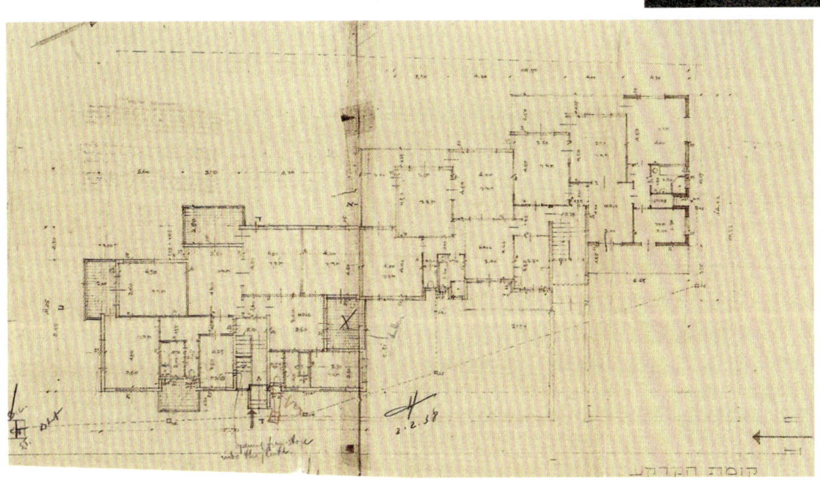

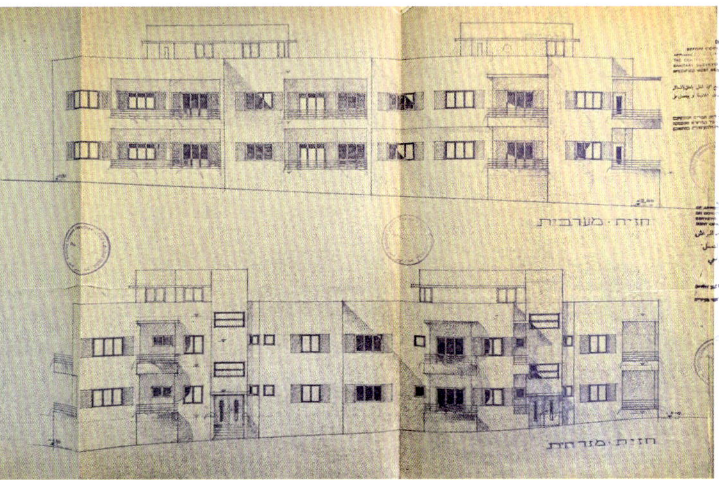

❸ Beit Aschner (1937): the rounded balconies as well as the handrails of the stairs indicate a changing design approach

stairs, and total reconfiguration of the interior layout. Klarwein added his signature features with the round handrail in the stairwell and rounded cornices. The facades are stone finished, probably because of municipal directives, the building frame is of a hybrid type which incorporates stone as well as reinforced concrete. This building has windows arranged in triplets, a motive widely used in modern architecture in Haifa which alludes to earlier local architecture.

But what conditions brought about the construction of these buildings? A very concise history of the urban development of Haifa and Mount Carmel, focusing on the Jewish neighborhoods until World War II, is given here as context.

Haifa Al-Jadida During Ottoman Rule

Haifa Al-Jadida (The New Haifa) was established in 1761 on a narrow coastal plain at the foot of Mount Carmel, by Zahir al-Umar al-Zaydani, Ruler of Acre and the Galilee. Situated on the south side of Akko Bay, Haifa was surrounded by a wall. It had two gates and a fortress, the Burj e-Salam, overlooking it. Zahir al-Umar's tolerant approach toward non-Muslims brought prosperity to the town during his rule.

During the 19th century Haifa started gaining economic and political importance, superseding Akko, which had been the main town on the bay until then. In the 1850s the first houses were constructed outside the town walls. The Muslim population generally built houses to the east of the walled town, while the Christian population expanded to the west.

In 1868 the Templars, who had a great impact on Haifa economically, socially, and culturally, established their colony just west of the walled town. Haifa's population was growing rapidly during the 19th century, shifting from a predominantly Muslim demographic to a more balanced community of Christians and Muslims, with a Jewish minority.

In 1905 the Hejaz Railway began operating from Haifa. This was a prominent route in the Ottoman Empire, and Haifa was its only independent outlet to the Mediterranean Sea. Thousands of pilgrims passed through Haifa on their way to Mecca, in addition to significant amounts of equipment used to construct the railway. Additionally, the railway was utilized to transport goods for export through Haifa. The administration and workshops of the Hejaz Railway were situated in Haifa, attracting many people from the region to search for work and business here. As a result, the town experienced unprecedented prosperity.

Shortly before World War I Haifa was a major town, with 20,000 inhabitants from diverse communities. It had a cosmopolitan character and a busy movement of passengers and goods.

❺ Beit Rachel (1938): detached house with rounded roofs over the balconies; demolished

❻ Beit Abraham (1939): after conversion by Klarwein

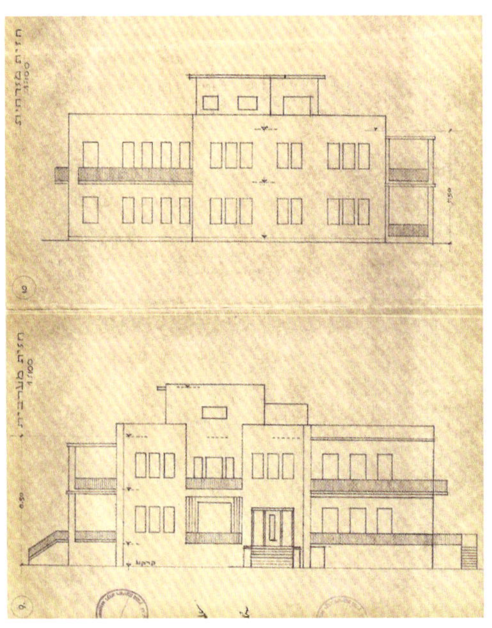

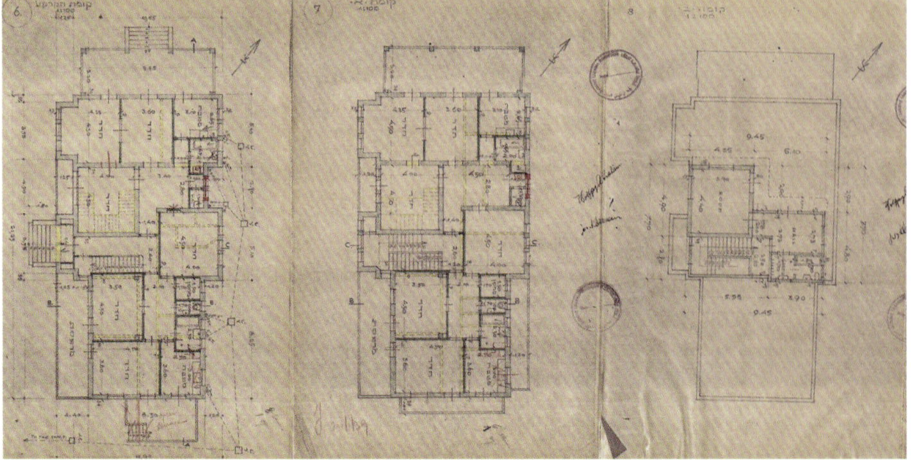

Jews in Haifa

A small Jewish community lived in Haifa in the Muslim quarter inside the town walls before the town expanded outside of its walls. In 1891 the first Jewish neighborhood outside the walls was established on the eastern side, known as Ard el-Yahud (the land of the Jews). In 1907 a garden suburb named "Herzliya" was established by a Jewish association on the Carmel slopes west of the town walls.

In 1908, the Jewish-German "Hilfsverein der Deutschen Juden" (Aid Association of German Jews) acquired a plot of land on the slopes of the mountain, just south of the walled town, with the help of the Wisotzky family. This area was intended for a technical school, which later became the "Technion". The land surrounding it was acquired gradually by Jewish immigrants and organizations.

Settlement on Mount Carmel

The area on top of Mount Carmel between the Carmelite monastery and the Druze villages was mostly uninhabited during Ottoman rule. In 1870, two years after the Templars arrived in Haifa, they attempted to establish a colony on top of Mount Carmel. However, they met with the resistance of the Carmelites who claimed ownership of the lands the Templars had set their eyes on. This ignited a conflict that was an expression of broader tensions between different lifestyles, Christian groups, and European powers. It was only resolved 17 years later following direct negotiations between the Pope and Otto von Bismarck, Chancellor of the German Empire. Eventually the Templars were granted permission to establish their colony on Mount Carmel. They named it Karmelheim. At the beginning of the 20th century mostly German emigrants and wealthy Arabs lived in Northern Carmel and Karmelheim.

The British Mandate Territory

In September 1918, Ottoman rule ended in Haifa. The land remained under British military rule until mid-1920, when the British Mandate was established. During the Mandate era the British developed Haifa as a pivot of geopolitical importance within the British Empire. This was manifested in three projects. The first was the mandate railway which was connected to the Hejaz railway in Haifa. The mandate railway headquarters were located here, and modern workshops were constructed in the Baylands near Haifa. The second project was the construction of Haifa port, which almost immediately became the main port of the land. This project included the reclamation of around 340 dunams (34 hectares) of land from the sea, on which the British government constructed a new modern business center for Haifa. The third project is the oil pipeline from Iraq to Haifa – a project that led to the establishment of the petrochemical industry in the Baylands and attracted more industries to the area.

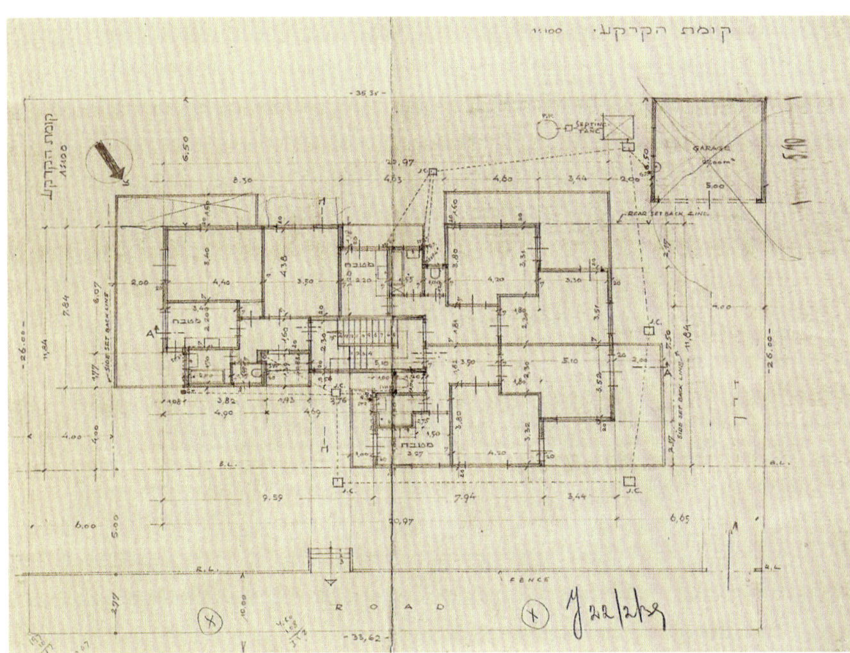

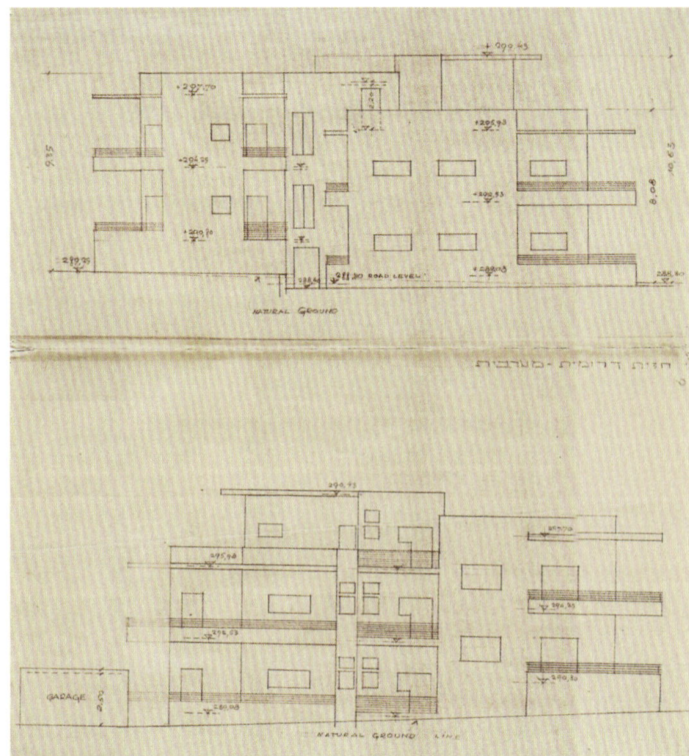

❼ Beit Bernstein (1939): variable ground plan with elegant architectural details

❽ Beit Kodesh (1939): detached house, demolished

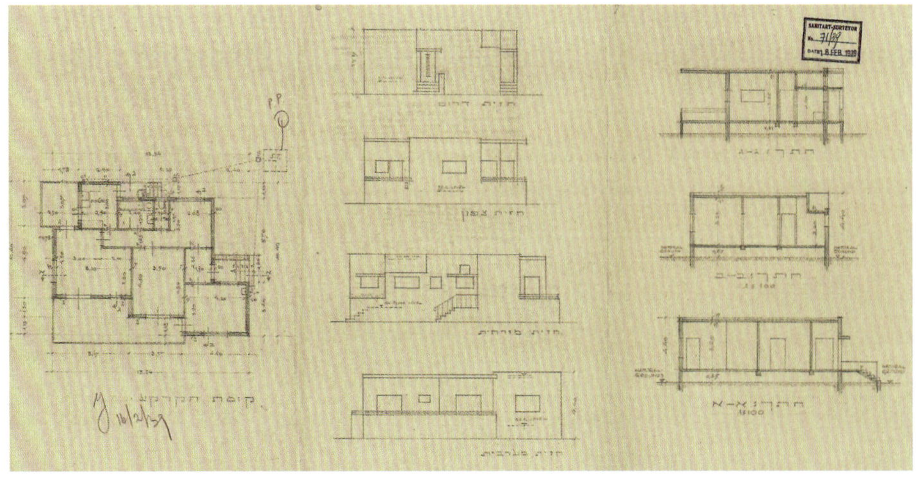

Hadar HaCarmel

The Palestine Land Development Company (PLDC) was a major player in acquiring land and planning Jewish neighborhoods in Haifa. The renowned town planner Patrick Geddes was invited to advise PLDC on new suburbs on Mount Carmel. In 1920 Geddes submitted a report on which Richard Kauffmann, then the head architect of PLDC, based his plans for the Carmel. Geddes proposed a layout in line with the principles the Garden City Movement which was being developed in Europe at the time.

Hadar HaCarmel was established in 1920-21, on slopes just south of the walled town, and the first houses in the neighborhood were built. During the 1920s the area retained the character of a quiet garden suburb and was gradually growing. Most houses were for single families, one or two stories tall and of eclectic architectural style. In 1925 the long-awaited opening of the technical school took place, at the heart of the neighborhood.

Disturbances in August 1929 were a turning point. Jews from mixed neighborhoods in the Old City of Haifa fled to Hadar HaCarmel in search of a safe place. Hadar became overcrowded with homeless families and was cut off from supplies, since the quiet garden suburb had no substantial market or food stores. As a result, Hadar changed into an urban quarter with apartment buildings and commercial uses. The first business center was completed in 1932.

The Immigration of Jews from Europe, especially Germany and Poland, in the 1930s brought great prosperity to Haifa, and to Hadar HaCarmel. Hundreds of apartment buildings were constructed, most of them designed in the International Style, brought from Europe by architects who were educated there. Joseph Klarwein was one of these. Many civic and commercial buildings were also constructed in Hader during this decade. One of them is Beit HaKranot, planned by Klarwein with the first phase completed in 1937.

During the Arab revolt in Palestine (1936-39) Hadar HaCarmel received two large waves of Jewish refugees who fled the mixed neighborhoods of Haifa. The demand for housing reached a record high, while more residential buildings were being constructed and the neighborhood was expanding. Beit Zang (Bialik St. 6) and Beit Gottesman (Nordau Ave. 4), which were designed by Joseph Klarwein, were constructed during that period. These plaster-finished buildings have shops on their ground floor, matching the urban character that evolved in the heart of Hadar HaCarmel at that time.

❾ Beit Gottesmann (1940): residential and commercial building in the city center

Design for a residential building. The arrangement of the furniture gives an idea of how cramped living conditions were at the time

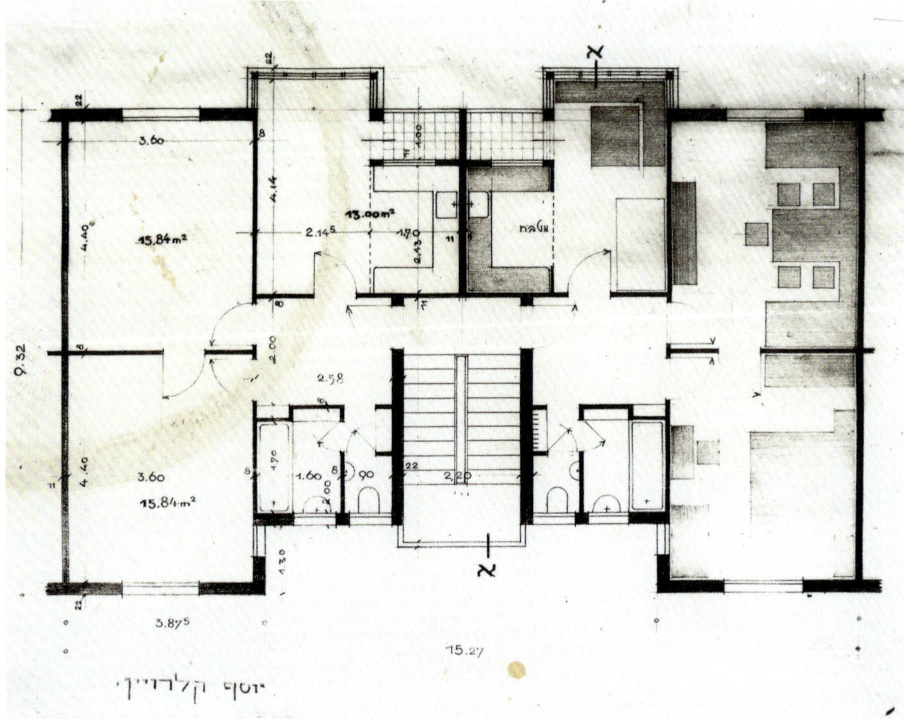

Neighborhoods on Mount Carmel

The neighborhoods on top of Mount Carmel evolved in a different manner to that of Hadar HaCarmel. At the end of World War I the Templars sold most of their properties on Mount Carmel to the PLDC and the Anglo-Palestine Bank. After the war, PDLC offered 150-200 plots for sale for residential development, but little development occurred. Only a few buildings were built during the 1920s on top of Mount Carmel, most of them in Northern Carmel, which was mostly in private hands, and around Karmelheim. The distance from the heart of the town and the steep topography delayed the development of this area.

During the 1930s many of the German Jews who immigrated to Palestine chose to settle in Haifa and on Mount Carmel. Apparently, the local climate and the views from the top of the mountain attracted them. Even though the Jewish population on Mount Carmel was relatively small, it had a significant influence on the economy and culture of the city. Residents there were in many cases business owners and professionals. The houses they built were mostly apartment buildings with plastered facades, intended to be let, designed in contemporary International Style, with spacious verandas and balconies facing the panoramas of the mountain or the sea.

A dominant characteristic of the neighborhoods on top of Mount Carmel is the man-made forest in which the buildings are immersed. This afforestation project was initiated by the Templars, in line with their view of this area as a place for recreation. The project was continued after the land was sold to Jewish organizations, which planted thousands of trees. This fitted in with the approach outlined by Geddes and drawn by Kauffmann, of surrounding every building on every plot with space for a garden, thus creating a unique urban character with a rural atmosphere.

The physical expansion of the city stopped when World War II broke out in 1939. During the war Palestine was cut off from Europe and Haifa port was used for military purposes. Private construction was halted because of a shortage of building materials and quotas set by the government. This brought an era of unprecedented prosperity and growth to an end.

NAHARIYA
A YEKKE SEASIDE RESORT

Sigal Davidi

Beit Ettlinger under construction and when completed in 1938

As children in Nahariya in the late 1970s, my classmates and I used to watch movies on Friday at 15:00 in the Hod cinema. Those shows became our (almost) regular routine. Many of my favorite shopping spots were located in the small commercial center near the cinema: Salon Trude, Trude and Fritz Eckstein's knitwear shop, Photo Nahariya, Dov Lazar's photography shop, Martha's lingerie shop, and David's ticket agency, where you could reserve tickets for shows across Israel. In sixth grade, our summer sports lessons took place in the Galei Galil pool on the beach, whose salty sea water made our eyes burn. Only recently have I learned that the architect Joseph Klarwein had designed all these familiar childhood landmarks. Not often does the professional meet the personal, and it is a pleasure to introduce Klarwein's Nahariya projects.

Early projects: A villa, a beach restaurant and a swimming pool

Nahariya is the northernmost town on Israel's Mediterranean coast. It was established in 1934 as an agricultural village by Jewish German immigrants, Yekkes, most of whom arrived from Offenbach, Breslau, and other towns in Hesse and Silesia[1]. They escaped Germany due to rising antisemitism and restrictions placed on Jews when Hitler came to power. As Zionists, they chose to immigrate to Mandatory Palestine[2]. Most of them were middle-class free professionals. In Palestine, they became farmers.

Immigrants from Germany often preferred architects of German origin, who shared their language and cultural background, to design their homes in Palestine. The residents of Nahariya were no exception. Most of the architects who planned buildings in Nahariya lived and worked in Haifa, a mixed Arab-Jewish city that experienced significant development momentum in the 1930s. Among them were the renowned architects Adolf Rading and Gideon Kaminka. Klarwein, who was living in Haifa at the time, was commissioned to build a home in Nahariya for the lawyer Fritz Shlomo Ettlinger, who arrived in 1937[3]. Those were times when many newcomers made their homes in the little village of Nahariya in the "Lift", a large wooden container used to transport their belongings from Germany. Others built small basic houses with tiled pitched roofs. The size and design of Ettlinger House stood out among the modest homes surrounding it. Klarwein used a distinct modernist vocabulary – square masses, a flat roof, and horizontal cornices. He also took the local terrain and climate into account.

He designed two terraces on the ground floor: one shaded by the floor above it, and the other by a large pergola. Another terrace on the first floor had a view of the sea. Unlike other buildings in Nahariya and modernist coastal buildings in Palestine, the house's walls were clad with sawed stone slabs rather than plaster, possibly as protection against the salty sea winds. The house was nicknamed "The Palace" for its size, design, and elegance.

Despite the prominence of Ettlinger House, Klarwein did not plan other residences in Nahariya. However, it seems that his acquaintance with Ettlinger helped him secure commissions for public projects there. In 1940, the newly established Nahariya Beach Development Cooperative Society (Galei Galil) raised funds to develop the beach and make Nahariya a resort town[4]. Ettlinger was one of the initiators of the cooperative and a board member. In 1944, the cooperative commissioned Klarwein to plan a beach restaurant named Casino, and in 1946, he was hired to plan a large public bath house by the beach and a swimming pool of Olympic dimensions.

This opened in 1950 and won high praise in the press. Presumably, Klarwein enjoyed working with the people of Nahariya who, like him, were new immigrants, spoke the same language, and shared similar traditions and culture – Klarwein, too, was a Yekke.

Twenty years after designing the Ettlinger House, Klarwein returned to Nahariya to plan the town's most important square.

Casino (1944) and swimming pool (1946)

A new civic square

In 1933, engineer Alfred Ciffrin and architect Grünwald, both from Haifa, laid out a master plan for Nahariya[5].

It envisioned a modern agricultural settlement with a system of straight streets that ran parallel and perpendicular to the coast. A main road along the Ga'aton River connected the Haifa-Beirut Road on the town's east with the coast in the west. Two centers were planned along this road: The one on the east, near the national road, was to feature workshops and industries, and the one on the west, near the coast, was intended for educational and cultural institutions and an agricultural research center[6]. The eastern center design comprised two rectangular squares surrounded by buildings on opposite sides of the Ga'aton road.

In Israel's first decade of statehood, Nahariya absorbed numerous new immigrants, and its population grew from about 1,500 in 1948 to 18,000 in 1958[7]. As early as 1950, the council's area of jurisdiction was quadrupled to enable accommodating 50,000 residents. A newspaper item from 1955 mentioned that every old-time citizen welcomed ten new immigrants[8]. New neighborhoods, schools, commercial and cultural facilities were built. Nahariya changed. While some residents continued farming, it primarily evolved into a small, highly popular resort town.

As part of the development momentum, the local council advanced the construction of the eastern center, which had not been built since the 1933 master plan, and was covered by trees. In 1956, the council invited Klarwein to prepare a detailed urban plan for the center, define its uses, prepare an outline plan, and design its buildings. Official documents and plans from that time mention it as the Civic Square, indicating the project's importance. Klarwein placed commercial buildings around the two squares' perimeters and a large public building in each. Rassco Construction Company was in charge of constructing the complex, beginning with the northern square. Klarwein was also commissioned to design all the square buildings.

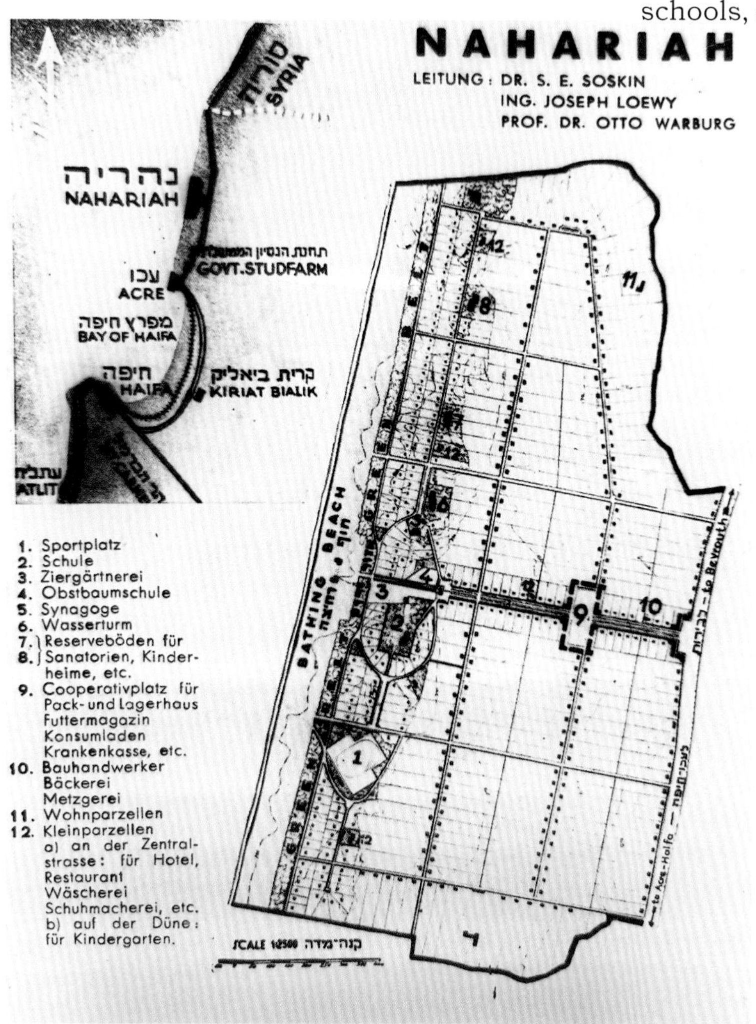

The masterplan for the overall development of Nahariya from the year 1933: on the left, the beach; on the right, the highway; and in the center, along the main Ga'aton Boulevard, the planned city center

The Rassco Center

The Jewish Agency German Department established Rassco (an acronym for Rural and Suburban Settlement Company, now a brand name) in June 1934 to provide housing for middle-class immigrants from Germany. During the British Mandate period, it mainly built agricultural settlements. After the State's establishment, it directed its resources to building urban neighborhoods. In the mid-1950s, Rassco turned to building small commercial centers in cities and villages that absorbed new immigrants with investments of wealthy Jews abroad[9]. It built commercial centers in towns across Israel, including Safed, Acre, Hatzor HaGlilit, Nazrat Ilit, Afula, Beit Shean, Tiberias, Eilat, and Nahariya. The financier of the new center in Nahariya was a Mexican investment group "Mexico-Nahariya Development Company". The outlines of most centers were similar: A U-shaped single-story building with an inner open space, often with a shaded arcade on the commercial ground floor. The centers became known as Rassco Centers, and many have kept their name to this day.

In Nahariya, the U-shaped building followed the Rassco centers' building type. The ground floor featured about 30 shops, and the first floor about 60 offices. Klarwein planned a simple, unassuming modernist building, typical of Israel's early period. He included various shading solutions in each wing. An arcade of round columns ran the length of the western wing, adding elegance to the building. Above the shops facing the street he designed shading cornices.

Ventilation was a central theme in the building. All the shop fronts had upper ventilation shutters in addition to the display

Eastern wing of the Rassco building

Western wing of the Rassco building with water basins, later converted to flowerbeds

windows. Large plant boxes and a small ornamental pond dotted the square. In 1959, soon after the completion of the commercial center's two wings, shops opened there, most of them for the benefit of the residents: a café, a shoe shop, a pharmacy, a butcher shop, women's lingerie, and a knitwear shop. It became the city's most vibrant commercial center.

The local council moved its offices to the first floor, awaiting the construction of its dedicated building. In 1961, Nahariya was officially declared a city, and in 1962, Klarwein began planning the second part of the civic square on the southern side of the Ga'aton road, now already a boulevard. In this square, he planned a town hall next to the commercial buildings. However, in the end, he did not receive the commission. His last prominent project in Nahariya was a large cinema house inaugurated in 1962 next to the northern side of the Rassco center.

Hod Cinema

Cinema Hod (Hebrew for splendor, majesty) fitted its name with its 1080-seat hall. It was another Rassco joint project with the Mexican investment group. The building of such a large and luxurious cinema was intended to establish Nahariya as the central recreation and entertainment town in Western Galilee. It was Nahariya's central hub for multiple purposes. In addition to films, it also hosted theater plays, concerts, lectures, and conferences, including political ones. Its symmetrical plan featured a spacious foyer on the ground floor with a snack bar and a café, a 640-seat hall, dressing rooms, a large stage, an orchestra pit (never built), and an underground shelter. The gallery had another 440 seats, restrooms, and a makeup room. Klarwein's interior design was classy, even European, and not typical of small, provincial Nahariya. Shiny, dark-and-light widening marble stripes covered the walls.

In his early plans, Klarwein also designed a symmetrical main facade that gave the building a static and stable look, recalling his other public buildings (Dagon Silo, the Knesset). He designed a rectangular mass with a central poster space and a balcony, and three lines of round openings on both sides. The building that was eventually constructed remained symmetrical but was more dynamic. It had diamond-shaped openings, possibly influenced by the design of Dagon Silo which he planned around the same time.

Afterword

By the 1970s, Nahariya had lost its Yekke character[10]. Almost none of Klarwein's fingerprints have survived in my childhood town's landscape and historiography. Over the years, Ettlinger House and Casino Restaurant were demolished. Hod cinema closed in the early 2000s. The building underwent changes that made it unrecognizable, and now houses stores and offices. Rassco Center still stands but has been neglected. Numerous additions mask the original building's qualities. My research on Klarwein's Nahariya projects, which began with only two, uncovered many others. Even the Municipality staff were surprised to learn that Klarwein was one of the town planners and contributed much to its early development[11]. The research and this exhibition bring to light Klarwein's diverse work of nationwide significance. Here I had the chance to share some of his peripheral work which is, in a way, a part of me.

1 Jewish German immigrants nicknamed "Yekkes" (or Jeckes in German) after their suit jackets (Jacke), rarely worn in Eretz Yisrael. **2** Palestine under the British Mandate (1920-1948). **3** Kreppel 2011, pp.230-232 (Hebrew). **4** Kreppel 2011, pp. 554-556; Lehmann 1960, p. 95. **5** Kreppel, Klaus (2005). Nahariyya – das Dorf der "Jeckes": die Gründung der Mittelstandssiedlung für deutsche Einwanderer in Eretz Israel 1934/1935. Tefen: The Open Museum, Tefen Industrial Park. **6** Efrat, Elisha (1977). "Has Nahariya remained a yekke town?" Horizons in Geography, 3: 141-150 (Hebrew). **7** Hauser, Shmuel. "Nahariya – from 1,200 to 18,000 people in ten years". Al Hamishmar, 20 June 1958, p. 8 (Hebrew). **8** "Every old-time citizen integrated ten new immigrants" Davar, 15 June 1955,

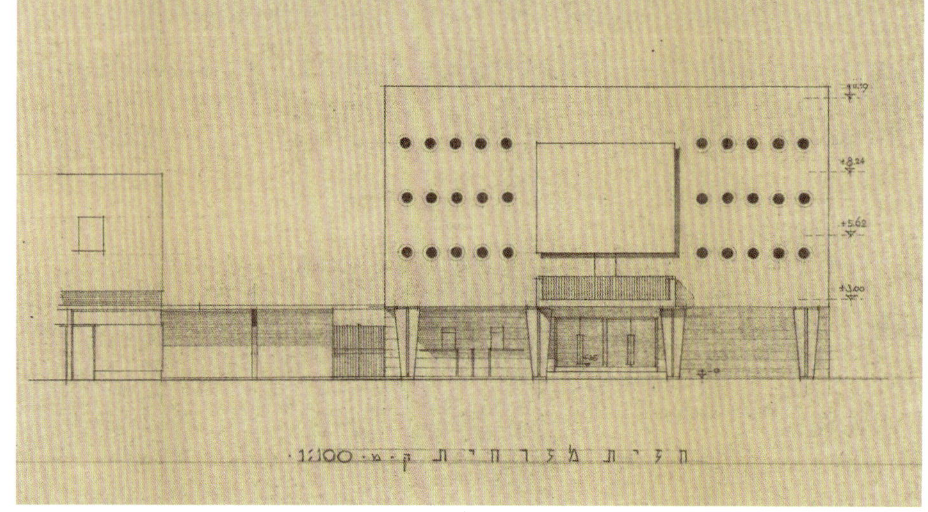

Cinema Hod (1962). Interior, main facade and elevation from the building submission

p. 2 (Hebrew). **9** Azai, P. "Rassco: half-jubilee and complete plans." Haaretz, 15 June 1955, p. 4. **10** Efrat, Elisha (1977). "Has Nahariya remained a yekke town?" Horizons in Geography, 3: 141-150 (Hebrew). **11** I thank Maor Turgeman, Head of Urban Renewal Administration at Nahariya Municipality, for his assistance in this research.

MEMORIAL ARCHITECTURE AND SANCTIFIED SPACE

Doron Bar

Unveiling of the tombstone of Chaim Arlozoroff (6 June 1934)

In many parts of the world, nations have used the tombs of visionaries, heroes, and leaders to shape national identity. Israel is no exception, with its approach reflecting the historical, cultural, and political contexts surrounding the state's establishment in 1948. The graves of prominent figures serve not only as memorials but also as sites of collective memory, reinforcing a shared narrative and fostering a sense of belonging among citizens.

In a relatively short span of time before and after 1948, numerous "holy places" emerged in Israel, all connected to the mythical Jewish past and Zionism. In this context, cemeteries played a crucial role, with the graves of renowned individuals becoming heritage sites and national symbols. The remains of exemplary figures were brought to Israel from the Diaspora and joined "local" notables buried in symbolic cemeteries in Tel Aviv, Jerusalem, Degania, and Kinneret. An important part of this symbolic and heroic landscape is represented by the graves of heroes and heroines who sacrificed their lives for Israel's independence. Their graves, along with the monuments erected nearby, have become prominent civic-Zionist pilgrimage sites.

The Jewish and the Zionist Traditions of Commemoration

Throughout the history of the Land of Israel, graves have served as a means of sanctifying space. Unlike Christianity, which often establishes holy places based on myths of miracles and revelation, Jewish believers have traditionally sanctified the land through the tombs of kings, prophets, and sages from the Mishnah and Talmud. This vertical connection allowed believers to reach back through historical layers, evoking the biblical and Talmudic eras.

Similarly, Zionism, since its emergence in the late nineteenth century, adopted this approach, consecrating space through graves and cemeteries. However, while Jewish sacred spaces developed organically from "below" over time, the Zionist graves discussed in this article were all part of a public initiative "from above." Before 1948, these initiatives were driven by Zionist organizations, and following the establishment of the State of Israel, they continued under the auspices of state organizations.

The intent behind designing these graves as national holy places was clear: they were meant to occupy a central role in the emerging symbolic landscape of the State of Israel and to appropriate it as distinctly Zionist. Unlike Biblical sites such as Joseph's Tomb or Shmuel's Tomb, which were not claimed by the Zionists, the graves that were emphasized included those of Zionist visionaries, heroes, and politicians, as well as the graves of the fallen—individuals who sacrificed their lives in heroic battles both before and after the 1948 War of Independence.

Joseph Klarwein played a significant role in this extensive and vigorous institutional activity. Although he did not immigrate to Palestine for explicitly Zionist reasons, he quickly became engaged in Zionist efforts and actively contributed to the establishment of the State of Israel. Klarwein designed some of Israel's most important civic symbols: In 1951 Mount Herzl, the resting place of Theodor Herzl, the visionary of the Jewish State, and in 1957 the Knesset building, the seat of the Israeli Parliament.

Commemorating Notable People in Tel-Aviv

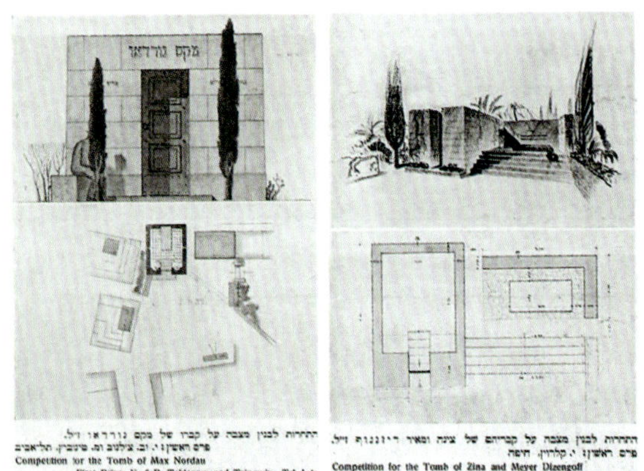

Graves of Max Nordau (left) and Meir and Zina Dizengoff (right). Publication of the entries to the respective competitions

The historic cemetery of Tel Aviv, "the first Hebrew city", is where Klarwein began his work in commemoration and remembrance. Many of the city's founders, along with writers, politicians, and prominent figures in the history of Zionism, are interred here[1]. Klarwein's inaugural public project in Israel was the design of a tombstone in this cemetery – for Chaim Arlosoroff, head of the political department of the Jewish Agency. Arlosoroff was murdered in 1933 on Tel Aviv beach, an event that sent shock waves through the country. His grave was placed in the western, "prestigious" part of the cemetery, next to that of Max Nordau, the first grave in the "Renowned People" and "Greatest of the Nation" section. In 1934, Klarwein won the competition to design Arlosoroff's tombstone in collaboration with Haifa architect Robert Friedmann. They created a simple rectangular gray stone block, devoid of decorations, likely influenced by the International Style that was popular at the time. The tombstone was placed asymmetrically atop the elevated grave surface and engraved with Arlosoroff's name, along with the dates of his birth and death[2].

Klarwein was also responsible for the adjacent tomb of Meir and Zina Dizengoff, the mayor of Tel Aviv and his wife, built in 1937. He designed the tomb as a narrow-elevated square with five steps leading up to it. The tombstone was placed on the right side of the square, surrounded by walls made of smooth white stones. On

Graves of Max Nordau (left), Meir and Zina Dizengoff (middle, both 1937) and Shaul Tschernichovsky (1943)

the middle wall, behind the tombstone, the names of the couple were inscribed in prominent bronze letters[3]. Klarwein received praise for this work, which was not only a significant professional achievement but also helped establish his reputation as a talented Zionist architect. Some even claimed that Dizengoff's grave was the most impressive tombstone in the cemetery[4].

When Shaul Tchernichovsky, one of the great Hebrew Zionist poets, passed away in 1943, he was interred in Trumpeldor Cemetery, as the old cemetery is also known, next to Dizengoff and Nordau. Tel Aviv Municipality invited Klarwein and Benjamin Chelanov (who designed Nordau's grave) to design Tchernichovsky's tomb. The monumental headstone consists of blocks of stone leaning against each other. The front part of the tombstone, sloping east, features Tchernichovsky's name along with the dates of his birth and death in protruding letters. At the family's request, many of the poet's manuscripts were placed in a marble box within the tomb's foundations[5].

Design study for the grave of Shaul Tschernichovsky by Klarwein

Klarwein had now designed three of the most prominent graves in the city's cemetery. Despite their simplicity and modesty—or perhaps because of it—the straight lines of the tombstones, along with the absence of carvings, decorations, and symbols, made these graves deeply moving, transforming them into significant Zionist symbols.

Cemeteries for the Fallen

Not only renowned Zionist humans warranted special graves; those who fell in the struggle for the realization of Zionism and the establishment of a Jewish state in the Land of Israel also deserved recognition. During the Yeshuv period (British Mandate period), dedicated burial plots were created across the country for those who died in battles and Arab revolts (meoraut). Following the 1948 Israeli War of Independence, military cemeteries were established nationwide to honor fallen soldiers[6]. Klarwein was actively involved in this process, designing two important commemorative sections in Nachalat Yitzhak Cemetery in Tel Aviv. Inaugurated in 1932 in East Tel Aviv, the cemetery became a significant Zionist (and later Israeli) commemorative space. Initially dedicated to the victims of Arab revolts and battles before 1948, it later honored those who fell during the 1948 War.

In 1942, Klarwein won a competition to construct a memorial for citizens of Tel Aviv who lost their lives during the 1936-1939 Arab revolt[7]. Klarwein designed a flight of stairs that leads to an entrance plaza, where a tall memorial monument was erected engraved with the inscription "To the Victims of the Riots". Another flight of stairs leads to an elevated plot, across which four rows of tombs are arranged in complete uniformity bordered by neatly shaped shrubs[8].

Klarwein also planned the nearby mass grave where the 128 victims of the bombings in Tel Aviv during World War II were buried. The ceremony to unveil the tombstones took place in August 1953. A modest memorial plaque was placed at the site, alongside seven rows of uniformly shaped graves.

Klarwein's designs for graves of the fallen in Tel Aviv had significant public impact and established him as a leading architect of memorial sites in Israel. This laid the ground for his most important work in this field: The memorials on Mount Herzl.

First design for the graveyard of the Tel Aviv victims of the 1936-39 riots, not realized

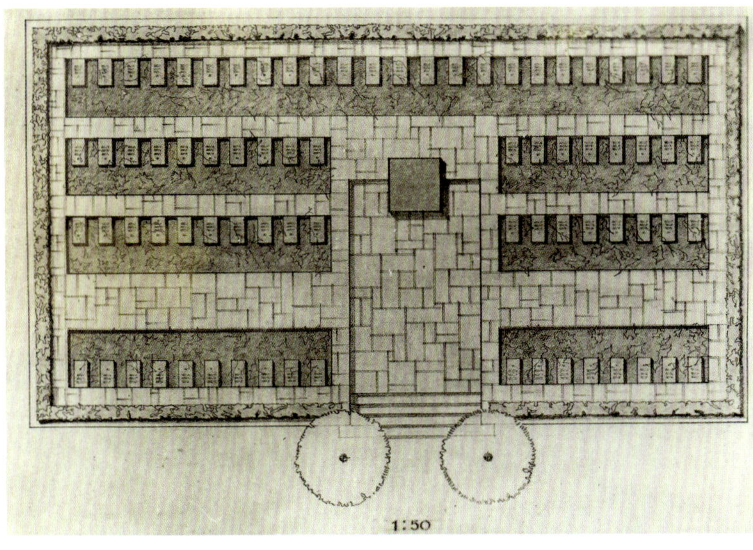

Second design for the graveyard of the Tel Aviv victims of the 1936-39 riots (1942)

Mount Herzl and the tomb of Theodor Herzl

Mount Herzl is Israel's most significant civic holy site. Located in Western Jerusalem, it is the final resting place of Theodor Herzl, the visionary of the Jewish state, as well as members of his family, Presidents of the Zionist Organization, and Ze'ev Jabotinsky, founder of the Revisionist movement. Klarwein was responsible for planning the tombs of all these prominent personalities.

Theodor Herzl passed away in 1904 and was buried in Vienna. In his will, he expressed a desire to be buried in the Land of Israel, but this wish was fulfilled only after the establishment of the State of Israel. In early 1949, it was decided that he would be interred at the top of the highest mountain in Western Jerusalem, which later became known as Mount Herzl. Due to the limited time before the burial ceremony, members of the "Committee for Bringing Herzl's Remains" opted not to construct a permanent structure over his grave immediately. Klarwein was tasked with planning the design for the grave itself, with the understanding that an architectural competition for the design of the tomb and its surroundings would be announced after the ceremony[9].

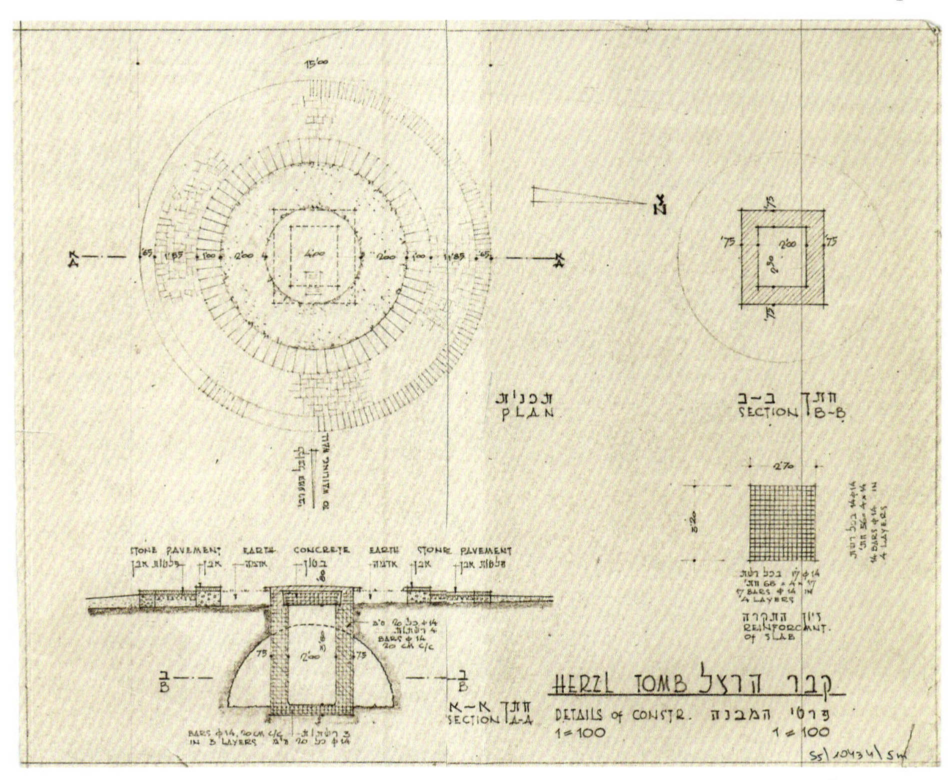

Burial chamber of the Herzl Memorial. Drawing by Klarwein (1949)

By August 1949 a large pit had been excavated at the summit of the mountain, and an "armored" concrete coffer was constructed within it. "This coffer is considered one of the strongest structures in Israel, surrounded by six tons of iron. It was designed to withstand even aerial bombardments, ensuring that the grave would remain secure", according to a report at the time[10]. In a distinctive design, Klarwein placed the tomb at the center of a circular raised stone structure. In accordance with Jewish tradition, the underground sarcophagus was oriented toward the east, specifically toward the Old City and the site of the destroyed Temple[11]. This circular design reflected Klarwein's desire to emphasize the tomb's unique location at the mountain's summit, highlighting the stunning panoramic view of Jerusalem and the surrounding Judean hills. Additionally, it appears that Klarwein had already envisioned the tent (Ohel), the building he wanted to construct over the tomb.

In 1932, while still in Germany, Klarwein had worked on a design for a memorial honoring the fallen German soldiers of World War I near Bad Berka. He imagined a domed structure with a diameter of 36 meters, supported by 48 pillars, and planned to place a black memorial monument at its center—described as "a sacrificial bowl of notable stones"—elevated above its surroundings[12]. Although this earlier plan did not come to fruition, it appears to have significantly influenced Klarwein when he designed the surroundings of Herzl's

Temporary canopy for the reinterment of Theodor Herzl on Mount Herzl on 17 August 1949

grave. In this case, he also envisioned a domed structure emphasizing the grave's importance.

Klarwein played a role in preparing the setting for Herzl's burial ceremony in August 1949. He designed a special wooden structure that was erected in advance over the grave. This canopy, adorned with plants and draped in flags, featured a unique facility on which Herzl's coffin was to be suspended before being lowered into the ground.

On 17 August 1949 Herzl's coffin was covered with 300 bags of soil brought from various cities, settlements and Kibbutzim around the country, and he was interred in the grave that had been prepared in advance. The tomb was now embellished by a circular flower bed, with poles and a chain marking the area where visitors could stand. A headstone at the site bore the inscription: "In this place will be erected the tent and the memorial for the grave of Herzl, who was brought here to eternal rest on the 2nd day of the month of Av, 1949"[13].

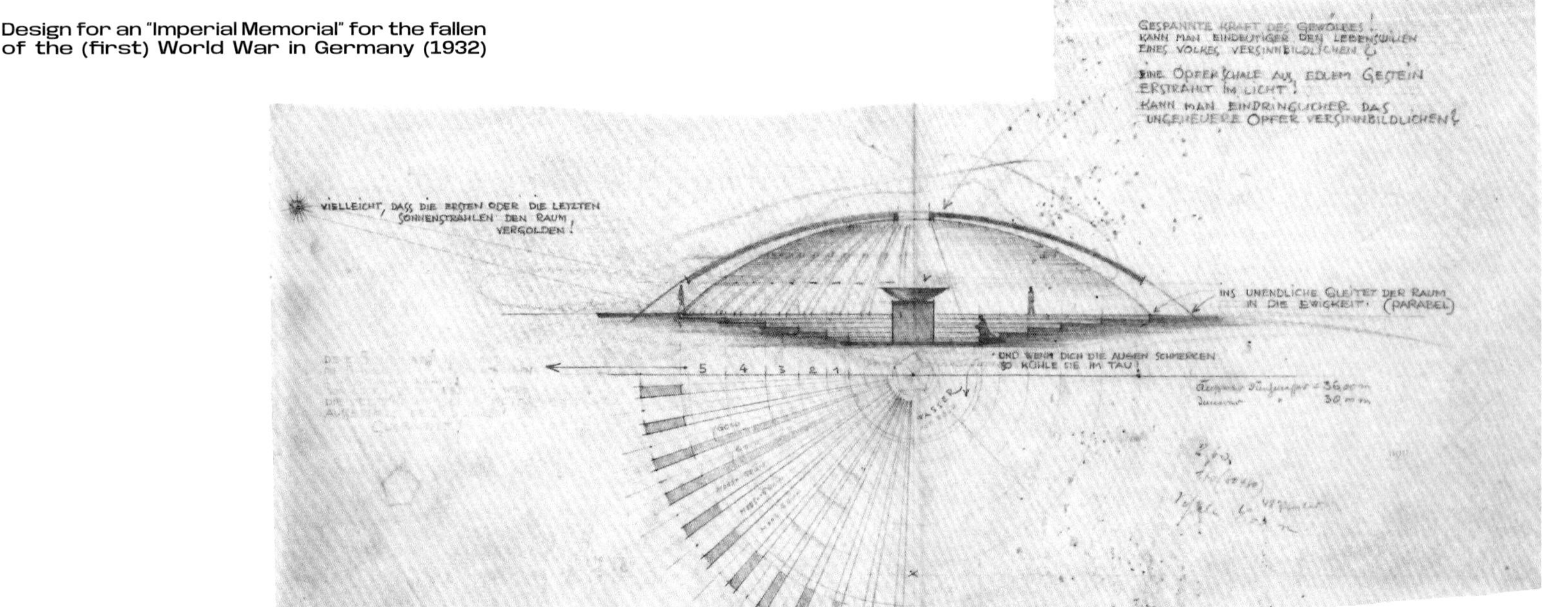

Design for an "Imperial Memorial" for the fallen of the (first) World War in Germany (1932)

Provisional grave of Theodor Herzl with flowerbeds (1949) / Models of the Herzl Memorial from the architectural competition (1951)

In September 1950, the World Zionist Organization announced a competition for the design of Herzl's grave, as well as the burial site for his successor in the leadership of the Zionist movement, David Wolffsohn. The plan was intended to express "the feelings of respect and admiration that the people of Israel have for Binyamin Ze'ev Herzl" and to integrate harmoniously with the landscape and history of Jerusalem[14].

More than sixty proposals were submitted. Klarwein's "ultra-modern and revolutionary" design was ultimately selected. The judges explained that "a grave containing the remains of a person who created such a unique idea and movement must also have a unique shape. This [Mount Herzl] is not the place for existing designs and traditional forms"[15]. Klarwein's drawings for the planned tomb did not survive, and we lack a written description of it. However, a photograph of the plan is preserved[16] as well as two models[17].

Klarwein revived his ideas from the 1930s, linking the memorial site he had envisioned in Germany with the one he proposed for Jerusalem. He planned to construct a dome six meters high and thirty-two meters in diameter over Herzl's grave, supported by forty-four arches – one for each year of Herzl's life. He designed the structure to include openings between the ribs, allowing for passage and views of the surrounding landscape. Under the dome, Klarwein proposed a round tombstone, elevated above its surroundings, situated at the head of a series of five circular steps. These steps symbolize the "Gathering of Israel" (Kibbutz Galuyot) from the five Diasporas, transforming future visitors into "pilgrims" who would come to venerate the sacred tomb.

Site plan of Mount Herzl with the grave in the center, competition entry by Klarwein

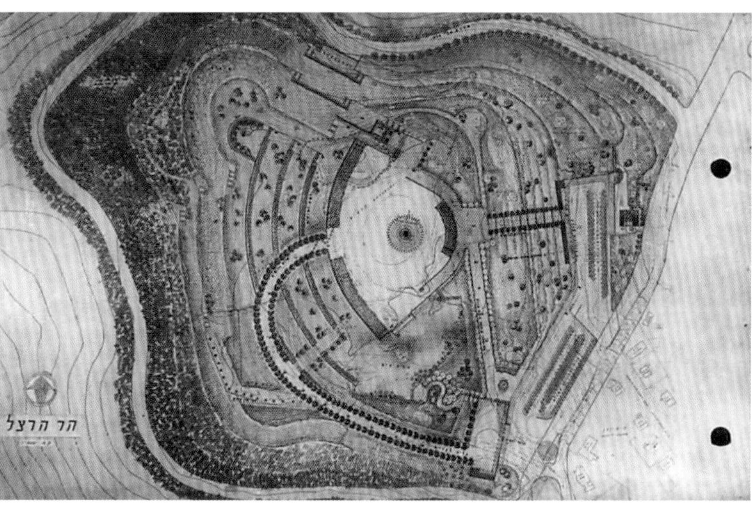

Klarwein proposed constructing the dome from reinforced concrete rather than local limestone, a material

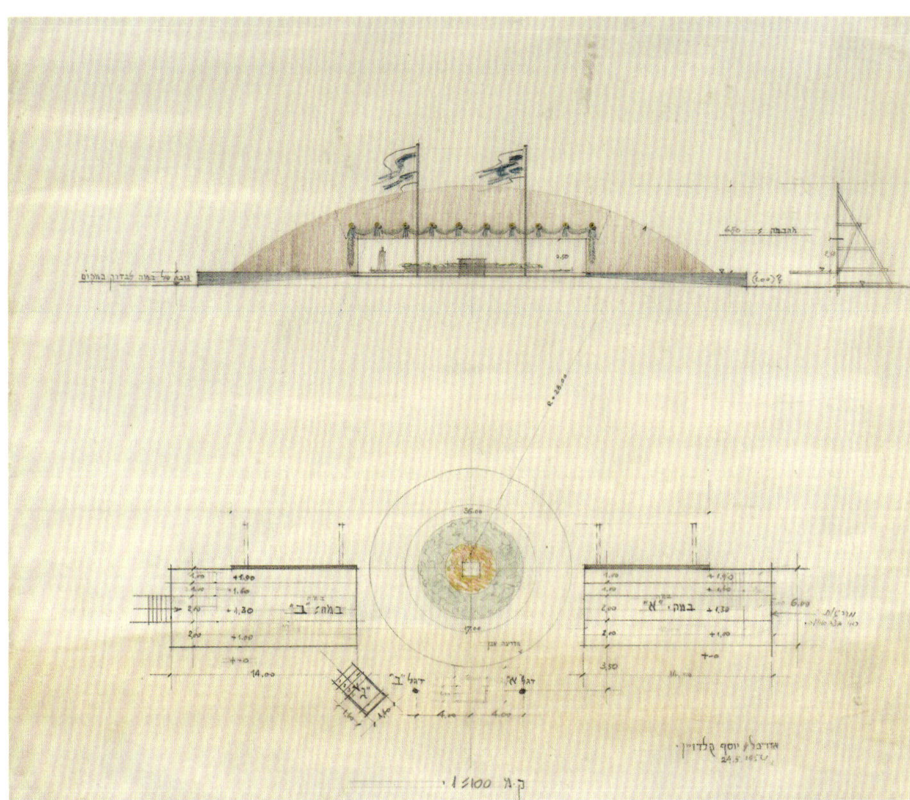

Ephemeral architecture for the commemoration of the 50th anniversary of Theodor Herzl's death, 1954 / Model of Mount Herzl, still with the dome, after initial replanning by Klarwein

Model of Herzl Memorial (around 1959) / Herzl Memorial – situation around 1964

favored by the Zionist movement. He envisioned covering the interior of the dome with mosaic. Klarwein also designed the surrounding, including a ceremonial staircase that would guide visitors from the gathering area at the foot of Mount Herzl to the tomb. He also incorporated a ceremonial path for formal processions, as well as a system of terraces and pathways to enhance the visitor experience of the surrounding views. At the summit of the mountain, he envisioned a semi-circular square facing Jerusalem, intended to serve as a ceremonial space.

Klarwein was also involved in arranging ceremonies at Mount Herzl. The 20th of Tammuz 1954 marked the 50th anniversary of

Herzl's passing and the start of "Herzl's Year." A ceremony attended by thousands took place next to the grave, with the setting designed by Klarwein. A wooden canopy decorated with flags was constructed over Herzl's grave, and above it, an arch was built, reflecting the dimensions and shape of the dome that was intended to be constructed[18].

During the mid-1950s, various development works were undertaken on Mount Herzl. The surrounding areas were improved, pathways were marked, and an entrance building featuring seven gates was constructed, symbolizing the seven stars on Herzl's flag. However, the main component of Klarwein's plan – the construction of the dome over Herzl's tomb – was not realized at that time[19].

The ongoing delays led Klarwein to develop an alternative plan. On 15 July 1960, marking the hundredth anniversary of Herzl's birth, the temporary sign was removed and replaced with a smooth black and square basalt stone over a black pedestal, engraved solely with Herzl's name. On that occasion, the ceremonial plaza at the top of the mountain was redesigned and expanded. The tomb was situated in the eastern part of the square, slightly elevated from its surroundings, and was surrounded by flower beds, open to the east. The central area of the plaza was expanded and designated for Independence Day ceremonies. The World Zionist Organization declared: "With the construction of the tombstone and the completion of the park, Mount Herzl has received its final form, and the planning work, which took about ten years, is nearly complete"[20].

Vladimir (Ze'ev) Jabotinsky's Tomb

Vladimir (Ze'ev) Jabotinsky, the founder of the Revisionist movement, head of Beitar, and commander of the Etzel underground, passed away in the USA in 1940. He was buried in the New Montefiore Jewish Cemetery on Long Island. In his will, he specified that he wished to be buried wherever he died and that his remains should not be transferred to the Land of Israel unless ordered by the eventual Jewish government of the country[21]. The implementation of Jabotinsky's request was delayed for many years and was completed only in 1963. In 1964, Operation "Ze'ev Jabotinsky Returns to the Homeland" was launched, led by a committee tasked with organizing the funeral of the Jabotinsky couple and their burial in Israel. The chosen location for their grave was in the western part of Mount Herzl, with a stunning view of the Judean mountains. The board of trustees appointed to put up a gravestone turned to Klarwein for the design of this section of the mountain, which extended over a dunam and a half (1500 sqm).

Klarwein designed the site simply yet elegantly: a flight of stairs leads to the tomb, which is positioned in the western part of the square on a raised platform. The headstone is composed of smooth black marble slabs stacked one on top of the other, with the names of Yohana and Ze'ev Jabotinsky engraved on the upper block. The grave was adorned with a bed of flowers, and Klarwein designed a paved ceremonial plaza around it[22].

Jabotinsky grave – current situation

Summary

Klarwein played a vital and active role in the commemoration of key figures in Zionism as well as of fallen soldiers. His contributions were instrumental in shaping the memorial landscape of the State of Israel. Participating in public competitions for designing tombs was essential for Klarwein. It enabled him to build his reputation not only as a designer of homes and public buildings but also as a key contributor to the foundational symbols of the Israeli nation. His expertise was further recognized through his role as a judge in several significant competitions, including the design of the tomb for Chaim Weizmann, the First President of the State of Israel[23].

In 1966, Klarwein served as the chairman for the Israel Prize Committee for Architecture, which awarded the prestigious prize to Al Mansfeld and Dora Gad for their design of the Israel Museum[24].

The tombstones and grave plots designed by Klarwein were a central and significant component of the Zionist-Israeli memorial landscape. He connected his professional work to the memory of visionaries and heroes in various dimensions—through the materials he chose, his unique architecture and style, the inscriptions he engraved, and the iconography he employed. Klarwein's approach to these memorial sites was intentionally modest; he avoided transforming the burials into colossal monuments, recognizing that the cemeteries he worked in represented a delicate interplay of personal and national-Zionist memory.

An exception is Herzl's tomb, which Klarwein initially designed in a rather monumental style, markedly different from the simpler tombs of Arlosoroff, Dizengoff, and Tchernichovsky. However, it soon became evident that the grand plan he envisioned for Mount Herzl, including a large dome, was not suitable for the 1950s Israeli reality and spirit. Over time, the design evolved to become much simpler and more modest, aligning it more closely with the other tombs he had designed. Ultimately, Klarwein emphasized the importance and uniqueness of the grave sites he designed not through architectural grandeur, but through simplicity. This approach fostered a meaningful connection between the tombs and their surroundings, allowing Klarwein to create a "sacred" space that stood apart from the ordinary. Through his skillful design, he crafted a Zionist and Israeli sanctified territory that resonates with significance and respect.

1 Maoz Azaryahu, A Place for Memory: The Creation of a national Pantheon at Tel Aviv's Old Cemetery in the Yishuv Period, Haifa: The Reuven Chaikin Chair for GeoStrategy, 2015. **2** "The unveiling of Arlozoroff's Z"L Tombstone", Yediut Tel-Aviv, 15.6.1934. **3** "Dizengoff Memorial Day", Davar, 13.9.1937. **4** "Dizengoff Monument Unveiled on First Anniversary of Death", Palestine Post, 13.9.1937. **5** "Unveiling Shaul Tchernichovsky's Z"L tombstone", Haaretz, 10.10.1945. **6** Maoz Azaryahu, The Architecture of the Military Cemeteries: The First Years, Tel Aviv: Misrad Habitachon, 2012, pp. 10-19. **7** "Declaration", Hatzofe, 28.1.1942. **8** "Results of the competition for the mass grave's tombstone in Nachalat Yitzhak", Yediut Tel-Aviv, 15.3.1943. "Final plan for the mass grave", Hatzofe, 22.10.1942. **9** For the transfer of Herzl's Remains, September 1949, CZA, S5/10416; for Klarwein's design of the tomb: CZA, S5/10434-5M. **10** "Work preparing Herzl's resting place is finalizing", Haboker, 29.7.1949. CZA, PHPS\1337489 for photos of construction. **11** "Herzl Tomb", 1:100, no date, CZA, S5/10434-5M. **12** Klarwein's drawing of the Bad Berka are stored in CZA, A a455/61. **13** CZA, KKL14\34-31 **14** World Zionist Organization announcement of the competition for the design of Herzl's tomb, September 1950, CZA, S5/10429 **15** "Exhibition of Herzl's tomb plans", Haaretz, 25.7.1951; International Design Competition for Herzl Monument (jfc.org.il) **16** ISA, G-5-5595 **17** YBZ_0651_062 **18** Joseph Klarwein, plan, 1:100, 24.5.1954, CZA, S113M/2752/2. **19** "Second stage in the building of Herzl's tomb is nearing completion", Davar, 11.7.1955. **20** "Memorandum", 16.2.1960, CZA, S5/11337. **21** Jabotinsky Institute Archive, A1-1/1/15, Yosef Lamm to Yitzhak Ben-Zvi, 7 May 1958. Another version of the will is kept in: ISA, N-9/2. **22** Klarwein's plans: S113M/2750, 3-7. **23** "Chaim Weizmann Memorial Committee", Al Hamishmar, 31.7.1953. **24** "Art (Architecture)", Hayom, 29.4.1966.

THE DAGON SILOS

LANDMARK OF HAIFA

Dafna Berger Shperling

Site plan from the official submission for the fourth and final extension of the silo (1968)

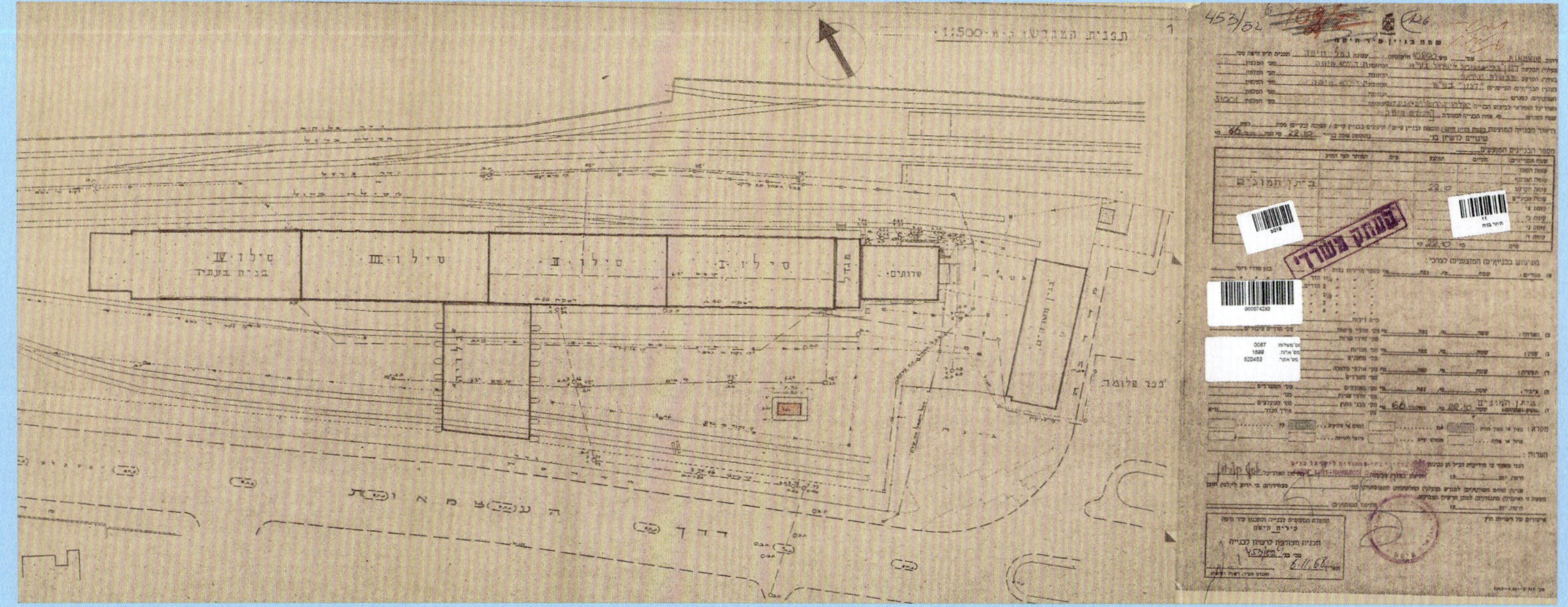

Dagon[1] Grain Silo is a uniform and massive industrial structure built of fair faced reinforced concrete – an iconic landmark of the port city of Haifa. It was the tallest building in Israel when it was first built from 1952 to 1955 and for decades the main entry point for grain imported by Israel. Even today, after about 70 years of operation, it is still considered an efficient facility of international standard. People who encounter this structure cannot remain indifferent: they either become enthusiastic fans – or think it should be demolished. The construction of the complex spanned decades, involving many professional engineers and architects, but its exterior design is attributed to Joseph Klarwein. This article will explore what Klarwein's contribution to this important project was.

Urban context

View across the Old Town and the harbor of Haifa with the Dagon Silos on the left edge

A town-planning scheme for the reclaimed area was prepared by the architects Albert Clifford Holliday (1897-1960) and Robert P.S. Hubbard (1910-1965). This included the design of facades of buildings on the northern side of Kingsway (today's HaAtzma'ut Road or Independence Road), stretching 800 meters where once there had been open sea. This urban design project gained international renown for its considerable scale and contemporary architectural style and details. It was constructed in less than five years starting in 1936 while maintaining cooperation between the public and private sectors, but never completed during politically and economically troubled times. On the western end of this scheme a new central passenger railway station was constructed in harmony with the design of Kingsway, fronted by a public square named in honor of Lord Herbert Plumer (1857-1932), the high commissioner of Palestine. Other buildings planned around Plumer Square included a post office, a hotel, a police station and a bank. Of these, only the latter was eventually built in accordance with the original scheme[2]. Today, the Dagon Silo still towers over the western side of Plumer Square.

Klarwein was not only in charge of designing the exterior of the silo, but also of town planning scheme no. 931[3]. This dealt with the

South elevation of the silos from the official submission for the fourth extension (1968)

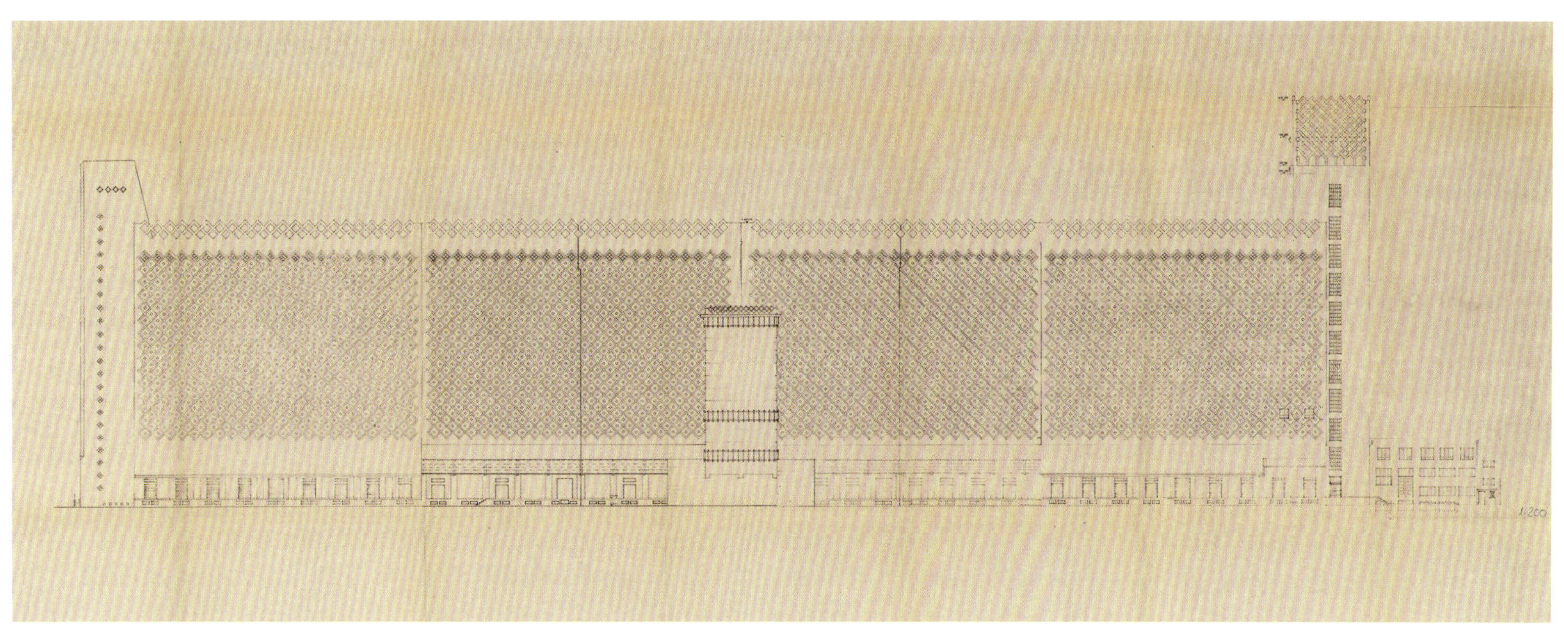

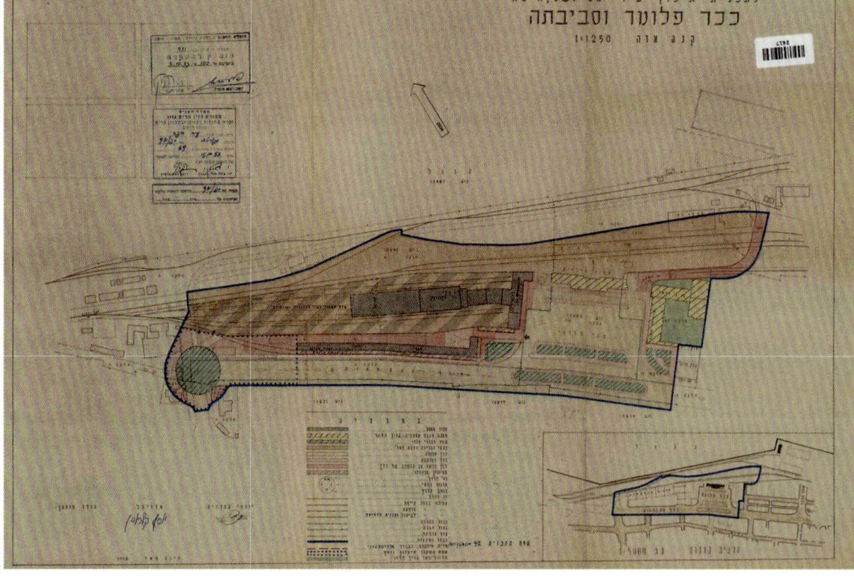

Site plan for the entire complex and urban surroundings

layout, volume and design of the buildings on the Dagon site, particularly those facing Plumer Square and HaAztma'ut Road (previously Kingsway). An early version of the scheme from 1953 shows the first phase of the silo with attached workshop building. A space for the expansion of about two-thirds of the silo (which was eventually built) is provided towards the west. An administration building adjacent to Plumer Square and buildings with arcades stretching along HaAtzma'ut Road seem intended to separate industrial activity from the urban environment. The scheme (which in the end was not approved) matches a perspective drawing of great expressive quality[4], which further clarifies Klarwein's architectural and urban vision for Dagon.

Klarwein's scheme is in effect a revision of Holliday and Hubbard's plans for Plumer Square, and an extension of their vision of Kingsway further to the west. Comparing Klarwein's vision to the Kingsway proposals one can see lower rise buildings of only 4 to 5 floors, as well as different proportions of built volumes and their spacing. Instead of an emphasis on accentuated street corners, Klarwein suggested clear corners leaving only arcades to tie the ribbon of buildings together.

Architecture

The Dagon Grain Silos have been realized in four construction phases on reclaimed land. They were built at different times while seeking to maintain architectural unity. The first phase of the silo was constructed in 1952-1955, when the Dagon company was already unloading grain at a temporary facility in Haifa port. The second phase was completed in 1960, the third in 1962 and in 1971, the fourth and final phase of the silo was completed. In its final stage, the Dagon Silo had a capacity of 100,000 tons[5].

In addition to the silo there are other buildings on the site. The workshop building (1956), which is connected to the silo's first phase, was initially also used as office space. Later, the administration building (1965) was connected to the workshops by a bridged wing. A guard house (1958) was integrated into the compound's

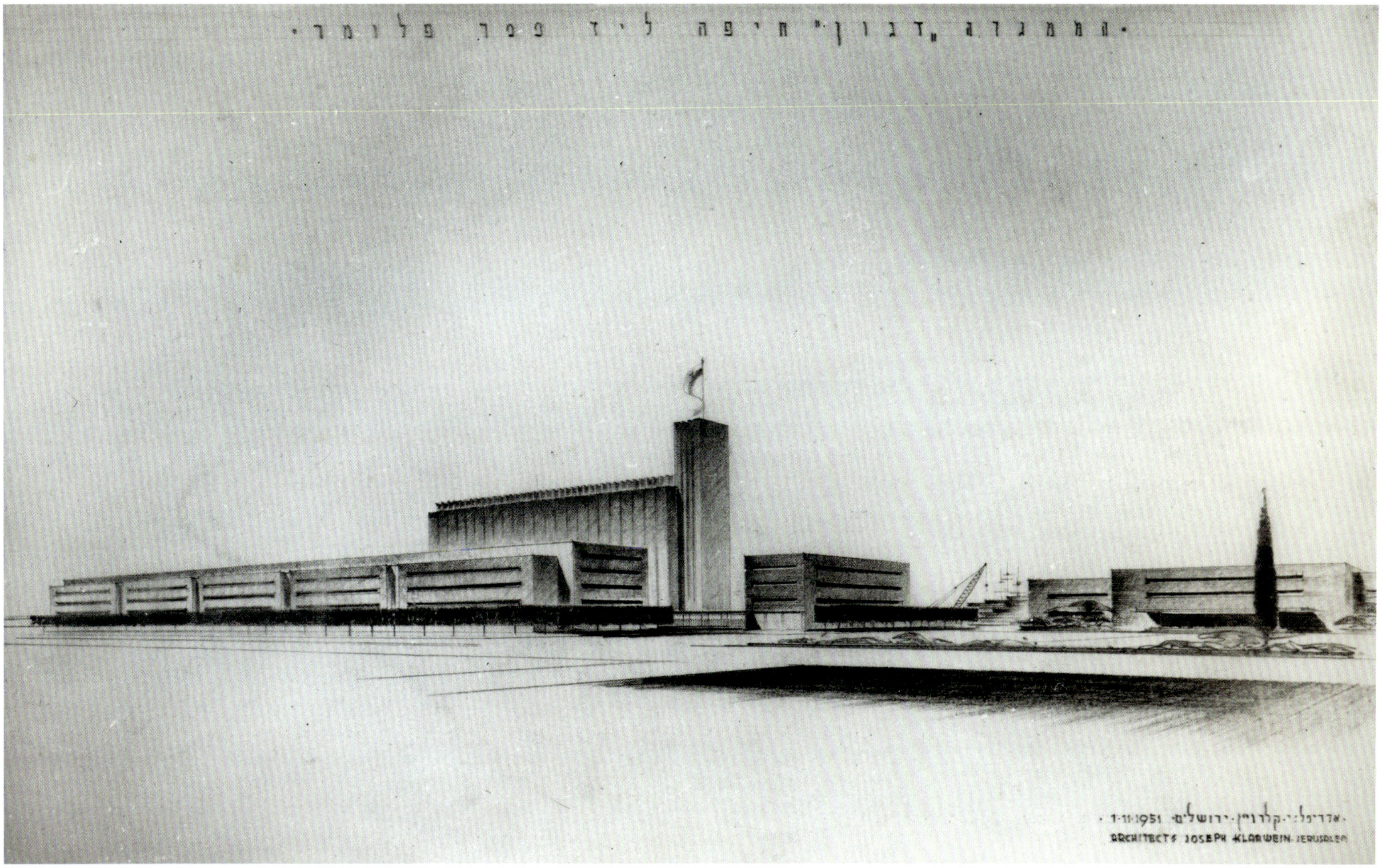

·הממגורה „דגון" חיפה ליד כפר פלומר·
·אדריכל·י·קלרוין·ירושלים· 1·11·1951 ·
ARCHITECTS JOSEPH KLARWEIN JERUSALEM

Sketch of scheme layout by Klarwein / architectural model of the first construction phase

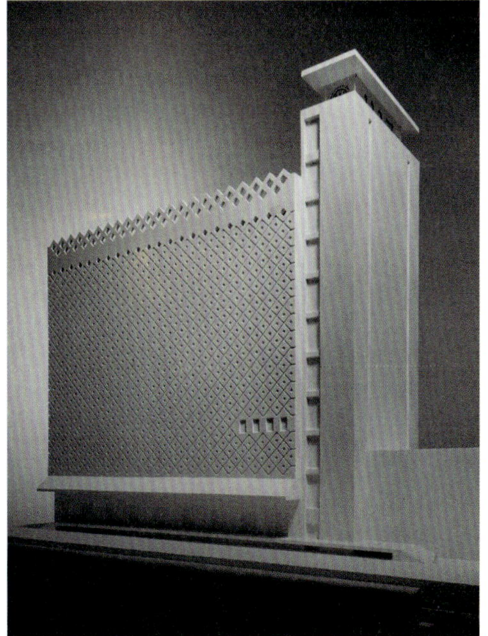

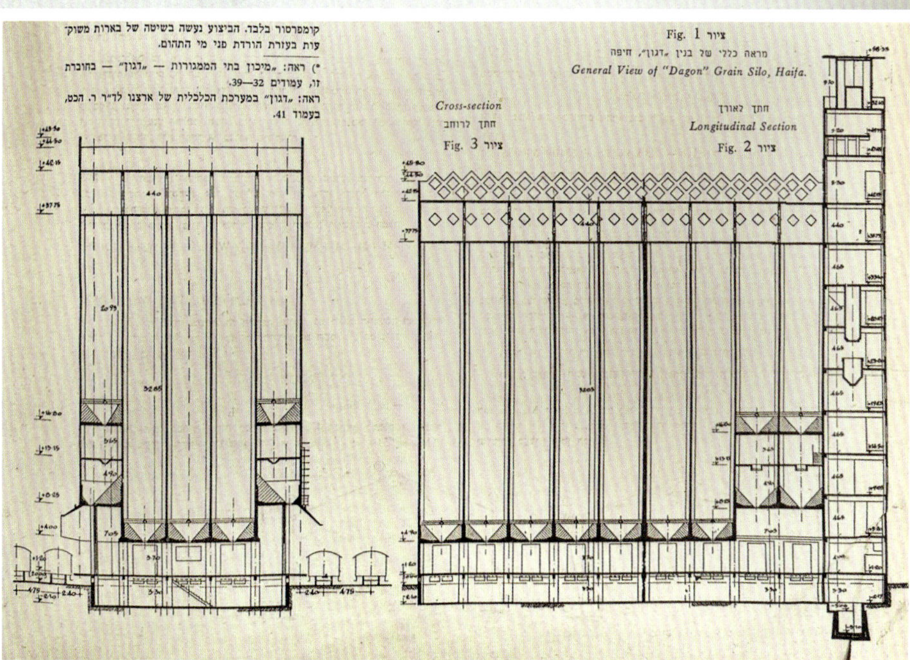

קומפרסור בלבד. הביצוע נעשה בשיטה של בארות משוק־
עות בעזרת הורדת פני מי התהום.
*) ראה: „מיכון בתי הממגורות — „דגון" — בחוברת
זו, עמודים 32—39.
ראה: „דגון" במערכת הכלכלית של ארצנו לד"ר ר. הכט,
בעמוד 41.
Fig. 1 ציור
מראה כללי של בנין „דגון", חיפה
General View of "Dagon" Grain Silo, Haifa.
Cross-section
חתך לרוחב
Fig. 3 ציור
חתך לאורך
Longitudinal Section
Fig. 2 ציור

Cross and longitudinal sections of the silo's first construction phase

Postcard showing the completed first building phase from Plumer Square (1955) and in the context of the conveyor belts connecting the silo with the harbor

Construction site of the third building phase with climbing formwork (1961)

The completed silos around 1973

wall, as was a truck control point (1968)[6]. In addition, three port-side cranes are connected to the silo by two bridged conveyors, transporting material from the ships directly into the silo.

The silo is operated as part of the Haifa port. The first modern port of Haifa, constructed by the British mandate government, was inaugurated in October 1933. Its construction included two breakwaters and the reclamation of 340 dunams (34 hectares) of land along the shoreline[7]. In 1936 Haifa superseded Jaffa as the main port of the British mandate territory, importing and exporting goods in quantities far exceeding projections made when the port was planned about a decade earlier[8].

The Enterprise

'Dagon' company was established in 1951 by Reuben Hecht (1909-1993), an industrialist and right-wing Zionist who was awarded the "Israel Prize for Exemplary Lifetime Service to the Society and State" in 1984. Born in Antwerp, his family migrated to Basle in 1919. The Neptun-Rhenania Group, established by his father and his uncle at the beginning of the 20th century, was one of the largest operators of river transport and logistics in western Europe. Unlike his father, Reuben Hecht was attracted to Zionism from a young age and was active in numerous Zionist movements including the Revisionist Zionist Party. Hecht visited Haifa for the first time in 1931. Influenced by Theodor Herzl's book 'Altneuland' he envisioned Haifa as an important urban center in the future Jewish state. In 1936 he immigrated to Palestine under British mandate. His offer to the British Government to establish a grain silo in the new Haifa port was turned down[9].

When the state of Israel was established in 1948, Hecht met in Basle with David Remez, Israel's first Minister of Transport. In 1950, with Remez's support and after grueling negotiations, Hecht was granted a concession by the Israeli government to build a grain silo in Haifa port. In 1951 "Dagon Batey Mamgoroth le-Israel" was established and the Israeli government signed a contract with the company. The construction of Dagon Grain Silo began in 1952[10].

Brochures and company reports attribute the planning of the silo to a team of engineers and architects, both in Israel and in Basle. Among them are architects Dan and Rephael Ben-Dor, the Jerusalem City Engineer Yehuda L. Berger and Gavriel Avidgor, the Dagon in-house engineer[11]. Klarwein's role is described as consulting architect in charge of the building's facades. In a 1952 report, Reuben Hecht mentions Klarwein separately from the planning team, and explains his role: "...We are fully aware of our tasks and responsibilities from the town planning and aesthetic points of view, as the Silo with its high tower will become Haifa's prominent landmark. The well-known Jerusalem architect, Mr. Joseph Klarwein, has undertaken to design a suitably dignified and imposing facade"[12]. In later documents Klarwein is listed in third place in the planning team of the first phase of the silo[13].

The facade design

Klarwein's architectural expression of the structure is manifested in the relief pattern that extends across the facades of all four phases of the silo. The geometric arrangement of squares rotated by 45 degrees and balanced on their vertices became the silo's hallmark. This design incorporates windows and extends to the roof parapets in a lace-like mesh made of reinforced concrete, comprising the upper edge of the massive structure. The construction method of climbing casing was chosen especially to allow the creation of this relief pattern[14]. This method was invented in 1900 in the USA for constructing silos and was first used in Israel in 1950 to build a silo in Kibbutz Gvat. Since then, the climbing casing method was adopted in the construction of many silos and other buildings because it proved to be comparatively economical[15]. At the time it was built, the Dagon Silo was the tallest tower in Israel at a height of 59 meters, including a rooftop canopy[16]. In 1961-62 its height was increased reaching almost 70 meters. The new modified tower's crown matched the geometric design of the structure[17].

Hecht explained the design of the geometric patterns of the silo facades as follows: "Just as the technical solutions needed to be adjusted to the specific needs of Haifa port, so special architectural questions arose, since the Dagon building is at the center of the city and a prominent feature of the Haifa skyline. The solution is based on the strong contrast between light and shadow in this land, which was utilized in the relief of the facade and is both modern and oriental as well as ancient in its shape"[18].

Warhaftig mentions[19] the similarity between the Dagon Silo pattern and the facades of Delmenhorst hospital near Bremen built in 1928 by Fritz Höger. Klarwein was a chief designer at Höger's architectural firm at that time. Höger is famous for his architectural style of Brick Expressionism achieved by setting building-bricks in patterns that create dynamic textures and a sense of movement. Interestingly, a variation of the relief pattern which is one of the main characteristics of Dagon Silo is featured in another building Klarwein planned – Hod cinema in Nahariya. The rotated square pattern also appears in early sketches for the Dagon administration building[20].

Reuben Hecht in front of the finished first phase with the decorated facade / detailed drawing of the facade decoration for the third phase, drawn by Klarwein

It seems that bricks, considered by expressionist architects as earthy local building material in northern Germany, were replaced by concrete in Israel, but the sense of locality and natural origin was retained. The dynamic textures of the facades were no longer created by meticulous, laborious bricklaying, but rather by advanced methods of casting concrete, reflecting progress and modernity in the realization of architectural structures.

View across Haifa through the grid of the facade

Administration building

The Dagon administration building, completed in May 1965, was planned by Klarwein in collaboration with Saadja Mandl. The interior architect was Refael Blumenfeld[21]. The old administration offices and dining hall were moved to the new building and their space in the old building converted into new workshops. The new dining hall was built as a bridge structure connecting the workshop and the administration building, covering a garden at ground level.

The architectural character and position of the administration building matches the vision laid out by Klarwein in his urban scheme for Dagon and its surroundings. Although it features no arcade facing Plumer Square, the building does pay tribute to the square as public space.

One of the most notable components of the administration building is the covered garden with its ribbed ceiling of fair faced concrete and natural rock paving. The site initially was proposed by Klarwein as an area specifically for truck maneuvering[22], but eventually was

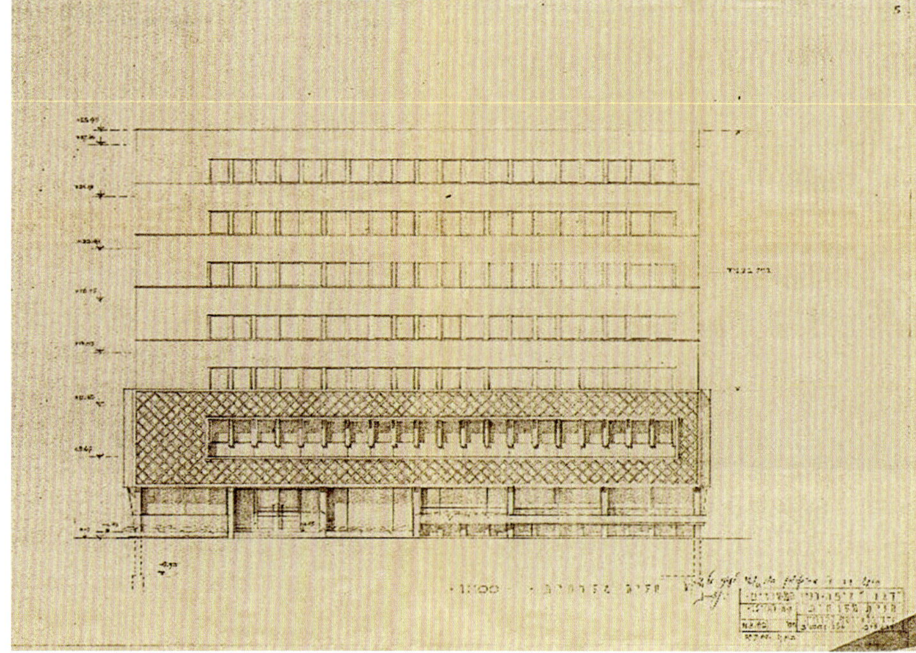

Preliminary design for the administration building, not realized

turned into a green space. Another dominant and extraordinary feature is the expressive colored glass-work, created by Naomi Henrik (1920-2018) that expands from floor to ceiling along the staircase in the hall. Its dynamic lines, light and color contrast with the weight and earthiness of the many stone and concrete textures inside and outside the building.

The facade of the ground floor incorporates sculptural artwork flanking a wide entrance to the Archeological Museum. The architectural details of the facades are a clear reference to details of the Kingsway and the central railway station design, but also give new meaning to them with a variation of the 1960s architectural style.

Archaeological Museum

Reuben Hecht was a dedicated collector of archeological artifacts since his youth, especially those that reflect the connection of the Jewish people to the land of Israel[23]. As an integral part of the Dagon site, he established the archeological Dagon Grain Museum, which gained an international reputation[24]. The purpose of this museum was to present the development of grain storing and distribution since ancient times (12,000 B.C.) to both students and the general public. Hecht believed in the importance of incorporating artwork and archeology in office and industry environments[25]. Therefore, the archeological collection was moved to the new administration building, with the intention of being open to the public.

Conclusion

The fourth and final wing of Dagon Silo was completed in January 1971. By 1973 another tower for machinery was completed on the western end of the silo and a second bridged conveyor built to connect the cranes with the silo. The facade of the second tower and the second bridged conveyor was designed by Saadja Mandl. In a December 1972 report Hecht refers to Klarwein's passing: "The deceased architect Joseph Klarwein designed the building to integrate into its surrounding, in its both modern and original style. Unfortunately, he did not live to see it being completed. Our friend Joseph Klarwein established a memorial to himself in the many buildings he planned, among the most beautiful in Israel, including the house of the Knesset"[26].

Rightfully Klarwein is credited with the design of the Dagon Grain Silo. He was involved in the planning at every stage. He created the geometric pattern that became the silo's hallmark, and which contributes to the architectural unity of the multi-part structure. The pattern clearly recalls impressions Klarwein brought with him from Germany. He laid out the general plan of the site and its interaction with the city, extending and revising the urban design of Kingsway-HaAtzma'ut Road. And finally, Klarwein took part in planning the administration building which, despite its unique features, nevertheless is well integrated into its surroundings as part of a masterplan which, unfortunately, was never completed.

Administration building on Plumer Square with the silos in the background (1965)

Colored glass window by Naomi Henrik along the staircase of the administration building (1965) / covered garden under the bridge linking the silos to the administration building

1 Dagan/Dagon is the West Semitic god of crop fertility, worshipped throughout the ancient Middle East. 'Dagan' was the Hebrew and Ugaritic noun for "grain", and the god Dagan was the legendary inventor of the plow. His cult is attested as early as about 2500 BC. (Britannica, T. Editors of Encyclopaedia (2024, August 26). Dagan. Encyclopedia Britannica. https://www.britannica.com/topic/Dagan). In modern Hebrew 'dagan' means 'grain'. **2** Herbert, Sosnovsky, 1993 **3** ISA גל-27/ 4009 **4** Central Zionist Archives (CZA) A455-12-3p **5** Israel State Archives (ISA), ג-10/ 292, p.76 **6** Original building file, Haifa city engineer archives **7** Buckton 1936 **8** Herbert, Sosnovsky, 1993 **9** Warhaftig 2007 **10** Warhaftig, 2007 **11** "Dagon" Silos for Israel Haifa, Newspaper of the Association of Engineers and Architects in Israel, July 1957, Tel Aviv; ISA (גל-1/7292) p. 64-65 **12** ISA (ג-21/5522) p. 337 **13** ISA (גל-1/7292) p. 64-65 **14** "Dagon" Silos for Israel Haifa, Newspaper of the Association of Engineers and Architects in Israel, July 1957, Tel Aviv **15** Aleksandrowicz 2019 **16** "Dagon" Silos for Israel Haifa, Newspaper of the Association of Engineers and Architects in Israel, July 1957, Tel Aviv **17** Original building file, Haifa city engineer archives **18** "Dagon" Silos for Israel Haifa, Newspaper of the Association of Engineers and Architects in Israel, July 1957, Tel Aviv **19** Warhaftig, 2007 **20** Original building file, Haifa city engineer archives **21** ISA (גל-13/6250) p. 91 **22** ISA (גל-27/4009) p. 108 **23** Warhaftig 2007 **24** Dagon Collection. Archaeological Museum of Grain Handling in Israel. **25** ISA ג-10/ 292 **26** ISA, גל-9/ 54765, P. 101-103

GIVAT RAM THE HEBREW UNIVERSITY CAMPUS IN JERUSALEM

Diana Dolev

Aerial photo of the university compound around 1970. In the background the National Stadium and the three ministry buildings, also by Klarwein

The idea of a Hebrew University (sometimes referred to as a Jewish University) emerged in Europe in the late 19th century and became a leading initiative of the Zionist Organization at the beginning of the 20th century. Its first chosen location was the summit of Mount Scopus, east of the Old City of Jerusalem, overlooking the Temple Mount and its mosques, the presumed location of the Holy Temple. The ceremony for the laying of the cornerstones in 1918 was celebrated by delegates of Jewish congregations from Palestine and abroad, and the symbolic connection with the site of the ancient Holy Temple inspired the various architects employed to design the campus.

In 1948, as result of the war and the division of Jerusalem, the unfinished Mount Scopus campus was evacuated and became an Israeli enclave in Jordanian-ruled territory. The university moved its facilities to rented rooms and buildings on the western side of the city, an arrangement that was understood to be temporary, because in Zionist ethos the Mount Scopus site had gained a status almost equivalent to the holy places around the Old City. It was – and still is – conceived as the real home of the Hebrew University. Therefore, the notion of returning to Mount Scopus obtained special significance and talk about an alternative campus was regarded as a betrayal of what the university stood for and of Zionist and national goals. Hence negotiations concerning a new location for the university were initially kept secret, including meetings with proposed architects.

Eventually a barren hill in the Givat Ram area was selected for a new campus, next to the proposed National Compound dedicated to the new Israeli national administration institutions. Since its founding, the Hebrew University had been conceived as an establishment of national significance, therefore the proximity to the nation's institutions was accepted without question. The laying of the cornerstones for the proposed new campus took place in 1954 in a relatively modest ceremony. Immediately after the 1967 war and the Israeli occupation of East Jerusalem, the university and the government took measures to "return" to Mount Scopus and a new campus was built there. Today the Givat Ram campus comprises several Hebrew University science faculties and various independent institutions, collectively known as The Edmond and Lily Safra Campus[1].

The Givat Ram building layout[2]

The Givat Ram university project was the most ambitious and prestigious of its time in Israel. Hence, it's exceptional importance for the architectural trends that would develop in the new state. On 27 April 1958 the campus was officially opened, although not all buildings had yet been completed. It is an enclosed compound, distanced from the city center, comprising a tightly knit complex of its own[3]. The architecturally up to date buildings are spread among lush gardens, designed by leading landscape architects. The layout of the buildings allows clarity and easy orientation for users all over the campus and offers the pleasure of relaxing in the spacious gardens. Following the masterplan, leading architects were in charge of designing the various buildings. Most of them belonged to the younger generation of local architects born in Palestine, some of whom were educated at Haifa Technion which had opened its architecture department in 1925. To this day, the resulting architecture is regarded as an exemplary achievement of high standard and good taste.

The masterplan architects

In 1951 three German-Jewish architects were nominated to design the new campus masterplan: Richard Kauffmann, Heinz Rau and Joseph Klarwein. All three were International Style modernists educated in Germany, where they had started their professional careers before emigrating to Palestine[4]. Although the nomination process was kept secret, as were all other proceedings dealing with the construction of the new campus, one may assume that Klarwein and Rau were appointed because they already held central positions in the planning of West Jerusalem after the establishment of the state in 1948. They obviously took an active part in choosing the Givat Ram site, so it was very much within their capacity in planning the new ruling edifices, that they teamed up to plan the new campus for the Hebrew University. In addition, Kauffmann resumed his former position as university planner which he had held between 1944 and 1948 for the Mount Scopus campus[5].

The masterplan

Examining the result of the team's plan, it is quite impossible to decipher what each of the planners brought to the planning desk, especially since no evidence of their discussions (in their native German, no doubt) is to be found. But we can deduce their intentions from the plans and the layout of buildings stretching along the terrain of the elongated mountain ridge, between the main entrance on the north and the students' dormitories on the south end. Special attention was given to the group of buildings immediately next to the entrance where five faculty buildings are lined up between the tall Administration Building[6] and the National and University Library[7]. Popularly referred to as the "campus heart", this group comprises a large park designed by US landscape architect Lawrence Halprin, while the faculty buildings on its margins are pushed back toward the slope of the hilly terrain. The "campus heart" cre-

Sketch by Klarwein of the basic campus layout (1953) / view across the campus heart towards the National Library with faculty buildings on the right (around 1965)

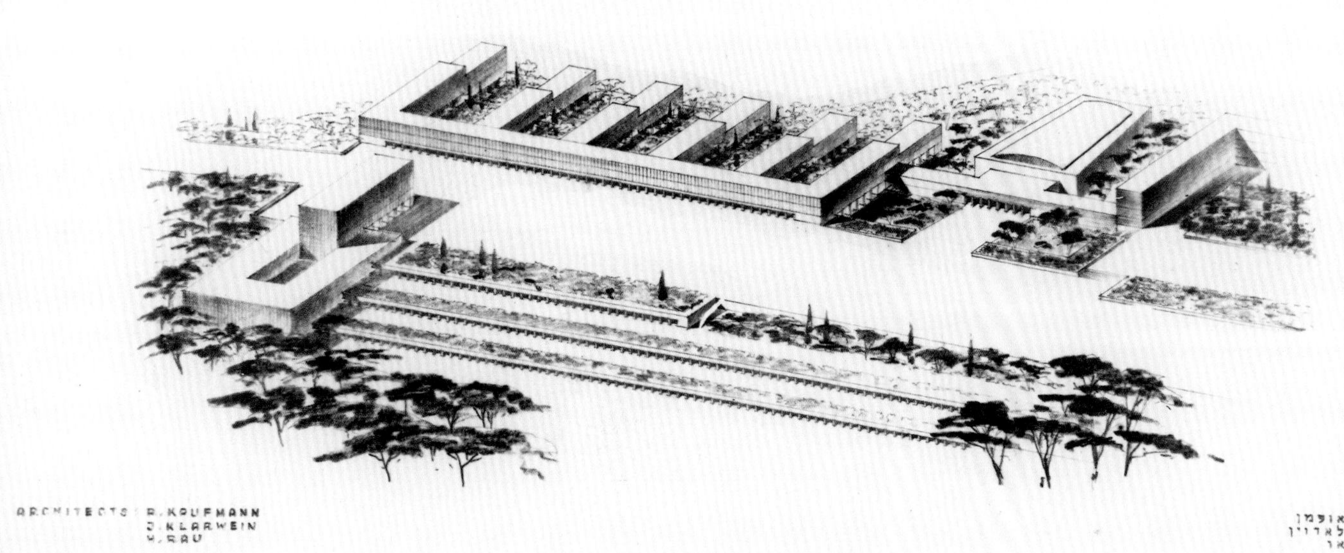

Isometric view across the campus heart by Klarwein. In the upper right the future Wise Auditorium

ated a self-contained ensemble of special significance, implying the Western idea of The University: between the sphere of matter exemplified by the Administration Building and the immaterial world of learning and research exemplified by the library lie the five faculty buildings each housing a different discipline of knowledge. These faculty buildings are equal in size and shape, thus indicating a non-hierarchical approach to the various fields of knowledge. Yet it must be said also that the uniformity of the design does not take into consideration the special needs each faculty may have in terms of number of classrooms, lecture halls and offices. It is therefore an example of the domination of the block form over other specific needs and preferences, which resulted in the necessity to improvise new solutions.

Further from the "campus heart" along the ridge and the slope toward the east the masterplan architects allowed diverse modern and post-modern styles of buildings. These accentuate the uniformity of style and the dominance of the block type of building within the "campus heart" and its singular significance within the campus.

The block in the early 1950s in Israel[8]

Block type buildings were popular with International Style architects since the 1920s and became even more widespread after World War II. It was believed to be a prototype that suits everyone everywhere, a design that provides optimal residence solutions for communities anywhere in the world, despite differences in ethnic, cultural and architectural heritage. In the effort to provide swift and affordable lodging solutions for the multitudes of immigrants who arrived in Israel after the war, local architects concentrated on the block style building. Apart from providing accommodation, it also served the Zionist goal of directing newcomers to adopt modern European standards. Officially, a "melting pot" policy was declared, with all Jewish immigrants merging their unique heritage to create a new society in their common fatherland. In fact, however, the aim was to erase the culture and traditions of immigrants from Arab countries. Furthermore, modern architecture in Israel constructed a barrier between the new Israeli entity and the past Palestinian indigenous environment. Devoid of decorations and without any extras being added to the simple and minimal modernist construction, the block implied detachment from local Palestinian architectural, cultural and religious heritage, as well as from the heritage of the newcomers (unless they arrived from western Europe). In short, the block served as the architectural embodiment of a new start for a new state and the creation of a new westernized Jewish society.

Indeed, the dominance of the block type in the "campus heart" has explicit similarities to other planning projects in the Givat Ram National Compound. Architects Munio Gitai Weinraub and Al Mansfeld designed a modernist style plan with remarkable affinity to the university campus.

Masterplan for the government compound by Weinraub/Mansfeld (1950)

Yet perhaps what connects the block type even more closely to the "campus heart" faculty buildings are Klarwein's government buildings on Derech Rupin Street, next to the university campus[9]. Those, too, were built in the early 1950s, and although they seem indifferent to their environment (as blocks usually are), they match the modernist West Jerusalem setting, particularly in Givat Ram, which was surrounded by new Jewish residential neighborhoods designed by Richard Kauffmann in the 1920s – Rehavia on the east and Beit Hakerem on the west. Standing in a line, on the edge of the National Compound are three out of the seven buildings that were originally proposed (the other four were never built). They consist of the Prime Minister's Office, the Treasury and the Ministry of the Interior, designed in a unified style that does not suggest their separate purposes.

Ministry buildings by Klarwein after heightening

The „campus heart"

Similar to Klarwein's government offices, the long walls of the faculty buildings in the "campus heart" are covered with standard rows of equal size windows that do not reveal the different interior spaces and their uses. They create a uniformity that expresses a matter-of-fact approach to the activity that takes place inside. The "blind"

Design for an unknown campus building

short walls at the buildings' ends are also common to the two groups of buildings. However, this is especially marked in the faculty buildings, since on the garden end of each, one would expect an opening towards the view. As is the case with the government offices, the only formal device that is contrary to the rigid block form is that the buildings are broken up into combined parts to make them fit the topography of the hilly terrain. The fact that architect Shimon Powsner, who played a major part in designing

Building of the Law Faculty by Klarwein (today Ross building). First study, perspective and existing building (1959)

the "campus heart", collaborated with Klarwein in some stage of designing the Knesset (the Israeli parliament) may explain the close affinity between the faculty buildings and the government offices.

When compared to Klarwein's Law Building, the resemblance to the faculty buildings is even more striking. It is as though one and the same mind designed them: they are similar in form as well as in the cut stone cladding of the exterior walls, which uses a vertical layout to avoid the impression that they are building stones (influenced by Erich Mendelsohn's buildings on Mount Scopus). In the seemingly egalitarian spread of the campus buildings, the "campus heart" stands out, very much due to Klarwein's input.

Conclusion

Overlooking the Holy Basin and dominated by its presence, Mount Scopus campus planners and onlookers could not avoid the impact of the Old City, the Temple Mount, and the Dome of the Rock (perceived by many as the ancient Holy Temple). The Givat Ram campus, in contrast, is remote from historical and religious places; its environment is entirely secular. There is nothing of significance to look upon from the summit of Givat Ram. And so it turns inward and allows people to stroll freely through buildings and gardens without any ulterior meaning attached. The campus provided a fertile ground for the typical modernist architectural trends connected to the goals of the new Jewish state. Furthermore, without the ties to ancient history, the Givat Ram campus could allow itself to focus entirely on what it was meant to be – an institution of higher education as well as an establishment of national significance.

The campus heart with the administration building in the background and the first faculty building on the left. In front one of the sculptures in the park designed by Lawrence Halprin

1 In 2005 the campus was renamed The Edmond Safra Campus following a donation from the Edmond Safra Foundation **2** For a comprehensive survey of the campus see David Kroyanker, Planning and Architecture 1953-2002, Edmund J. Safra Campus Givat Ram, Jerusalem, 2002. See also Diana Dolev, 'The Architectural Design of the Giv'at Ram Hebrew University Campus", in Yfaat Weiss and Uzi Rebhun (eds.) The History of the Hebrew University of Jerusalem; The Nation-State and Higher Education, (Hebrew), Jerusalem 2024, pp. 260 – 293. **3** Both in its Mount Scopus site and in Giv'at Ram, the Hebrew University campuses were detached and enclosed, and as it was the only university in Israel since it opened in 1925 until the establishment of the Tel Aviv University in the mid-1950s, it set an example for all other universities to come **4** Kauffmann (1887 – 1958) was born and educated in Frankfurt, where he started his career, before emigrating to Palestine in 1920. Rau (1896 – 1965) was born and educated in Berlin and emigrated to Palestine in 1933. Together with his architect David Reznick, who was his partner at that time, Rau designed the campus synagogue, which was not initially in the masterplan. **5** Richard Kauffmann was the senior among the three with an impressive career behind him. Since his arrival to Palestine in 1920 and until 1948 he planned hundreds of Kibutzim, Jewish agricultural settlements and urban neighborhoods. Klarwein collaborated with Kauffmann before, when he designed the Biology Building for the Mount Scopus campus (the construction was not finished when the campus was evacuated, and the unfinished building had been demolished when a new campus was erected there after the 1967 war). **6** Designed by architects Dov Karmi, Zvi Meltzer and Ram Karmi. **7** Designed by architects Ziva Armoni and Hanan Hebron who were joined by architects Shulamit Nadler, Michael Nadler and Amnon Alexandroni. **8** For a comprehensive history and analysis of the block type in Israeli architecture, see Zvi Efrat, 'Block', in The Israeli Project; Building and Architecture, 1948 – 1973, (Hebrew), Tel Aviv, 2004, pp. 167-186. The book has been translated to English under the title The Object of Zionism; The Architecture of Israel, Leipzig, 2018 **9** Klarwein also prepared a general outline for the National and University stadium in the valley on the east border of the campus, while the more detailed plan was in the hands of the Department of Public Works, which also actually built it.

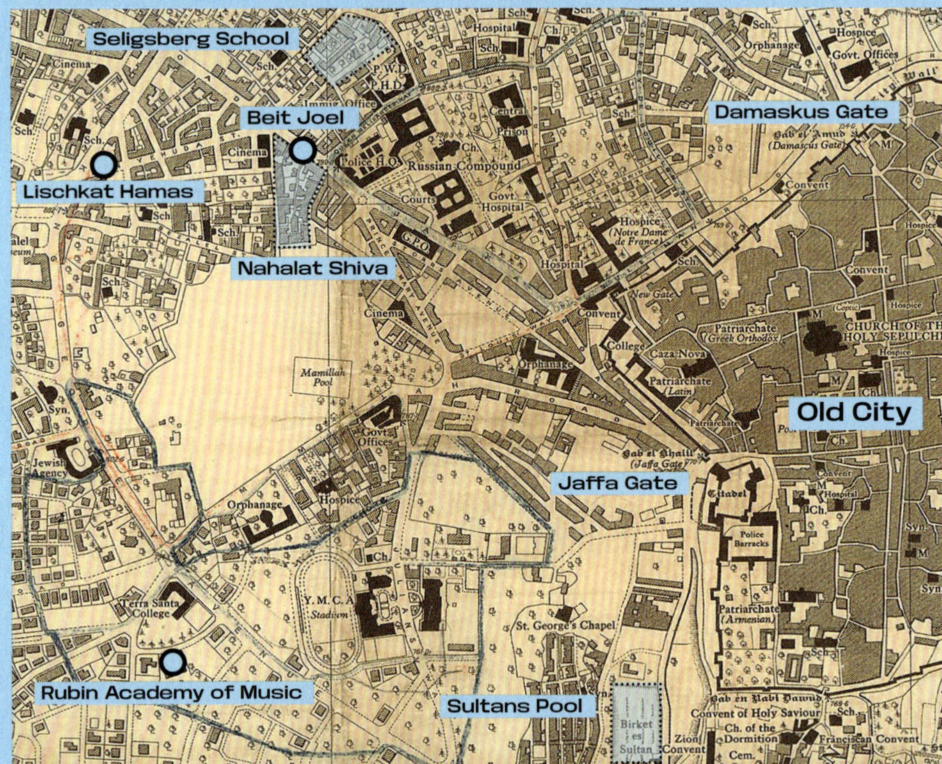

Klarwein's architectural and urban planning projects for "East Jerusalem" until 1967. After the founding of Israel in 1948 the area of Givat Ram far west of the Old Town had become the centre of Israeli Jerusalem. The historic Jewish suburbs west of the Old Town like Jaffa Road were considered to be "East Jerusalem" at the time. This changed after the 1967 war

CONTESTED MODERNISM

PLANS FOR EAST JERUSALEM 1947–1965

Noah Hysler Rubin

‚A godforsaken neighborhood was Nahalat Shiva, which was almost completely removed. Crowded and stacked, with old buildings and dilapidated infrastructure, it was an obstacle in all urban plans from the Mandate period onwards and doomed for destruction. In its place, the planners wished to build the "City" of Jerusalem. The one who went farthest of them all was Arch. Klarwein, whose plan was approved in 1963, and according to which the neighborhood was to be razed to the ground and replaced with office buildings, with commercial centers, a park, and roads. The first stage of the plan was carried out with the building of Beit Yoel, which brought on the destruction of about 10 of the old neighborhood buildings, including the remains of the house of Yoel Moshe Solomon, who gave the building its name. However, in the 1960s, the world and Israel saw the need for rehabilitation rising. That which had been considered a burden that must be removed turned, in time, into an asset that must be conserved and preserved. In 1986, all plans for the destruction of the neighborhood stopped, and an overall plan was prepared for its conservation and embellishment'[1].

Not many accounts have been written on the controversial rehabilitation of Nahalat Shiva, one of the earliest Jewish neighborhoods in New Jerusalem. It was established at the end of the Ottoman era. During the British Mandate period, it was considered ‚slums' and destined for complete demolition and subsequent reconstruction. After the establishment of the State of Israel and the city's division in 1948, it was set for rehabilitation and, finally, preserved as a historic neighborhood. In the short text quoted above, Yitzhak Yacobi, then the head of the Company for the Development of East Jerusalem, and Nahum Meltzer, the architect responsible for preserving the neighborhood in the 1980s, situate Joseph Klarwein at the heart of the controversy.

Klarwein's detailed plan for the area, which was approved in 1960 as part of massive planning efforts for the rehabilitation and reconstruction of Jerusalem city center, stood at the epicenter of the controversy regarding Israeli urban reconstruction and preservation and perhaps marked the turning point of discourse and practice. Indeed, Klarwein's long involvement in the area, known as ‚East Jerusalem' between 1948 and 1967, reflects the main motivation for intervention from the beginning of the British Mandate until the late 1960s. The ideology of modernization and the identification of older urban fabrics as ‚slums' due to their high density, traditional layout, or simply underdevelopment drew on the newly established modern planning practice and was a reaction to poor living conditions in industrial cities and to British experience throughout the Empire. It was shared by early Israeli planning authorities striving for uncompromising modernization and overall renewal. These concepts were expressed in Klarwein's modernist architecture and cast aside all that was traditional, non-Western, and, in the case of Jerusalem, also holy.

Perhaps nowhere else was Klarwein's work as a modernist architect more controversial, juxtaposing the universal and the local and evaluating urban landscape between modernist and traditional development and between conventions of the East and West. In this crucial area, Klarwein's architectural values were initially highly sought after and later utterly disputed. First, during the mandate period and the early Israeli period, Klarwein's plans disregarded local fabric, demanding its adaptation to universal standards and enforcing a foreign architectural language. However, it was also here that, eventually, the local prevailed over the universal. The local character was always present and dominant, and inhabitants, by way of objection, insisted on local particularities.

It is challenging to trace Klarwein's involvement in the planning of Nahalat Shiva and his overall impact on East Jerusalem[2]. In the absence of a unified body of information, the Klarwein-estate at the Central Zionist Archives containing valuable modernist plans for sites in the eastern tip of the new city, and documentation of the local District Planning Committee, as well as a rich public discussion in current media, serve to trace Klarwein's critical role in shaping the area and in negotiating between the modernist architectural mainstream and the particular, historic landscape.

Early rehabilitation during the British Mandate period

Nahalat Shiva was established in 1869 by seven Jewish families from the Old City, who started the Jewish settlement westwards along Jaffa Road. Fifty years after its establishment, with the beginning of the British mandate, Jerusalem had expanded significantly. The British, who took it upon themselves to protect and conserve the Old City while modernizing and developing the growing city around it, did not appreciate the neighborhood's ingenuity[3]. The master plan by Clifford Holliday in 1930 labeled most of the old Jewish neighborhoods in Jerusalem, including Nahalat Shiva, as areas for reconstruction, describing them as uninhabitable for their poor physical state, traditional layout, and cheap building materials. Detailed plan no. 549 'Development Scheme of Nahlat Shiva Quarter', approved in October 1939, condemned the whole neighborhood to demolition. It proposed a large building around an inner courtyard, with a commercial ground floor and six floors of offices above[4]. It was claimed that the proposals were being assessed according to their 'usefulness to the public' and that the plan's purpose was to 'clear and develop the area'[5].

Inhabitants, landowners, and their descendants rejected the plan. Concerns about the existing urban fabric, its heritage, and its society were all manifested in August 1939 in objections by the wardens of neighborhood synagogues, which were all condemned to be destroyed: "The main reason on which our objection is based is that the building which is to be demolished is a synagogue and a holy place. This synagogue was constructed over 70 years ago by pioneers who founded the new city. This synagogue has been a religious center for many years and is a historical place in Jerusalem outside the city walls. Therefore, we request to alter the above scheme to avoid the demolition of the synagogue or any damage caused"[6]. The negotiations yielded a plan devised by the Solomon

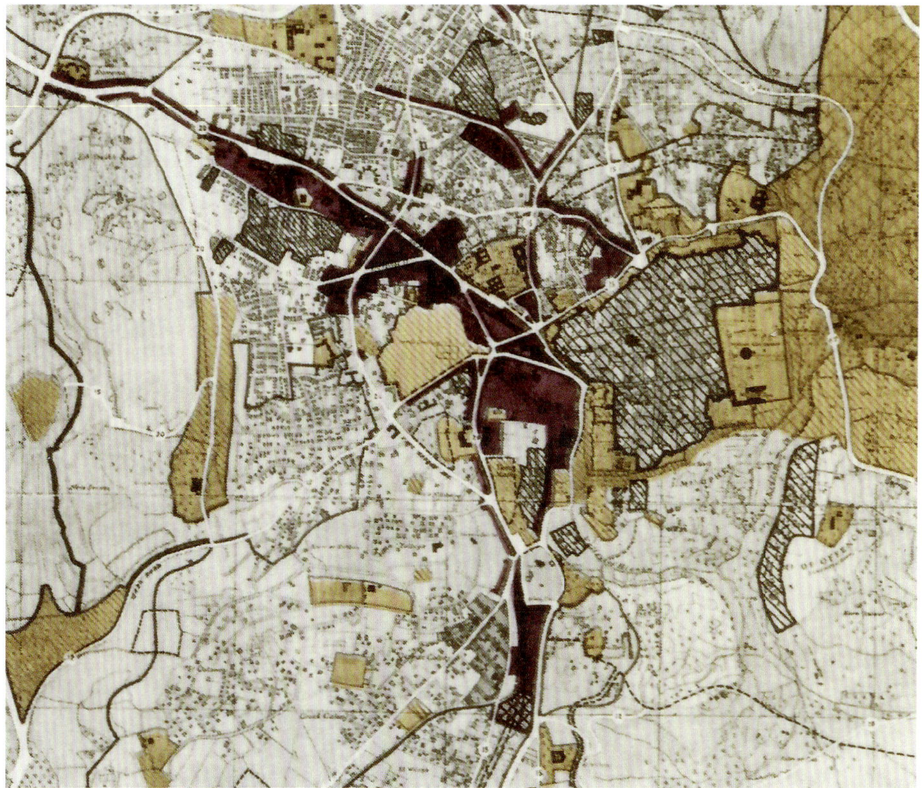

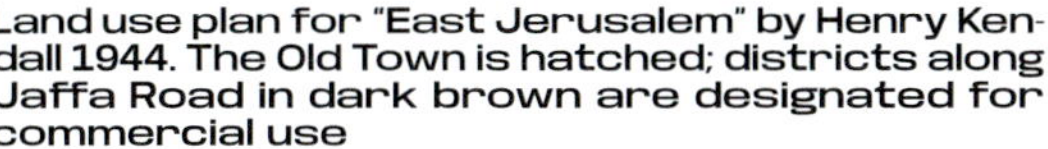
Land use plan for "East Jerusalem" by Henry Kendall 1944. The Old Town is hatched; districts along Jaffa Road in dark brown are designated for commercial use

family and its partners for a "House of Beit 'Joel'" designed by the architect Abramovitz, to be built on the front of the neighborhood facing Jaffa Street, named after one of the original seven builders[7].

While plan 549 was ratified by Henry Kendall, the urban planner of the Mandate Authority, in 1944 and later annulled, two sets of plans found in the Klarwein collection at the Central Zionist Archives attest to other British intentions for rehabilitating the area. One of them was prepared for the Sultan's Pool (Birket es-Sultan), an ancient water basin to the west side of Mount Zion, part of an ancient water supply network for Jerusalem. It was renovated several times and received its shape at the time – a water reservoir and dam – during the Mamluk period. On 12 November 1947, a representative of Jahshan Brothers, a Jerusalem motor company, wrote to Klarwein stating that if the company were granted a concession for development of the site by the Municipal Corporation of Jerusalem, Klarwein would be asked to prepare a plan[8]. Indeed, the Central Zionist Archives hold three perspective drawings depicting a striking plan for a square pool ending in a dam, which is enlarged into a vast empty square. Flat roofs mounted on pillars are situated on both sides of the square. Arcaded platforms surround the pool itself. The organization, the order, and the emptiness, as well as the masses of the planned structure, stand in stark opposition to the ancient surroundings, which are prominent in the background: The mixed neighborhood of Sham'a, established just south of the dam in 1900 by Mizrahi Jews, and further south, Abu Tor, which was developed as a residential quarter in the late 19th century by Muslim and Christian Arabs from Jerusalem, later adjoined by a Jewish community. While Mt. Zion is adorned with white modernistic buildings, the Jewish neighborhood Yemin Moshe, established in 1892 on the west of Birket es-Sultan, is not depicted in the drawing.

Next to the plan may be found an undated photograph of the site showing its traditional setting and uses. It depicts men dressed in traditional clothes, accompanying loaded horses and donkeys as they descend gradually to the water, perhaps on their way to or from Jaffa Gate. The striking differences between the photograph and the perspective attest to the great transformation the latter proposes for the landscape and its uses.

Finally, it seems Jaffa Gate itself was a candidate for complete remodeling. In the Klarwein estate, five undated photographs of a model named "Jaffa Gate market – preliminary view" accompanied by two plans and two perspective drawings show a semi-circular shopping center along a major road, with an inner courtyard and arcades. In front of the market is an oval square with a cenotaph. Here, the immediate surroundings of the plan are altogether missing, leaving the model entirely out of context, out of time, and out of place.

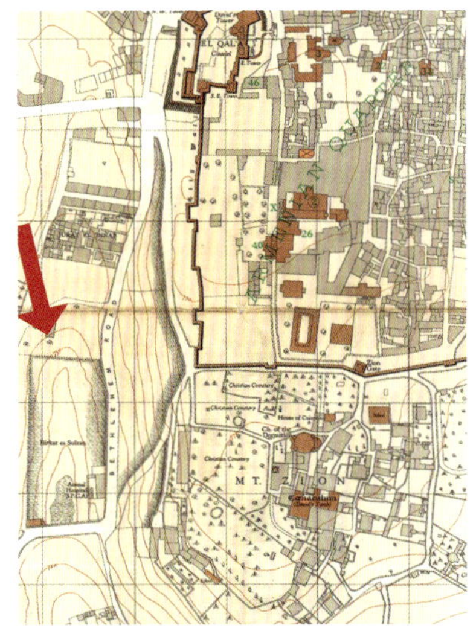

Position of Sultan's Pool at the foot of Mount Zion near the south-western corner of the Old Town (arrow) / Historic photo with the dam and the Ottoman fountain on top / Architectural model and elevated view of Klarwein's project, not realized

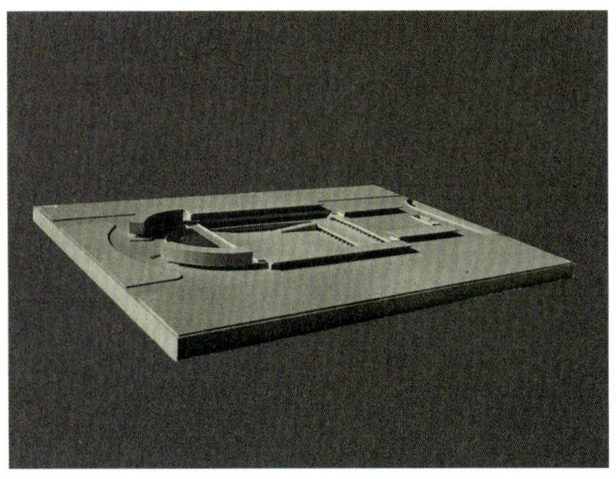

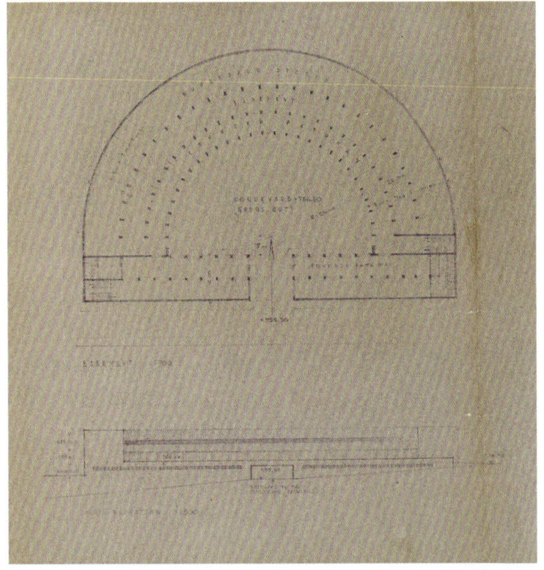

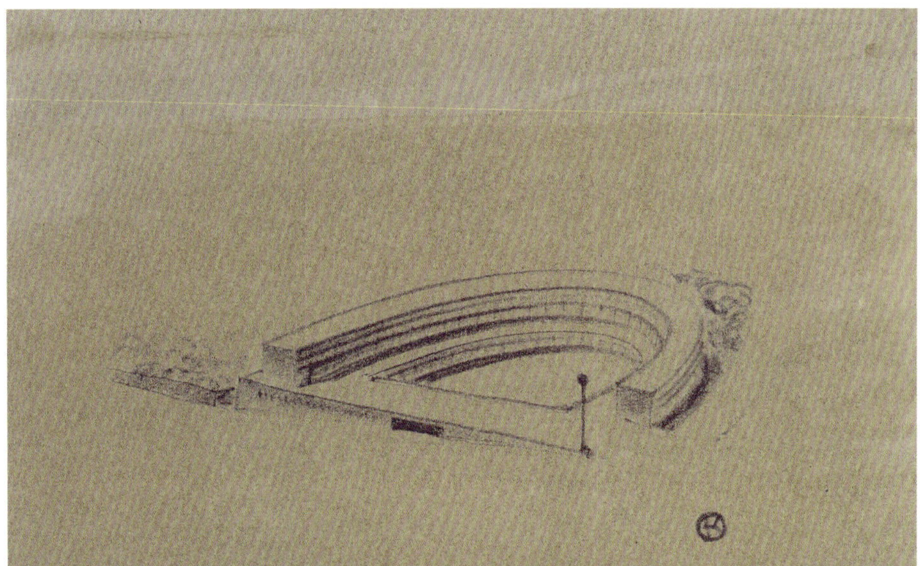

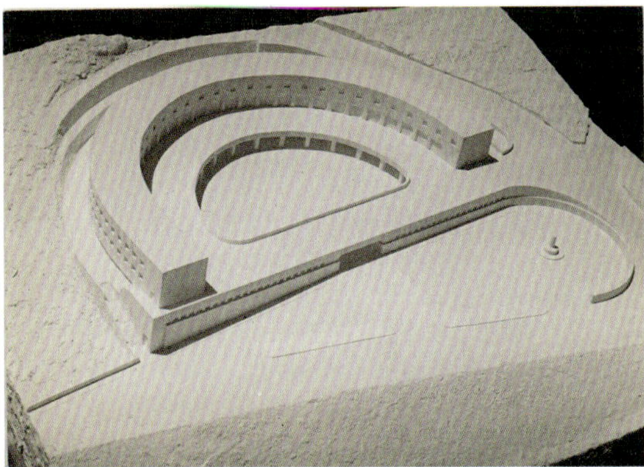

Project for a wholesale market near Jaffa Gate; ground floor, elevated view, model and perspective

1960: Klarwein's rehabilitation plans for Jerusalem's downtown

Planning Nahalat Shiva during the 1950s and 1960s was part of the Israeli efforts to recreate the urban center of Israeli Jerusalem[9]. According to Israel Kimhi, the plan was meant to dramatically change the image of Jerusalem's urban center and grant it monumentality fit for the state of Israel[10]. This transformation was one of the significant challenges faced by Israeli planners at the time in redesigning the Israeli part of Western Jerusalem which had previously been the center of the city and now was at its eastern end.

In 1954/55 architect Michael Shaviv, the technical adviser to the Jerusalem Local Town Planning Committee, led a planning team in preparing a new masterplan for Western Jerusalem. In line with the previous British planning discourse, the issue of slum clearance was crucial. Already in his extensive plan for Israel of 1951, Arieh Sharon, the leading Israeli architect of the time, stated regarding Jerusalem: "One of the purposes of the plan is the rehabilitation of the present city, which, except for a few recent quarters, consists of extensive built-up areas almost entirely lacking in green wedges or sites for public institutions"[11]. In July 1955, the Association of Urban Engineers conference was held to discuss Slum Clearance Policy in Israel[12]. Shaviv explained the criteria for defining slums in Jerusalem and listed eleven such areas; within these, he listed three areas doomed for destruction, including Nahalat Shiva and Sham'a[13].

The draft plan includes some proposals for rebuilding Nahalat Shiva and the adjacent Mamilla Park. These proposals involve demolishing all built-up areas and replacing them with modernist, continuous building blocks that make up long fronts along Jaffa Street and form huge empty plazas between them[14]. The plans are described in local papers, highlighting the rational architecture of the proposed modern housing[15].

Joseph Klarwein's detailed plan no. 856 for the urban center of Jerusalem was published in 1960. Nahalat Shiva is designed anew around a ‚green strip' 40 m wide and 80 m long, connecting the newly established Independence Garden to Jaffa Street[16]. The plan was, explains Menachem Levine, head of Jerusalem Municipality Historical Archives, to surround all commercial areas with arcades and keep an open view of the Garden of Independence, built along the outskirts of the historic Moslem Mamilla Cemetery. Solomon Street, one of the main roads, was intended to be widened while additional wide roads surrounding the neighborhood completed its transformation[17]. Klarwein's private collection includes perspective drawings for the built-up area, which give magnitude and meaning to the two-dimensional plans and the accompanying text. The first one, dated 1958, shows a symmetrical plan for a colossal plaza defined by two blocks of buildings, five to eight floors each, with the first floor supported by pillars, serving as a commercial urban center, offices, and other similar uses. An obelisk stands on the horizon in the back of the square[18].

Development plan No. 856 for the area south of Jaffa Road with Mamilla Park by Klarwein (1960). Nahalat Shiva is demarcated by dotted blue line

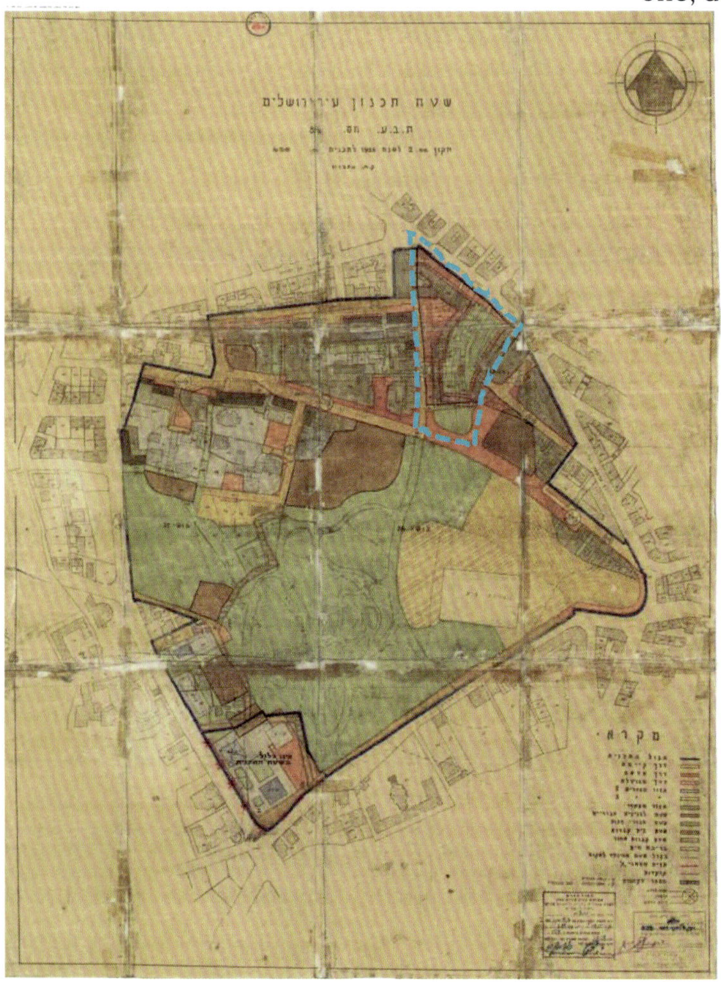

The plan was fiercely criticized. It sparked a discussion about Nahalat Shiva's primacy and its inhabitants' pioneering nature. Yossef Rivlin, a descendant, celebrated it as a historic materialization of a great idea: It occupied real historical grounds; it showed the way to the Jews of Jerusalem, the fame of "the Old Yishuv"[19]. The Religious Committee in Jerusalem voiced its urgent disquiet regarding the proposed destruction of the central synagogue in Nahalat Shiva; the mayor replied, hoping that Hachsharat HaYishuv, the building company, would take it upon itself to rehabilitate it[20].

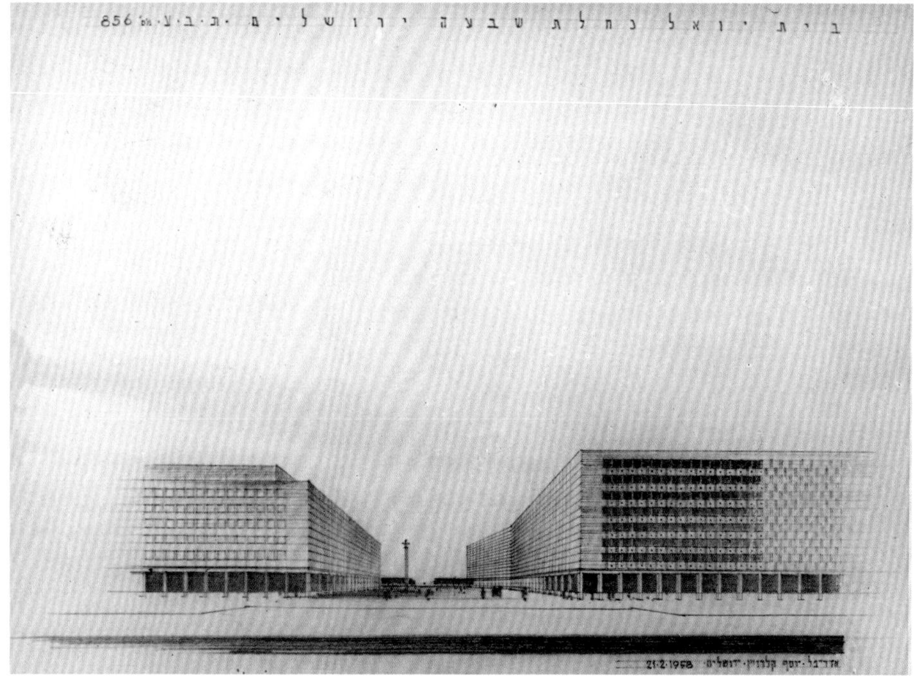

Perspective drawing of Nahalat Shiva development by Klarwein

In a letter to the newspaper Ha'aretz, Eli Mezger a reader, warned against the destruction of the neighborhood, reminding planners that Nahalat Shiva was now the oldest quarter of the city. "Although it isn't the first outside the Walls, it still has a great part in the history of new Jerusalem. In her narrow alleys, it is also a memorial to the old city [..] In my opinion, destroying this neighborhood, especially now, is not only damage to an important historical asset of Jerusalem but also, and perhaps even more importantly, a harsh moral sin, as long as the Old City is not in our hands"[21].

New perspective drawings were presented in 1963, yet they were just as wide-ranging. In the first, a long vista composed of symmetric blocks of buildings on both sides can be seen, this time a large building of about six floors at the front and two identical tower blocks above it. An ornamental water fountain may be spotted between them in the background, just before the garden. In the second, a continuous building block following the plot's outline is adjoined by another rectangular block with an inner courtyard. This time, the central piazza is blocked by a building separating Jaffa Street and the Garden like a screen. The main element in the piazza is a water pool. The obelisk is moved to a bend created by the continuous building along the plot contour. The two buildings along Jaffa Street, one of which is the rectangular building, are lined with pillars, somewhat reminiscent of early suggestions for the Knesset building.

The massive plans were celebrated in the daily papers. They were described as the future local equivalent of the City of London[22], or of the New York Rockefeller Center[23]. Adopting the reconstruction discourse, reporters describe the existing site as a nuisance that will prevent the new buildings from being built[24]. They praise the new company hired for the job as "developers of urban centers instead of slums, which are being destroyed in London and in other cities"[25]. The papers also list the proposed tourist attractions planned for the site, including entertainment places, a hotel, playgrounds, and

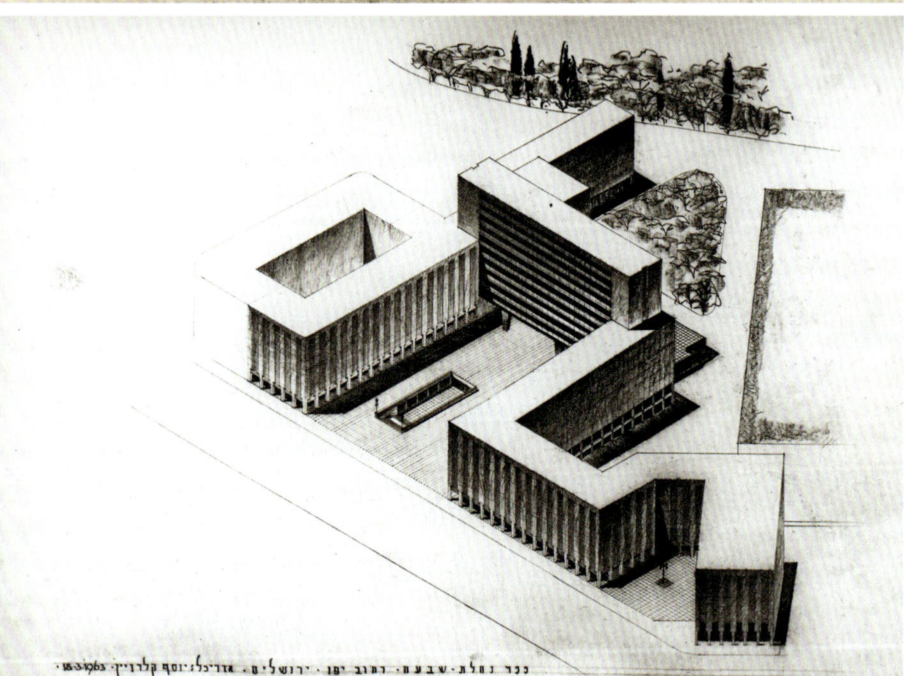

Various design approaches to the future architecture of Nahalat Shiva

holiday dwellings[26]. They hail the suggested observation tower, ‚equipped with binoculars,' which would compensate for the lack of the Old City and the access to the east: "From the watch tower, one would be able to view the Mediterranean Sea on one side, the Dead Sea, the old city and Ramla on the other"[27].
The connection to the past—whether the historic endangered neighborhood or the lost Old City—was indeed discussed. The new English developer demonstrated some sensitivity to the endangered synagogues, as he suggested leaving them "as an enclave, which will be a historical souvenir"[28]. Similarly, "in memory of Nahalat Shiva, the first neighborhood outside the Walls, it has been agreed that in the 'City,' a small garden will be planted and in its midst will remain the two synagogues of the neighborhood as historic sites. All the other old buildings will be destroyed"[29].

The final picture in Klarwein's archives relating to Nahalat Shiva is an undated photograph of Beit Joel: the only building completed before public outcry brought the project to a halt, and the neighborhood was spared. The structure retains many of the features suggested in the perspective drawings, including the rectangular, simple mass, and pillars supporting the first floor. Nevertheless, it also bears the name of one of the seven founders of the neighborhood, as suggested back in 1939 by his family[30].

Beit Joel, first building phase (1960)

Klarwein's modernism in a modernizing country

The architectural historian Zvi Efrat describes Klarwein's plans for the Knesset as the epitome of Statism, which he defines as "a unifying, flattening, and hollowing slogan, providing a common meta-cultural objective and an instant collective identity to an emerging society of immigrants, exiles, and settlers, a group allegedly too heterogeneous and feeble to survive as a body politic"[31]. Inbal Ben-Asher Gitler and Anat Geva similarly described Israel's built environment as a continuation of pre-state architectural culture, which aimed to convey the perception of Israel as progressive and as home to an advanced new Jewish society that is part of Western culture. They attest that the adaptation of Western architectural culture and technologies to the national policy of establishing a new, unified Jewish society entailed ignoring immigrants' cultural collective memories and often disregarding Israeli regional or local environments[32].

Joseph Klarwein's largely uncredited work for East Jerusalem from the end of the mandate into the early years of Israeli statehood may reflect the young state's needs and environmental cost. However, the idea of placelessness or internationality[33] rendered in his plans and sketches for East Jerusalem could not withstand the weight of history of Nahalat Shiva and its adjacent sites, especially when it was considered as a substitute for the Old City itself.

1 Nahum Melzer and Itzhak Yacobi, Nahalat Shiva is renewing; in: 120 Years to Nahalat Shiva (1869-1989), Eli Shiller and Menachem Levine (eds.):Jerusalem 1989, p61 **2** Eldad Brin and Igal Charney: Planning as political declaration: reappraising the first Israeli outline scheme for Jerusalem; in: Town Planning Review, 89 (6) 2018 https://doi.org/10.3828/tpr.2018.42 refrain from mentioning Klarwein's name for lack of certainty regarding his official role. **3** Noah Hysler-Rubin: Arts & crafts and the great city: Charles Robert Ashbee in Jerusalem; in: Planning Perspectives 2006, Vol. 21 (4), 347-368; Geography, colonialism and town planning: Patrick Geddes' plan for mandatory Jerusalem; in: cultural geographies 18 (2), 231-248, 2011 **4** Israel Kimhi: "Planning Nahalat Shiva"; in: 120 Years to Nahalat Shiva (1869-1989), pp. 67-69. **5** Minutes of meeting no. 22 of the District Town Planning Commission, 12 May 1939, ISA 4162/33-m: Development Scheme of Nahlat Shiva'a (digital file 000af3s). **6** Wardens of "Nahlat Jacob" synagogue at Nahlat Shiva Qr." 13 August 1939 ISA 4162/33-m (000af3s). **7** letters from S. Horowitz and. Co., Jacob Solomon, Abraham Levin, Naftali Lipscutz, and Nehemis Solomon to A.K. Park, City Engineer, 25 November 1947, ISA 4162/33-m (000af3s). **8** invitation letter from Arab company asking for the plan – (private archive) **9** Noah Hysler Rubin, Israel Kimhi: Planning Jerusalem, 1948-1968: Between the City and the Nation; in: Jerusalem Book Series, 1948-1973; Amnon Ramon, Arnon Golan, Assaf Zeltzer and Reuven Gafni (eds.), Jerusalem 2023, pp. 59—84. **10** Israel Kimhi: Planning Nahalat Shiva; in: 120 Years to Nahalat Shiva (1869-1989), p. 69. **11** Arieh Sharon: Jerusalem Outline Scheme; in: Physical Planning in Israel, 1951, p. 25. **12** Yossef Cohen, M. Amiaz, M. Shaviv, Eng. Yaacov Ben-Sira and A. Brutzkus: Suggestions for Slum-Clearance Policy in Israel; in: Megamot 1955 (4), pp. 346-361 **13** Shaviv, ibid, pp. 351-2. **14** 1955 plan draft; in: Noah Hysler Rubin and Israel Kimhi, ibid. **15** Haaretz, 6 October 1955; Slum clearance in the Capital, Haaretz 13 October 1955. **16** https://apps.land.gov.il/IturTabotData/tabot/jerus/1006733.pdf, last visited 24 November 2024. **17** Menachem Levine: The Development of Nahalat Shiva; in: 120 Years to Nahalat Shiva (1869-1989), Eli Shiller and Menachem Levine (eds.); Jerusalem 1989, p. 55. **18** Israel Kimhi: Planning Nahalat Shiva; in: 120 Years to Nahalat Shiva (1869-1989), ibid, p. 69. **19** Yossef Rivlin: Fifty years to the first neighborhood out of the Walls, Haaretz 6 February 1960. **20** A plan for the rehabilitation of Nahalat Shiva in Jerusalem, HaZofe 29 February 1960. **21** Eli Mezger: Nahalat Shiva, Haaretz 15 March 1959. **22** Yossef Harif: Nahalat Shiva will turn into the "City" of Jerusalem, Maariv 20 January 1963. **23** Three large building plans are being prepared for the center of Jerusalem, HaZofe, 25 January 1965. **24** Haaretz 9 September 1963; Extensive development plans in Jerusalem: Nahalat Shiva will be rehabilitated and a new entertainment center built, HaZofe 19 May 1963. **25** A negotiation is being carried out for the rehabilitation of Nahalat Shiva in Jerusalem, HaZofe, 24 Tevet 5763 (20.1.19). **26** Haaretz 19 May 1963; HaZofe 19 May 1963 Extensive development plans in Jerusalem: Nahalat Shiva will be rehabilitated and a new entertainment center built. **27** Lamerhav 19 May 1963 **28** A negotiation is being carried out for the rehabilitation of Nahalat Shiva in Jerusalem, HaZofe, 24 Tevet 5763 (20 January 1963). **29** Yossef Harif: Nahalat Shiva will turn into the "City" of Jerusalem; Maariv 20 January 1963. **30** CZA File A455-55 also contains detailed plans of the buildings but they are signed by Arch. Daniel Levine. **31** Zvi Efrat, The Object of Zionism: The Architecture of Israel; Leipzig 2019, p. 388. **32** Inbal Ben-Asher Gitler and Anat Geva (eds.): Israel as a Modern Architectural Experimental Lab, 1948-1978; Bristol/Chicago 2020, p. 4. **33** Ben-Asher Gitler and Geva, ibid.

THE KNESSET
BALANCING SPACE AND DEMOCRACY

Charcoal drawings by Klarwein of the proposed Knesset building from the architectural competition

Talia Margalit

Joseph Klarwein's winning design for the Knesset building in Jerusalem sparked intense professional and public criticism when first made public in July 1957. In the following years, he found himself isolated, facing the Architects' Association, whose members vehemently argued that his plan was monumental, neoclassical, even fascist, and therefore inappropriate for a democracy, especially in Israel. Over time, this influential group of architects successfully intervened to alter the plan. This essay will not detail the relationships, decisions, and changes that led to the building's completion[1], but will instead focus on the disparity between Klarwein's vision and that of the association, and how forcefully this association promoted a staunchly European Modernist style as the sole expression of the young nation's values.

After the establishment of the state, the "Capital"—Israel's governmental center—was planned in western Jerusalem as a spatial expression of the separation of powers, with designated areas for the Knesset (parliament), the judiciary, and the executive branch

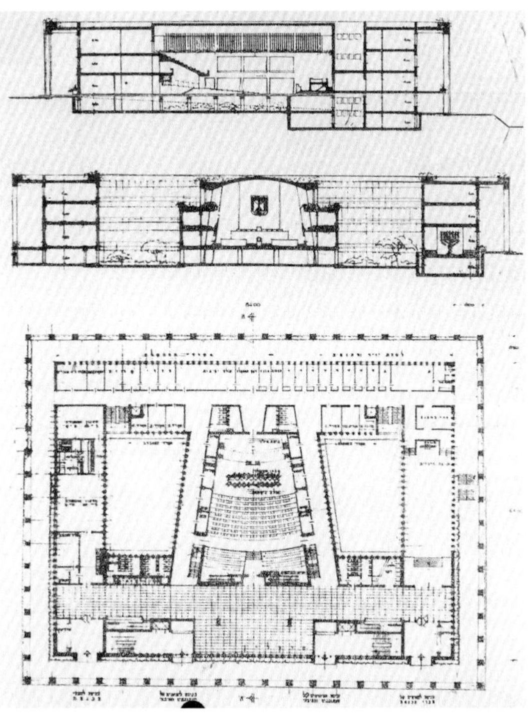

Floor plan and sections of Klarwein's entry to the competition / Model of Klarwein's entry

(government ministries). The Knesset site was chosen on a prominent hill to emphasize its importance as the center of democracy. On 25 July 1956, an open architectural competition for a permanent Knesset building was announced. The judges included the Minister of the Interior, Knesset members and staff, government representatives, and prominent, active members of the Architects Association. On 22 July 1957, Prime Minister David Ben-Gurion announced a donation from the estate of the late James de Rothschild for the new building's construction, and the judges soon announced their selection of Klarwein's proposal. This design featured a single, rectangular building with the plenary hall situated centrally between two internal courtyards, and the four facades lined with tall pillars (Figures 1,2,3), which Klarwein explained were an allusion to the columns of the ancient Temple.

The judges' statement declared the winning building would be "a magnificent symbol of the State of Israel," adding that "the use of classical allusions in the architectural composition lends the building a certain majesty that inspires respect in all who approach it"[2]. They also praised the building's modesty, stating that it "beautifully serves its unique purpose through its placement on a site of moderate proportions... and through the dignified appearance of its structure from all sides." The judges found no other submission close enough in merit to award second prize.

Articles published in the following days celebrated the win, also emphasizing Klarwein's choice of local historical symbolism:

"Before him loomed the Gothic spires of German and Austrian government buildings, the Italian Renaissance mausoleums, soaring minarets piercing the sky, and meticulously carved stone fortresses like those of London and Paris, as well as the immense dome crowning the American Capitol building. He turned his back on all of these. He preferred the ancient city walls, studying their curves and projections through his binoculars, spending hours examining the Herodian tombs. He sought to understand the secrets of the anonymous architects of Suleiman the Magnificent and decided that his design would be a fusion of acropolis-style architecture against the backdrop of the Jerusalem landscape..."[3].

Klarwein saw no contradiction between modernism and historical, even oriental, or Middle Eastern, influences in his design approach. When a journalist asked him "Why the Jerusalem walls?", Klarwein replied: "They are built of straight, simple lines. Simple, austere stones like the stones and rocks around them. It's always beautiful, modern, and beautiful." Yet, it was also noted that Klarwein "loathes modernism. He himself lives in a 90-year-old curved house in Jerusalem.... Here there's atmosphere, says the creator, there's ambiance; an architect can't work without drawing inspiration, and what finer inspiration is there than the curves above my head, an ocean of architectural ideas."

This text, along with the published building plans, likely fueled the opposition from the Architects' Association. Like Klarwein, they all came from Europe, but while he lived in Jerusalem, most of the Association members resided in Tel Aviv and advocated for a purely modernist style devoid of historical, local and Middle Eastern influences. Two weeks after the judges' decision, this was already hinted at in another article about the victory[4], which noted "Many of those who read the decision disagreed with it... Those who saw the plan that won third prize... began to consider whether it wasn't a more successful example, at least formally. The building's facade is pan-

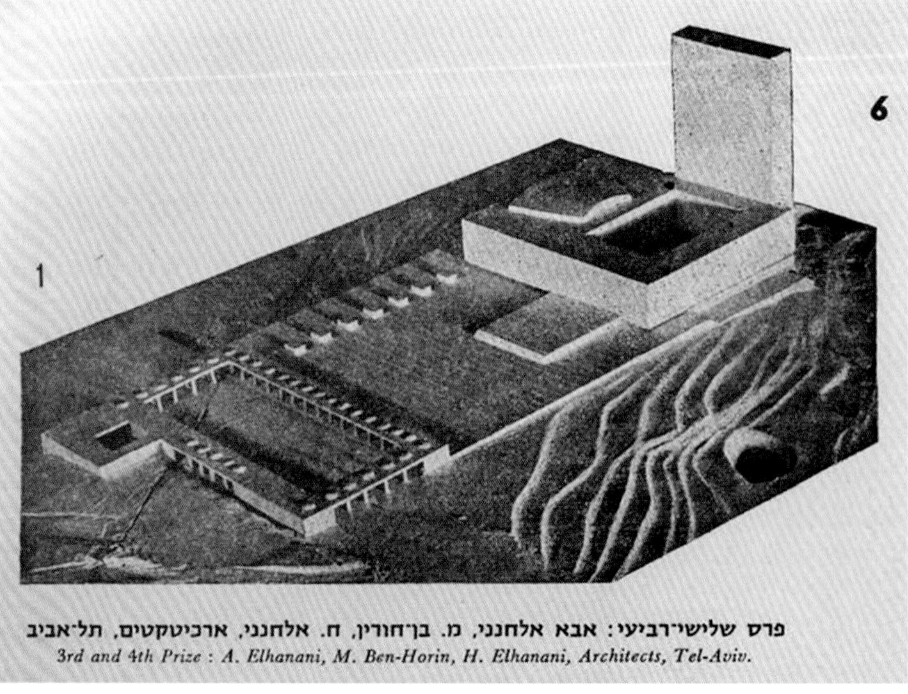

Entry by A. Elhanani, M. Ben-Horin, H. Elhanani, awarded joint third and fourth position

בית הכיפה. תוכנית זו, אחת מ־35 התוכניות שהוגשו לתחרות ושמונה מהן, בין המעניינות ביותר, מתפרסמות בעמודים אלה בסדר מקרי, מציעה פתרון אופייני למספר רב של תוכניות: המשרדים, השרותים, אולמות המשנה, מסודרים מסביב לחצר פנימית והאולם המרכזי, אולם הכנסת, בנוי בהמשך המיבנה. תקרת אולם מליאת הכנסת, בתוכנית זו, מכוסה בכיפה גדולה ומקומרת, הבולטת כלפי חוץ.

1

מבוך. האדריכלים רובין ופרידמן מירושלים זכו עבור תוכנית זו בקניה שלישית. התוכנית מצולמת מאחור, מצד הכביש המוליך אל קרית הממשלה. הפתרון בתוכנית מדגיש את אולם הכנסת בצורת אולם קולנוע הבולט מעל רחבת הכנ… …ת קטנות משני צידיו. המשרדים … …ין צורה בלתי מסודרת.

2

בית המעלות. בנין בן עשר קומות מוצע בתוכנית בה מופרדים המש־רדים מן האולם, הנמצא בגוש נפרד לגמרי שצורתו דומה לסופג־דיו הפוך. הבנין המפוצל דומה יותר למרכז מסחרי אזרחי מאשר למיבנה מייצג כ־בניין הכנסת … מקשה ללא צורך על הע־בודה בבית … צורת פני השטח בקריה.

3

פרס שלישי. האדריכלים לוטן, מור ותורן מתל־אביב זכו בפרס השלישי־רביעי עבור תוכנית זו „שהיא פשוטה ביותר אך יחד עם זאת לא הצליחה לתת ביטוי מתאים לייעוד הבניין," קבעה וועדת השופטים בהערכתה ל־תוכנית. גם בתוכנית זו, כבתוכנית מספר 1 בעמוד זה, מסודרים גושי בניני המשרדים השונים סביב חצר, ואולם הכנסת מתנשא מעל לבנין כולו.

4

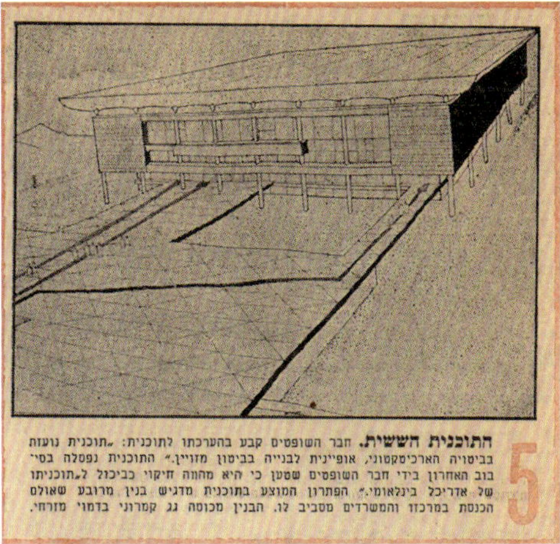

התוכנית הששית. חבר השופטים קבע בהערכתו לתוכנית: „תוכנית נועזת בביטויה הארכיטקטוני, אופיינית לבנייה בביטון מזויין." התוכנית נפסלה בסי־בוב האחרון בידי חבר השופטים שטען כי היא מהווה חיקוי כביכול ל„תוכניתו של אדריכל בינלאומי." הפתרון המוצע בתוכנית מדגיש בנין מרובע שאולם הכנסת במרכזו והמשרדים מסביב לו. הבנין מכוסה גג קמרוני בדמוי מזרחי.

5

בית הכיפה 2. בקניה שניה זכה האדריכל הצעיר מנחם כהן, שזכה לפני זמן לא רב בפרס הראשון בתחרות על בנין בית עירית תל־אביב. כהן לא הצליח ביותר בפתרון תפקידיו של הבנין שבצורתו מזכיר את התוכניות 1 ו־4 המופיעות בעמודים אלה. גם לבנין של כהן ישנה כיפה מעל לאולם הכנסת, והמשרדים מסודרים מסביב לחצר פנימית שבצד האולם הראשי.

7

Six further entries by mostly unknown participants; no. 7 is the project of Menachem Cohen

eled with glass... The office wing rises 18 stories and is prominent from afar... The distances for movement are balanced and elevators are used".

Reading this article, the impression is that Klarwein already felt attacked and began justifying his choices using modernist terms. Unlike his earlier pride in his sources of inspiration, he now explained the colonnade as "a natural and simple solution for shielding against the sun's rays," claimed his was the most economical proposal submitted, and stated that "I didn't specifically seek Oriental inspiration; perhaps I drew inspiration from the simplicity of Egyptian temples, but the style I've designed here belongs to no specific period, it belongs to all periods."

In the following days, several architects hinted at conspiracy and corruption in the competition. An emergency meeting of the architects took place, and they called for the cancellation of the decision. Subsequently, the association's chair, leading architect Arieh Sharon, sent a letter to the Knesset presidium requesting an urgent meeting and a delay of practical steps related to the Knesset construction plan until that meeting.

Even before a response from the Knesset arrived, the Architects' Association's discussion was detailed in the provocative newspaper ‚Ha'olam Hazeh')This World). On 8 August[5], a bold headline announced "The Knesset Building Scandal," with a sub-headline explaining that the controversy stemmed from "suspicions of favoritism, poor judgment, hints of bribery, and expressions of malignant cronyism." However, the article offered no evidence of corruption, instead focusing on stylistic and ideological arguments against the design: the building was deemed out-of-date; "The spirit of the twentieth century, which created new approaches to building art, is not reflected at all in this plan, which ignores even the latest achievements in building materials and design." It lacked "the spirit of the land and its nascent development," presenting "static rigidity" instead of dynamism and progress; the design's uniformity, "rooted in a desire for monumentality," was criticized as monotonous; the building was "alien and detached from its surroundings"; and, most critically, "the building's style displays a tendency towards neoclassicism, typical of authoritarian regimes."

This harsh criticism, twelve years after the end of World War II and the Holocaust, was meant to firmly reject Klarwein's design as not modernistic and therefore unsuitable for Israel. The style was described as representing a "conservative neoclassical approach," with architects, "mostly from the older generation," filling city streets with symmetrical, columned buildings. Such styles, the article argued, were favored by authoritarian regimes, from the pharaohs of Egypt to Hitler, Mussolini, and Stalin, who wanted their buildings "to project an aura of menacing power" to all who saw them. The article concluded by showing designs that had done well in the competition, alongside positive descriptions of Modernist plans that emphasized different functions through the separation of building blocks or the use of reinforced concrete.

The comparison of Klarwein's design to fascist architecture was repeatedly made in the press, citing architects and architectural academics. Shlomo Shaag from the Technion was quoted as claiming that "Klarwein's plan follows the examples of buildings erected by Hitler and Mussolini...all those horrifying columns... this alone is an affront to our national sentiment."[6] Journalist S. Itur[7] reported on a meeting between the Architects' Association and the head of the competition's judging panel, where critics argued that "a building with columns is alien to the spirit of Judaism and reflects Greek style instead," claiming that the columns "would inspire feelings of insignificance and powerlessness in all who enter or see the building." It was also reported that "the most extreme critics see the colonnaded building as an expression of tyranny; they point to them as columns of thugs and note that the fascist style favored colonnaded buildings—and we have no need to emulate this style." Architect Mordechai Ben Horin, disappointed that his high-rise design only won third prize, wrote to Ha'aretz on 12 November 1957, about the winning building: "Its style is pseudo-classical. Tyrants and despots seeking to gain power over people choose the pseudo-classical style for the facades of their public and government buildings. A Knesset building in this style is alien to us and to the spirit of democracy."

By this point, the association had withdrawn its calls for the cancellation of the win and downplayed earlier suggestions of corruption. A professional article in The Bulletin of the Association of Engineers and Architects in Israel[8] claimed that the judges acted "to the best of their ability and conscience." The article presented both Klarwein's and the third-place designs, arguing that a significant

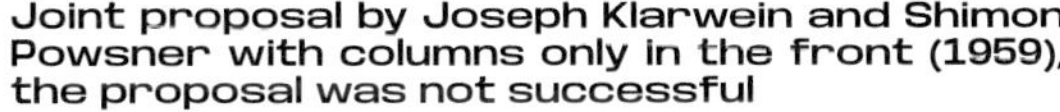

Joint proposal by Joseph Klarwein and Shimon Powsner with columns only in the front (1959), the proposal was not successful

portion of the architectural community, committed to modern architecture, viewed Klarwein's design as connected to "the shadows of the past" and to a "narrow path, rejecting what they considered the dawn of a new era in construction." While advocating for strict modernism as the only path, the architects confidently expressed the belief that this was also public opinion: "The public began to fear that the building would not be suitable for them or the times, and anxiously awaited the outcome of the debate, as covered in the press," leading to pressure on the Knesset presidium to "increase its responsibility."

Although they themselves saw no fault in the plan and believed, it would resonate with the public, Knesset officials struggled to address the criticism and they referred the plan for further review to a subcommittee of foreign experts, and even sent Klarwein on a study tour abroad. This led to years of delays in the planning process. Klarwein was joined by a consulting architect, Shimon Powsner, who rotated the building's entrance from north to south and significantly altered the plan while Klarwein was abroad.

Klarwein strongly opposed this, and the Knesset Speaker ultimately decided to revert to the original location. In the end Powsner was replaced by the architects Dov and Ram Karmi with Bill Gillit, who, along with Klarwein, finalized the plan. The colonnade remained, with a flat cantilever concrete roof added above. The building was raised above three stories of terraced offices; the interior plan was revised, and numerous artworks and sculptures representing Jewish culture and tradition were placed inside and around the structure. Most of the building was clad with stones from various regions of Israel, although fair faced concrete was also used, particularly in the pillars.

Ultimately, the insistent demand for a modern, open, and airy Knesset building was not realized. The final structure is, in fact, far more monumental than Klarwein's original design, and it also incorporates historical influences). Researchers suggest[9] that the need to create a visually impressive building, along with the numerous pressures and changes under time constraints, resulted in a blend of Karmi's and Klarwein's ideas. Conversely, Karmi's later buildings show a tendency towards monumentality that likely influenced his contribution to the Knesset' design.

At a time when freedom of speech in Israel is threatened and autocratic forces are working to curtail democracy and abolish the separation of powers, the story presented here alludes to the inherent difficulties in Israel's hegemonic democratic discourse from its very beginning. As shown in the architectural context, this discourse promoted a single, uniform style, condescendingly dismissing Klarwein's complex vision and instrumentally manipulating the memory of the Holocaust. Furthermore, the discussion of democracy was elitist and exclusive, ignoring Middle Eastern cultures, Arab citizens, and Knesset members.

The Knesset building opened at the end of August 1966, with a state ceremony and celebrations that lasted several days. The following year, Jerusalem was changed with the conquest of the East City. From that point forward, the face of the country also changed completely. However, the limitations inherent in the early dominant discourse, including the discourse of the Architects' Association presented here, laid the groundwork for deep-seated conflicts that have cast, and continue to cast, a shadow over Israeli society and politics.

Inauguration of the Knesset building on 30 August 1966

1 For a detailed account of this process, see: Rolef (2000) and additionally "Knesset Planning: Additions to the Article," Cathedra 105, 2003, pp. 171-180. **2** The judges' decision, 24 July 1957, Knesset Archives. **3** Yonatan Amir, "The Owner of Plan Number 13," Maariv, 26 July 1957, p. 2. **4** The House of Representatives," Davar, 2 August 1957, p. 23. **5** Ha'olam Hazeh, issue 1034, pp. 7-9. **6** Ha'aretz, 16 August 1957. **7** S. Itur, "The Storm Around the Tall Columns," Maariv, 21 August 1957, p. 2. **8** Bulletin C, Volume 15 October 1957, pp. 2-8. **9** See endnote 1.

Current situation of the Knesset with exposed concrete pillars and reddish stone cladding

OSSIP KLARWEIN ANNOTATED CATALOG OF WORKS

Johannes Cramer

Preface

The work of Klarwein has, in light of his life's achievements and his significance in the development of the State of Israel, remained surprisingly overlooked. There is no monographic literature. Wikipedia lists two German and one English page[1], all with contradictory, incomplete, and partly incorrect[2] information. In the context of the discussion on exile architecture, Myra Warhaftig[3] was the first to compile information about Klarwein's life and work in Palestine/Israel, later followed by Minta[4]. Klarwein himself repeatedly compiled lists of his works, though these are clearly focused on major buildings. Many smaller projects, especially entries to competitions, have been forgotten[5]. The buildings and projects Klarwein worked on while at the Höger office are extensively discussed by Turtenwald[6] as designs by Höger—only occasionally mentioning Klarwein's co-authorship. His architectural activity in Palestine/Israel can be recon-

structed from building records, notes, and documents in family archives as well as Klarwein's own estate, which is held under the reference number A 455 at the Central Zionist Archives (CZA) in Jerusalem. However, it contains only a relatively small number of fully developed architectural drawings. The collection primarily consists of sketches and (model) photographs.
Israeli research, even for his major works, has so far failed to produce monographs. It focuses on the design of the memorial for Theodor Herzl (1949–60)[7], the competition and construction of the Knesset[8] from 1957–66, and his urban planning projects for the Hebrew University[9] in Givat Ram and the government district Kiryat HaMemshala[10]. The now thoroughly researched contributions of "Bauhaus architects" to the development of Tel Aviv, for example, completely ignore Klarwein[11].

This body of material has been expanded through extensive personal research in German and Israeli archives and through extensive fieldwork, especially in Israel. Nonetheless, completeness cannot be expected. In the estate, there are numerous sketches and even fully rendered perspectives that have yet to be assigned to specific building projects. At times, it remains unclear whether they were created before or after emigration.

Altogether, 63 constructed and 41 unrealized buildings, as well as 7 urban planning projects and 15 other works, totaling 126 projects by Ossip/Joseph Klarwein, are currently documented. In addition, there are sketches for many other buildings that cannot be clearly attributed. Of the constructed works, more than half still exist—albeit often in significantly altered form. This should suffice to bring the work of an architect, unjustly largely forgotten, back into public awareness.

1 https://de.wikipedia.org/wiki/Ossip_Klarwein (created 20 November 2012 by Ulf Heinsohn – accessed 1 Februar 2024); https://dewiki.de/Lexikon/Ossip_Klarwein; www.archinform.net (15 April 2024); https://en.wikipedia.org/wiki/Ossip_Klarwein (1 Februar 2024); as well as numerous other pages with fragmentary references. **2** For example, the ZOA (Zionist Organization of America) House in Tel Aviv is repeatedly attributed to Klarwein. In fact, it was designed by Ibn Gabirol, Rosenblum, and Dubnow (Mozes 1952). Klarwein did win the competition but did not receive the commission. Similarly, the Israeli Pavilion at the 1958 World's Fair in Brussels was designed by Arieh Sharon, B. Idelson, and Arieh Elhanani. **3** Warhaftig 1996, pp. 294–99, and Warhaftig 2005. **4** Minta 2004 and 2013. **5** CZA A 455/7; comparison with Klarwein's office cash books from 1952 to 1967 confirms that mainly small projects are not listed. **6** Turtenwald 2003. Sources cited there, as well as publicly available online information, are not listed again here. **7** Maoz 1996, Bar 2016 and 2020. **8** Hattis Rolef 2000. **9** Dolev 2006. **10** Dolev 2000. **11** Stabenow/Schüler 2018, Boness 2012, Stephan 2019.

Printed caption: Motto: Polygon 3rd Place Arch: J. Klarwein Bremen, Handwritten: Water tower for Varel i/Old 1911 (more likely 1912/13)

VAREL (OLDENBURG), WATER TOWER 1911 COMPETITION

Source: CZA A455/61
Project

This document depicts a 12-sided, almost completely closed high tower, topped with a fully windowed dome for the water tank. The stairway to the tank was envisioned on one side of the building. The foot of the tower is encircled by a single-storey residential home with a hipped roof in reform architecture style. I The tower was completed in 1914 according to the plans of a different architect.

HAMBURG-BARMBEK, BUGENHAGEN CHURCH 1925 COMPETITION

Source: CZA A455/7 and 61, Turtenwald #14
Project

According to a Klarwein-compiled catalog of works, he took part in a 1925 competition for the new construction of Bugenhagen Church in Hamburg-Barmbek. There are contradictory accounts as to whether he did this while already working in the Höger office. Only five architects were invited to take part in this competition, including Fritz Höger but not Klarwein. It seems likely that Klarwein was already working for the Höger practice in 1925, but an account of Distel/Grubitz from November 1926 contradicts this. Perhaps Klarwein worked for both at the same time? There is nothing in Klarwein's estate that relates to the two designs from the Höger studio sketched by Turtenwald. So it remains unclear what Klarwein's role in this project was. I The monumental building was completed by Emil Heynen from 1927-29.

HANOVER, NATURAL HISTORY MUSEUM 1927 COMPETITION, PURCHASE

Source: CZA A455/7; Turtenwald #162; ZB 1927, p312 u. 570, Volkswille 192
Project, Condition: extant

A competition was run for architects based in the province of Hanover, with three special invitations issued to Kreis (Dresden), Straumer (Berlin) and Bonatz (Stuttgart). Straumer won the contest, and Höger received a partial purchase but the project was never completed. I Klarwein records the purchase derived from the competition as his achievement, with no mention of Höger. There is an undated newspaper clip in the estate with an illustration that records Höger as author of contribution No. 12. Furthermore, there exists a hand-drawn sketch by Klarwein just like the abovementioned one in the newspaper article.

Sketch from the competition

HAMBURG-WANDSBEK, REEMTSMA TOBACCO FACTORY EXTENSION 1926–27/29

Walddörfer Str. 103
Source: Turtenwald #169; Bucciarelli p122-23
Condition: extant

Possible preliminary sketch. The head of the pilasters is similar to the completed building / Historic photo

In 1926 Höger was commissioned by the Reemtsma brothers to extend the existing factory building by Klophaus & Schoch (1925). The monumental, five-storey block features a functional grid facade. This is structured by prominent pilasters of spirally arranged bricks with column heads similar to capitals. It is also effectively ordered by protruding and receding clinker elements. The window panes were originally made of domed glass. ❙ The second phase of construction was completed immediately after the first. The basic design principles remain the same, albeit with reduced and more abstract clinker decoration. A semi-circular stairwell towards the courtyard was added. ❙ Klarwein claims the building as one of his own. No sketches or drawings with a clear connection to this project have yet been found, although two studies for large office buildings may be related to the Reemtsma building.

FRANKFURT AM MAIN, HEAD OFFICE OF I.G. FARBEN 1928 COMPETITION, SECOND PRICE

Sources: CZA A455/34; Turtenwald #187
Project

Charcoal study and sketch for the entire complex by Klarwein

A limited competition was held in April 1928 for this building project between six invited architectural practices (Paul Bonatz, Martin Elsässer, Fritz Höger, Jakob Koerfer, Ernst May and Hans Poelzig). The result was that Höger and Poelzig were asked to revise their submissions. In the end, Poelzig was given the nod and Höger had to settle for second place. Poelzig completed the building in 1931. ❙ Klarwein lists the project in his catalog of works with the note "(Hoeger)". Photos of several sketches, a site plan and a model are included in the CZA, which do not correspond in detail to the final approach. The design, which can be attributed to Klarwein based on his drawing technique, features a long, straight, connecting structure on the trapezoid site in Grüneburgpark, across which five high office wings are asymmetrically arranged. The highlight of the building complex is a high-rise on the opposite side. The basic layout has similarities with both the Bonatz and Poelzig approaches. All of the facades of the block-shaped cubes have strict vertical divisions which also detract from the heaviness of the overall structure. ❙ The basic ideas of the building composition are reflected in the 1953 master plan for the Hebrew University in Jerusalem.

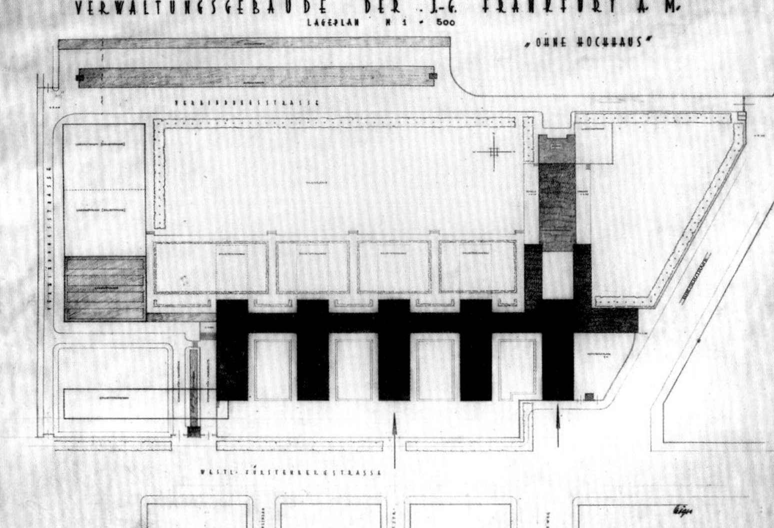

Model and site plan of the complex

HANOVER, THE ANZEIGER ("GAZETTE") HIGHRISE 1927–28

Goseriede 9
Source: CZA A 455/7 and 33; Turtenwald #171; Bucciarelli p128ff
Condition: extant

Historic view of the building after completion (1928)

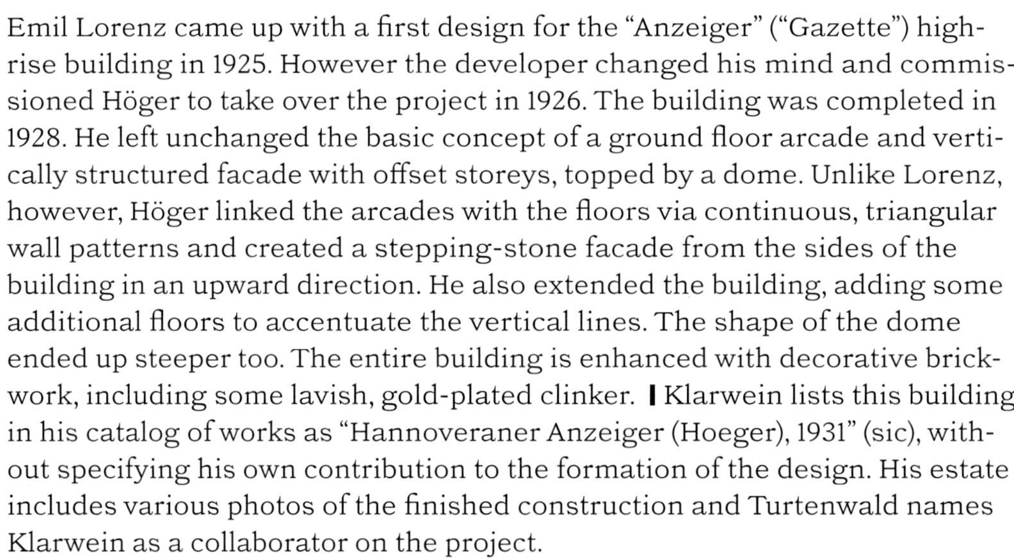

Emil Lorenz came up with a first design for the "Anzeiger" ("Gazette") highrise building in 1925. However the developer changed his mind and commissioned Höger to take over the project in 1926. The building was completed in 1928. He left unchanged the basic concept of a ground floor arcade and vertically structured facade with offset storeys, topped by a dome. Unlike Lorenz, however, Höger linked the arcades with the floors via continuous, triangular wall patterns and created a stepping-stone facade from the sides of the building in an upward direction. He also extended the building, adding some additional floors to accentuate the vertical lines. The shape of the dome ended up steeper too. The entire building is enhanced with decorative brickwork, including some lavish, gold-plated clinker. ❙ Klarwein lists this building in his catalog of works as "Hannoveraner Anzeiger (Hoeger), 1931" (sic), without specifying his own contribution to the formation of the design. His estate includes various photos of the finished construction and Turtenwald names Klarwein as a collaborator on the project.

HAMBURG-EPPENDORF, STATE HIGH SCHOOL 1926–28 COMPETITION

Hegestr. 35
Sources: CZA A455/7; Turtenwald #146; Bucciarelli p118ff
Condition: extant

An initial competition was run for the project in 1919, which Höger won, but the project was not completed due to allegations of plagiarism. The second competition was held in 1925. Höger was successful again, and this time he was commissioned to build the school. Planning began in 1926. The building complex consists of three different-sized cubes for the entrance, the hall and gymnasium and the classrooms together with science labs. It is dominated by a huge tower at the juncture of the hall and the classrooms. The tower and the two wings have a hipped roof, while the classrooms have a flat roof to allow for open-air classes. The early perspective drawings, which may have originated from the second competition, include lavish facade decoration in the style of architectural expressionism, which was increasingly toned down in the course of further specification – perhaps under the influence of Klarwein, who joined the practice in 1926? – in favor of a more block-like structure. The interior (turquoise green?) tiling requested by the teachers for the stairwells was dropped as a cost-saving measure. ❙ Klarwein lists the school in his catalog of works as “Staatliches Lyzeum in Hamburg-Eppendorf (Hoeger)”. There are no known sketches by Klarwein relating to this building. Turtenwald names “Müller” as his colleague on this project.

The complex composed of massive cubes of different sizes after completion in 1928

HAMBURG-LANGENHORN, ST ANSGAR’S CHURCH 1928 COMPETITION

Source: CZA A455/61; Turtenwald #198
Project

Development of the design from first sketches to the final model

The competition to design this church was run in 1928. Turtenwald refers to documents in Höger’s estate which point to Klarwein’s involvement in the design: “… while working on the church competition for Langenhorn, I (i.e. Klarwein) came … up with the idea of a shape similar to a pillared gable… but it was dropped for being too grandiose and monumental …”. The significance of style photos discovered as part of the estate, depicting an unusually conservative approach with a steep pitched roof and a block-like tower with a sharply pointed spire, is unclear. Perhaps a style photo attributed by Turtenwald to Winterhude is also a more modern version of this project. ❙ Herrmann Geißler and Otto Wilkening completed construction of the church by 1930.

"STADTKRONE" 1928

Source: CZA A455/7
Project

Charcoal drawings labelled "Stadtkrone" presenting the town hall of Rüstringen/Wilhelmshaven (left) and the church at Hohenzollernplatz, Berlin (right)

In his 1919 publication of the same name, Bruno Taut introduced the term "Stadtkrone" – "City Crown" – to architecture with the intention of providing cities with a profound design. The words and images of this publication became a point of reference for expressionist architecture. In his catalog of works, Klarwein lists "Stadtkrone 1928" without giving any indication of what this means. It remains unclear whether this may have been a reference to an architecture competition launched in 1927 and decided in 1928 to design a new landmark building for the city of Halle.

HAMBURG, SPRINKENHOF 1927–29/32/(43)

Burchardstr. 8
Source: CZA A455/7; Turtenwald #178; Bucciarelli p138-43
Condition: extant

View of the first phase (1929) with diagonal facade decoration similar to the future Dagon Silo in Haifa / Stairwell with original colouring based on findings by restorers

Sprinkenhof is a building complex which was completed in three phases. The aim was initially to alleviate the housing shortage by building small apartments which later might be converted into offices. The first building, completed in 1929, was designed with a rectangular floorplan as a closed, nine-storey cuboid with a large inner courtyard. The windows with domed glass are organised in a strict grid pattern. It is only the large driveways and rounded stairwell tower in the courtyard that soften the overall severity. The ground floor at street level is divided into large openings by clinker pillars with rounded, protruding capitals. The entire facade features a diagonally arranged diamond pattern, in the middle of which individually crafted, figurative brick medallions have been inserted. The interior design, in particular of the stairwells, is very colourful. The second phase, completed in 1932, picks up the design features of the first building, but replaces the diamonds with squares and dispenses with any figurative depictions on gilded brick medallions, which now are also squares. The third construction phase was not completed until 1943. **I** The sole indication of Klarwein's involvement with this project comes from his own records. But he can have referred to the first two phases only, as the third was planned after his forced emigration. The sketches found in his estate include a few drawings of large, block-like office buildings but they cannot be definitively linked to the Sprinkenhof complex. Two sketches, given an earlier dating by Turtenwald, of a pronounced vertical facade structure might relate to the Sprinkenhof project and can possibly be attributed to Klarwein. **I** Research concludes unanimously that Höger and the studio of Hans and Oskar Gerson were responsible for the first phase.

HAMBURG-GROSS BORSTEL, ST PETER'S CHURCH 1929; PARTIALLY BUILT 1932
COMPETITION, PURCHASE

Schrödersweg 1
Source: CZA A455/61; Turtenwald #208 and #235; ZB 1929, p524
Project; parish hall extant

The competition for construction of St Peter's Church was held in 1929. Although Höger was only given a purchase award, he was still commissioned to build the church. Financial difficulties however prevented construction of the church, so only a single-storey parish hall was erected in 1932 as a temporary church. It was given the name "Christus über den Wogen" ("Christ above the Waves") and is still in use today, in largely unaltered form. The actual church was not built until 1959 based on plans by Otto Andersen. **I** The significant involvement of Klarwein in this project is indicated in the first instance by his mention in the report on the competition results. In addition, four sketches have been found in Klarwein's estate, three of which are marked in his handwriting with the word "Borstel". What is more, his estate also includes photos of two models with different layouts and a precisely drawn floor plan. In all of these drafts, the huge church nave with vertically structured side walls is the dominant feature, along with a high, laterally positioned tower. In the course of development, the initially comparatively low pitch of the church roof became increasingly steep. The small parish hall appears in all versions as a side wing adjacent to the altar area.

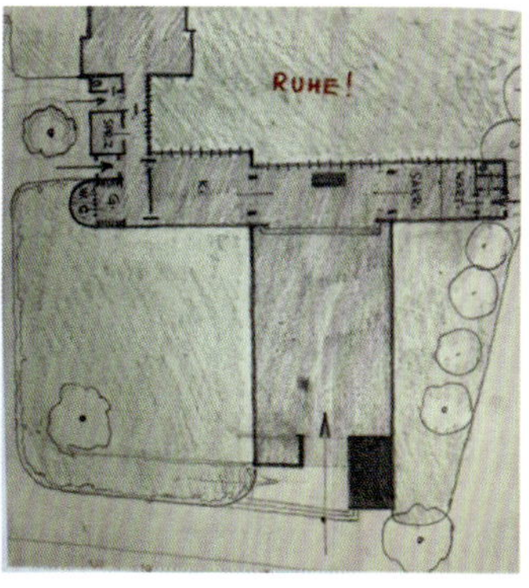

Two sketches, elaborate model and a precise floor plan of the project. Only the small rounded annex to the church was built before World War II broke out

HAMBURG-HAMM SÜD, WICHERN CHURCH 1929 COMPETITION, SECOND PLACE

Wichernsweg 16
Source: CZA A455/61; Turtenwald #214; Bucciarelli p164-65
Project

The site of the Wichern parish is opposite a broad green area on Droopweg and these days features extensive planting, with a simple church and parish offices constructed in 1954. It replaced a building destroyed during the war,

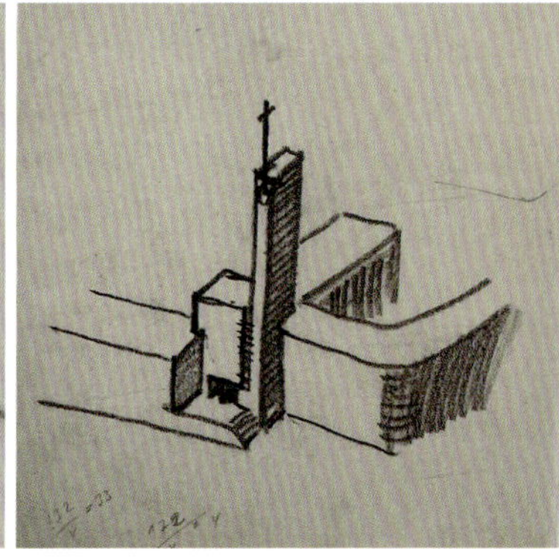

Sketches presenting the various solutions from ultra-modern to neogothic discussed in the Höger studio / At the bottom a sheet from the entry to the competition with the main elevation. Similarities to the Church at Hohenzollernplatz are evident

which had been erected as a temporary structure after a competition in 1929 in place of the large church building planned by Höger. ❙ Three very different projects were developed for the competition. One proposed a church nave as a cuboid on the corner of the site with windows on both sides parallel to Droopweg, with the tower on the west side. The two other proposals put the tower in the center of the site on Droopweg with the nave extending into the depth of the site. The more "modern" version of these two extends the corner of the plot into an open space, making the oversized tower visible along the street from afar. The conservative, neogothic design proposed a facade with a soaring, triangular front towering over the adjoining buildings. The overall urban effect results from the significant height and the unconventional shape. For this version, two models were also built. ❙ The involvement of Klarwein is evident on the one hand from his catalog of works, as well as from numerous sketches found in his estate. Five sketches show the "modern" option, four plus a model photo labeled by Klarwein relate to the "Gothic" version; one drawing in this project may well stem from Höger. ❙ Both Turtenwald and Buccarelli name Klarwein as a colleague on this project.

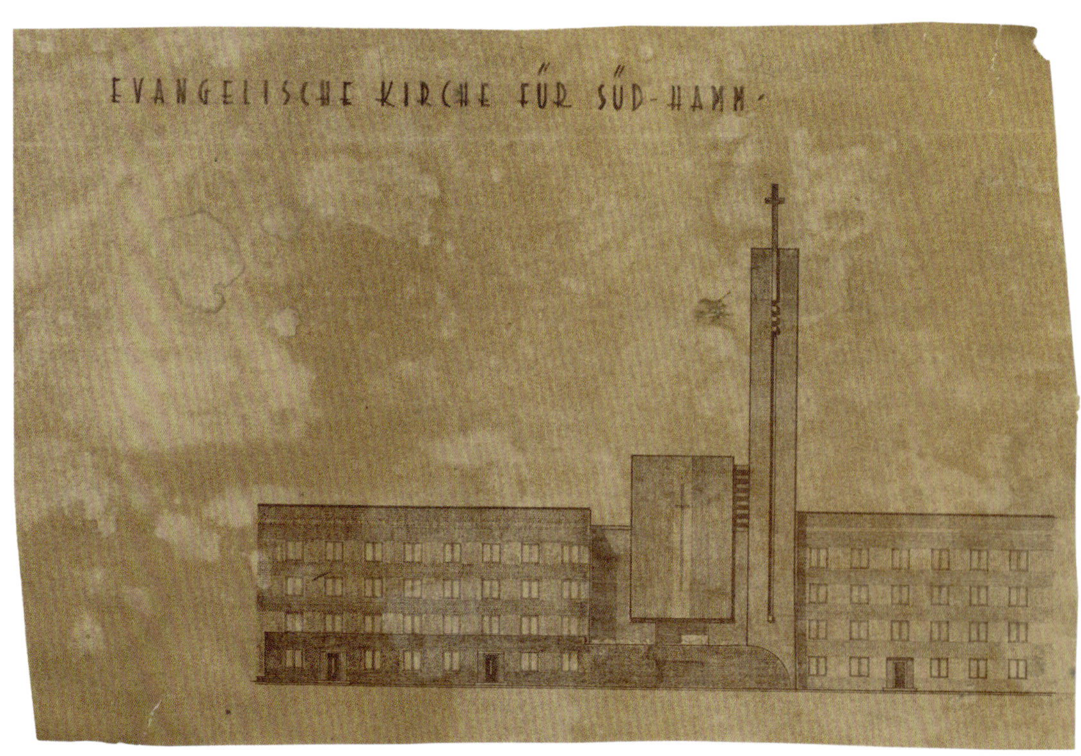

NURENBERG, TOWN HALL
1929 COMPETITION, SHORTLISTED

Source: CZA A455/7; Frankfurter Zeitung und Handelsblatt, 16.11.1929
Project

In his works catalog, Klarwein includes a submission to the design competition for a "Town Hall" in "Frankfurt". This no doubt relates to the nationwide competition run in 1929 by the city of Nuremberg, in which Klarwein participated. An article in "Frankfurter Zeitung" notes that Klarwein's submission made it onto the "short list". Klarwein probably confused the two cities when compiling his catalog of works in the fifties. The project was never realized.

RÜSTRINGEN (LATER WILHELMSHAVEN) TOWN HALL
1926–29 COMPETITION, FIRST PRIZE

Rathausplatz 1
Source: CZA A455/61; Turtenwald #177, p76ff; Bucciarelli p134
Condition: extant

Early sketch by Klarwein, undated / View of the entire complex with the water tower in the center / Stairwell with turquoise lining and colorful details

After much preliminary work done before Klarwein joined his office, Höger's studio was commissioned to build the town hall as the winner of a 1926 competition. The completed building was handed over to the client on 11 October 1929. The "Seaside Fortress" echoes the classic town hall structure with its massive tower in the center, which also serves as a water tower. Two wings with stepped floors house offices. The council chamber is located at the back of the building as a separate extension. The whole complex is structured by pilaster strips, which find their conclusion in a triangular shape on the tower. The notable features of the interior are the stairwell, lined with turquoise wall panels and the striking use of the colors red, black and beige, more muted today as a result of restoration. Evidence of Klarwein's participation in this project is provided in the first instance by his own claims. In addition, his estate includes several sketches with handwritten notations, which show all the design features

that were later realized, and some model photos and images of the completed building. The clear architectural composition also points to his involvement.

BERLIN-FROHNAU, ST JOHN'S CHURCH 1930 COMPETITION

Source: CZA A 455/61; Turtenwald #224
Project

Sketches signed by Klarwein with different solutions for the main facade and the position of the clock tower

The competition for construction of the church was held in 1930, with Höger/Klarwein not listed among the winners. Johannes and Walter Krüger were given the nod. The fact that Klarwein was involved in the project is evident from at least four perspective drawings with handwritten markings by Klarwein dated 1930. The church building is centrally positioned on the semi-circular Zeltinger Square. The sketches show different options for the monumental front. The flat-roofed nave is block-like with vertically divided side walls. The high tower is positioned to the side or above the altar.

BERLIN-LICHTERFELDE, MARTIN LUTHER CHURCH 1930 COMPETITION

Source: CZA A455/7; Turtenwald #224
Project

Model and sketch of the compound with church and rectory

The competition for construction of the new Martin Luther Church was decided on 13 May 1930. The design submitted by the Höger firm was unsuccessful. Fritz Schupp and Martin Kremmer were given the nod. **|** Klarwein does not include the project in his catalog of works. Nevertheless a sketch and two model photos were found in his estate. The three illustrations present different options for both the layout on site as well as the position of the church building and tower. All three designs share a block-like nave dominated by a soaring, cuboid tower. In the most detailed model, there is an undeniable similarity to the Church at Hohenzollernplatz which was being designed at the same time.

HAMBURG, WEMPE OFFICE BUILDING 1931

Source: CZA A455/61; Turtenwald #181; KuBi
Project

Nothing is known about the background to this project. The proposed building covers the entire corner site of an unknown Hamburg Jungfernstieg plot with a rounded facade. Based on the handwritten notes of two sketches, the work was commissioned by Oskar Wempe. **|** A color sketch dated 19 January 1931 bears Klarwein's unmistakable handwriting. A second, more detailed drawing was made by a different person. It remains doubtful whether a third sketch with a tower-like corner design relates to the same project.

HAMBURG-WINTERHUDE, CHAPEL 1932 COMPETITION

Source: CZA A 455/7; Turtenwald #234
Project

Model from the competition

In 1932 the Paul-Gerhardt parish ran a competition for the design of a new church, which the Höger firm also entered. In the end the parish decided to have just a small chapel erected in 1933, which today serves as the parish hall. The actual church was not completed until 1962. **|** Klarwein includes a design for this project in his catalog of works: "Project: Protestant Chapel for Winterhude, 1932", which was clearly never built. A model and four slightly varying sketches for an unknown project might relate to the dimensions of the site in question.

LEIPZIG, KONSUMZENTRALE 1929-32 COMPETITION, FIRST PRIZE

Industriestr. 95
Source: CZA A455/61; Turtenwald #204; Bucciarelli p158
Condition: extant

Sketch of the complex with handwritten remarks by Klarwein / General view of the complex / Historic photo soon after completion in 1932

This extensive building project was awarded to the Höger firm as the result of a 1928 competition and completed in 1932. Besides offices for the central administration block, a warehouse, workshops and car garages were requested. The office building is located on Jahnstrasse (now Industriestrasse), with the other buildings arranged behind it around a completely enclosed inner courtyard accessible only via a wide driveway. The facade of the office building features horizontal bands of windows, interrupted by emphatically vertical stairwells. The facades reveal an intriguing play on

Multicolored stairwell

different-colored clinker brick, artfully laid to produce a variety of patterns. The main entrance and driveway are given prominence in the overall design of the building. ❙ The public areas of the interior are characterized by bold colorful elements, with red handrails and stair posts, and large turquoise tiles on the walls. Numerous design details complement the overall effect. ❙ The involvement of Klarwein is indicated by his own catalog of works, as well as a sketch bearing his handwriting and dated 1928; Turtenwald also names him as a collaborator.

NORDENHAM, FISHERY PLANT 1932

Source: CZA A455/7 and 61
Project

The "Fishery Plant of North Sea Fisheries in Nordenham, 1931-32" is listed in Klarwein's self-compiled catalog of works as his own design. The Central Zionist Archive Jerusalem contains two design sketches marked "North Sea". It seems entirely plausible that both pieces of information belong together. Ship owner Adolf Vinnen commissioned the construction of the only private fishery port in Nordenham in the late 19th century and acquired a fleet of fishing boats. Until the start of World War II, the fishing industry was booming, so the plan for a new building seems completely realistic. However, there is no detailed evidence of this – partly because in competition with Geestmünde, Nordenham Fishery Port was abandoned after World War II and the harbor basin filled in. So the impact of this project remains unclear.

Sketch by Klarwein

"IMPERIAL MEMORIAL" FOR THE FALLEN OF THE WORLD WAR 1932 COMPETITION

Sources: CZA A455/7 and 61; Turtenwald #243, p185; Die Gartenkunst, 6/1932; Hilbig 2006, Project

The idea of honouring fallen soldiers with a central "Heldenhain" (Heroes' Grove) for the Reich had already emerged during World War I. After much debate, the crest of a hill near Bad Berka in Thuringia was selected as the location and a public competition was launched for the design. The jury had 1828 submissions to choose from and, after meeting on 12 May 1932, announced a shortlist of 153 designs. From that pool, 20 were selected for further refinement in a second phase and 20 other designs were purchased. It is not known where the Höger submission was placed, but it was not among the prize winners. ❙ Turtenwald assumes some involvement by Klarwein, who included the competition in his catalog of works. There are numerous sketches, dimensional plans, photo montages and a model photo of the project in the CZA archive. This all points to Klarwein making an essential – and perhaps the most significant – contribution to the design. He envisaged a flat dome 36 meters in diameter, open on the sides and with a large opening at the top above a "Sacrificial Bowl of Precious Stone" resting on a pentagonal pedestal within a pool of water five steps below the ground. ❙ The project was never carried out. Klarwein revived these ideas in his design for Theodor Herzl's grave in 1951.

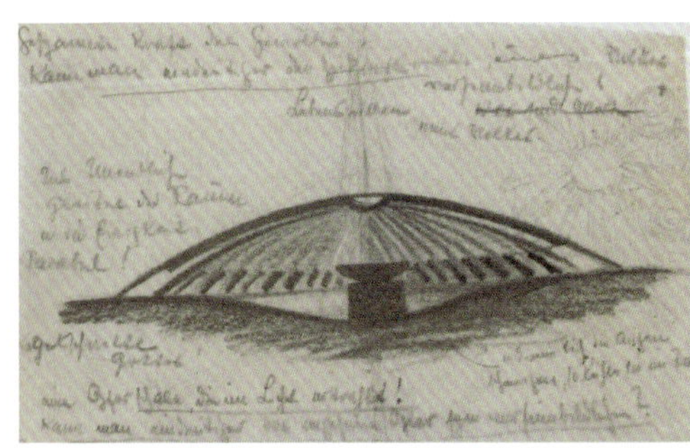

Sketch of the design with explanatory remarks / Situational study for the memorial in the forest

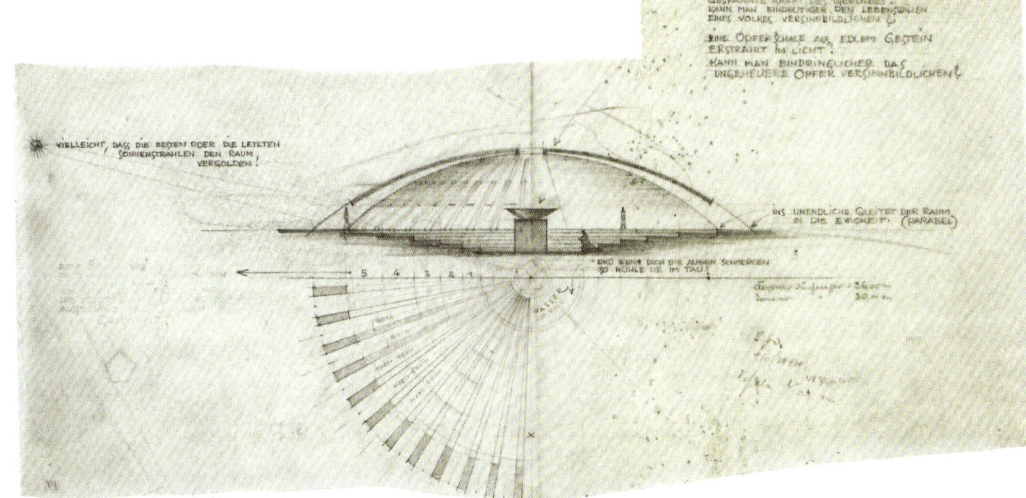

Elaborate drawing, section of the memorial with romantic annotations

DAS WACHSENDE HAUS / THE GROWING HOME 1932 COMPETITION

Sources: CZA A455/7; Turtenwald #236; Wagner 1932a, Wagner 1932b, Fröhlich 2008

Model of the starter home and its first extension

In view of the ongoing housing shortage in the late 1920s, Berlin City Planning Director, Martin Wagner, was keen to explore the idea of small, expandable houses, largely to be assembled on an industrial scale in a workshop. In conjunction with renowned architects, he formed a working group to develop the idea and carried out a competition entitled "The Growing Home" in 1932 with the Berlin Exhibition and Trade Fair Office. Designs were invited for a basic home with 25m² living space which could be gradually expanded to 80m². There were 1079 submissions. According to Turtenwald, the Höger firm was one of the contestants, with a project designed entirely by Ossip Klarwein. That design was purchased. **|** The starter home with flat roof and large glass doors would be erected in the centre of the building site. It could be extended on both sides by an additional room; if needed, a glasshouse could be added in front. **|** According to an article in the Palestine Post on 21 June 1937, Klarwein in cooperation with other colleagues applied his ideas for this project in 1937 to the development of a one-room home that would cost no more than 250 Palestine Pounds, the prototype for which was displayed at a trade fair in Haifa.

BERLIN, REICHSBANK 1933 COMPETITION

Source: Turtenwald #246; Secret Agreement Project

After lengthy preliminary work, the German Reichsbank (Central Bank) ran a competition in 1933 among 30 renowned architectural firms, including Höger, to extend its office space in Berlin-Mitte. In the end, however, on the instruction of Hitler, Heinrich Wolff was commissioned to do the work, regardless of the jury's suggestion. I No documents to do with Höger's contribution have been found. I However, the project is still relevant to the work of Klarwein and his position within the Höger firm, because there is a handwritten "Secret Agreement" dated 24 February 1933 among the Klarwein compensation files, where both parties agree that Klarwein, even after his resignation from the Höger firm, should continue to work on the project. However, for various and obvious reasons, nothing became of this agreement.

BERLIN, EVANGELISCHE KIRCHE AM HOHENZOLLERNPLATZ 1928–33

Nassauische Str. 66/67 and Hohenzollerndamm 202/203
→ Article Johannes Cramer; Source: Turtenwald #206
Condition: extant, some wartime damage, modernized

The Lutheran Church on Hohenzollernplatz with parish offices and parson's residence was the last project Klarwein worked on in the Höger Studio. His urban planning studies document an attempt to give concrete expression to the various different functions following the ideas of the International Style. In parallel to political developments, the architecture is gradually adapted from being avant-garde to markedly more conservative.

First approach with flat roofs, strip windows and no externally visible stairwells; later elaborate spire and finally high hipped roof over church and parish house

UNIDENTIFIED CHURCHES

Source: CZA A455/61
Projects

Apart from project related sketches, numerous additional studies can be found in the estate for presently unidentified church buildings (in Germany?). Apart from their broad sweep they also demonstrate a preference for clear volumes and often surprising compositions.

Berlin, Kirche am Hohenzollernplatz

The big Arlozoroff grave in the front, on the left the Nordau memorial, obscured Dizengoff and in the background on the left Tschernichovsky

TEL AVIV, TRUMPELDOR CEMETERY; MEMORIAL FOR CHAIM ARLOZOROFF 1934 COMPETITION

With Robert Friedmann
→ Article Doron Bar
Condition: extant

Chaim Arlozoroff (1899-1933) was born in Ukraine and studied in Berlin. In 1924, he emigrated to Palestine and was chosen in 1926 as representative of the Jewish community to the League of Nations. Subsequently, he played a major role in the founding and building of MAPAI (socialist party) and as an adviser to Chaim Weizmann. On 16. June 1933 Arlozoroff was murdered in a politically motivated assassination. I His memorial, reminiscent of a sarcophagus, is hewn from a single block with a smooth surface. It is placed asymmetrically on the gravesite. The incised inscription is almost obscured by the rim of the grave. I This gravesite was the first project Klarwein completed in Palestine.

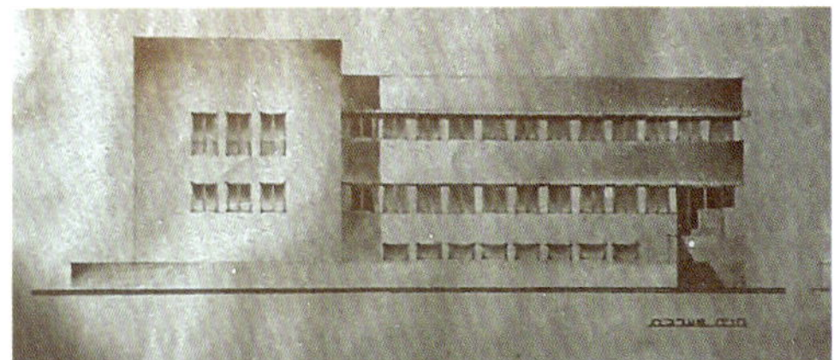

Competition entry 1934 / Stand frame from a film on the occasion of the laying of the cornerstone 1935

TEL AVIV, BEIT HAMEHANDES / ARCHITECTS AND ENGINEERS ASSOCIATION 1934 COMPETITION

Dizengoff St. 200
Source: CZA A455/61
Project

In 1934 Klarwein in cooperation with his colleague Robert Friedmann from Hamburg participated in the competition for "Beit HaMehandes", the seat of the "Association of Engineers and Architects in Israel". A drawing marked "Architect – Eng. House, Tel Aviv, first prize, OK 1934" ("Architekten – Ing. Haus, Tel Aviv, 1. Preis, OK 1934") is the first known work by Klarwein in Palestine. It shows an ensemble composed of shallow cubes including an assembly hall. After the completion of the selection process a dispute developed between the two participants about the authorship. The building for which construction started in 1935 differs substantially in design and execution from the competition entry. It remains unclear whether one of the two was actually responsible for completion of the project.

HAIFA, BEIT ZANG 1935

Bialik St./Ibn Sina St.
→ Article Dafna Berger; Source: CZA A455/7; Haifa City Archive
Condition: extant, without major changes

The residential and commercial building consisting of three floors is situated in the Old City. This type of building was preferred by many immigrants, comprising shops on the ground floor – which originally was left largely unenclosed – as well as rental apartments in the upper floors to ensure a regular income. The first residential project by Klarwein in Haifa.

TEL AVIV, HABIMA THEATRE 1933–45

Source: CZA A455/29 and 61; YBZ 0651_089
Condition: substantial changes

Early sketch from 1934 and a model of the complete complex comprising the Habima Theater (Kaufmann/Klarwein), the early Helena-Rubinstein-Museum (Karmi/Z.u.Y. Rechter) and the Charles Bronfman (formerly Fredric R. Mann) Auditorium (Karmi/Z.u.Y. Rechter) after a first redesign

In the Klarwein estate can be found a perspective sketch as well as numerous photos of models showing a building with a semicircular facade, a raised stage tower and a stepped rear. These are clearly preparatory designs for the Habima Theater in Tel Aviv, which was constructed from 1934 based on plans by Oskar Kaufmann. Klarwein and Kaufmann arrived in Palestine at almost exactly the same time. Possibly, Klarwein earned his first pounds as a collaborator in this project. All designs by Klarwein show the earliest stage of development before changes that led to the facade with columns in 1939.

HAIFA, BEIT ASCHNER 1937

13 Lotus St.
→ Article Dafna Berger; Source: CZA A455/7; Haifa City Archive; residents
Condition: extant, without major changes

The apartment building comprising three floors has a projecting flat roof and a lively appearance with bay windows and rounded balconies. In the family archives there is a framed perspective drawing of the building, signed in the lower righthand corner by Klarwein.

HAIFA, BEIT HAKRANOT 1935–37 / 1940 / 1954–56

Source: CZA A 455/7
Condition: slight changes

Klarwein constructed this office and commercial building on behalf of the two foundations Keren Kayemeth (Jewish National Fund) and Keren Hayesod (charity organization) in the Jewish quarter of Hadar HaCarmel, founded in 1920 on the slopes of Mount Carmel. Just above the site lies the original building of the Technion Haifa, constructed in 1912 based on designs by Alexander

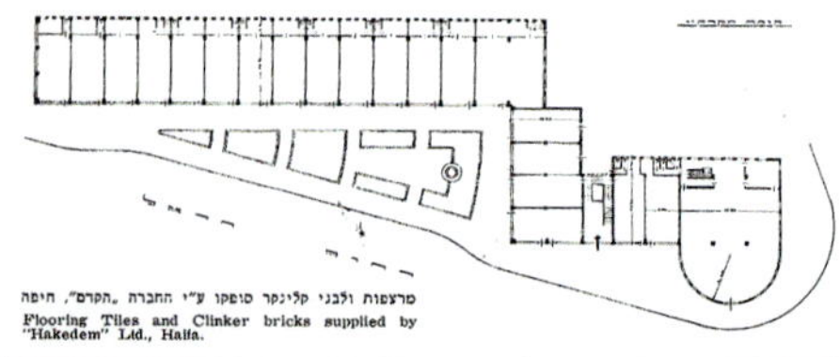

Floor plan and general view of the first building phase / Sketch by Klarwein dated 1935. There were major subsequent changes and this was only partly realized. In the background the original Technion building / Present situation

Baerwald of rough-hewn limestone, as well as the Hebrew Reali School in a similar style. A sketch by Klarwein from 1935 already shows an extensive complex of several buildings. However, only two floors of the foundation building complemented by a semicircular entrance building could be realized by 1937. The building with a smooth limestone facade had shops on the ground floor, offices in the upper floor. Klarwein had his own architectural offices there in 1938. He described the building as the "shopping center of the Technion". By 1940 at the latest, a long, double-storey shopping wing was added to the south-east. **I** Klarwein also designed the addition of two floors in 1954-56, with the balustrade of the flat roof being used as a link to the next floor. The shopping wing, too, was given two additional floors. Since then, HaKranot obstructs the view of the older buildings above it, which gave rise to some criticism. Later building additions were not planned by Klarwein.

HAIFA, BEIT KARSEBOOM 1937

8 Yitzhak Elhanan St.
→ Article Dafna Berger; Source: CZA A455/7; Haifa City Archive
Condition: Extant, with modifications

The apartment building, originally comprising two storeys throughout, is characterized by a particularly lively design with numerous balconies. The complex extending well into the depth of the site is divided into two wings with two apartments in the front part of each wing and a single six-roomed apartment at the rear. The well appointed, large apartments are luxurious both in size and fittings.

TEL AVIV, TRUMPELDOR CEMETERY; MEMORIAL FOR ZINA AND MEIR DIZENGOFF. 1937

→ Article Doron Bar
Condition: extant

Meir Dizengoff (1861-1936) came from what today is Romania. In 1892 he tried for the first time to establish himself in Palestine, but failed. In 1905, he finally settled there, was a major participant in the founding of Tel Aviv and its first mayor. His wife Zina (1872-1930) and he himself were jointly buried in 1936. **I** The comparatively elaborate memorial consists of a rectangle enclosed by high limestone walls, with the inscription placed on the rear facade. In front of this, the massive block of the gravestone has been positioned asymmetrically.

Current situation of the Dizengoff grave between Max Nordau (left) and Shaul Tschernichovsky (right)

TEL AVIV, TRUMPELDOR CEMETERY, GRAVE MAX NORDAU 1937

→ Article Doron Bar; Source: Jerusalem Post, August 30,1966
Condition: extant

Max Nordau, born Max Simon Südfeld (1849-1923) was born in Pest and was a doctor (e.g. family doctor for Herzl in Paris) and a journalist. Since 1892 he actively promoted Zionism. He lived in Madrid, London and Paris, where he died in 1923. In 1926, his remains were transferred to Tel Aviv and buried on 5. May in an honorary grave in Trumpeldor Cemetery. | The burial chamber extant today was clearly planned as a unit with the grave of Meir and Zina Dizengoff and only built in 1937. According to the Jerusalem Post, the ensemble was the product of a competition that Klarwein had participated in.

HAIFA, BEIT RACHEL 1938

2 Keller St.
Originally: Beit Shulamit Sola and Aharon Hochfeld
→ Article Dafna Berger; Source: CZA A455/15
Condition: demolished

The two-storey single family home consists of two large cubes of different size with plastered facades that are position adjacent to each other. Towards the street, windows have been narrowed into hatches and slits, while at the back, panorama windows and cutouts for porches dominate. The substantially projecting roof with its rounded corners together with the round arch of the entrance door make for a special character common in the architecture of Palestine in the thirties. The building was demolished in 1980 in favour of a building providing heightened utilization of the site.

NAHARIYA, BEIT ETTLINGER ("PALACE"), PLOT 85 1938

→ Article Sigal Davidi; Source: CZA A 455/7; Kreppel 2010, p335-36
Condition: demolished

Klarwein was apparently given this commission by applying for it in writing. The client, the lawyer Fritz Shlomo Ettlinger (1889-1964), had immigrated to Palestine in 1936. The double-storey house with a flat roof and underground garage is influenced by the Bauhaus movement and responds to the challenges of the climate by having a substantially projecting roof as well as a veranda and a terrace. The facade was clad with large slabs.

HAIFA, BEIT WOLFGANG ABRAHAM 1939

113 HaTishbi St.
→ Article Dafna Berger; Source: CZA A455/7; Haifa City Archive
Condition: extant, but modified

In 1939, Klarwein was commissioned to add a viewing floor to this initially double-storey building built by a third party in 1934. In addition, major changes to the layout of the two main floors created two two-roomed apartments on each floor, accessed through a lobby joining the two. The main facade of roughly hewn natural stone was part of the original building.

HAIFA, BEIT BERNSTEIN 1939

8 Megiddo St.
→ Article Dafna Berger; Source: CZA A455/7; Haifa City Archive
Condition: Substantial modifications

The three-storey building with three two-roomed apartments on each floor is characterized by its pronounced stratification and the numerous balconies of varying sizes, which over the years have mostly been enclosed. As a result, the appearance of the building has been changed so as to be unrecognizable.

HAIFA, BEIT KODESH 1939

6 Nahlieli St.
→ Article Dafna Berger; Source: CZA A455/7; Haifa City Archive
Conditon: demolished, replaced by an apartment block

The raised, single-storey building was situated in Bat Galim, a suburb set up in 1921 according to plans by Richard Kauffmann in the style of a Garden City. In the north, it borders directly on the sea. Its character was formerly determined by generous single-family homes on large plots. The building with its elaborate design was characterized by a harmonious interplay between interior and exterior spaces.

Sketches, place and date unknown

HAIFA, SYNAGOGUES AROUND 1940?

Source: CZA A 455/61
Projects

The population of Haifa grew significantly in the thirties due to immigration. New synagogues needed to be built. Klarwein appears to have applied for such commissions. Two very different proposals are preserved. One project has been executed in colour and signed by Klarwein, showing a building stepped back in three levels above a massive base, not immediately recognisable as an assembly building. The second proposal consists of a roof extending well beyond the building supported by two slim columns and is reminiscent of a temple with a portal. The sides are marked by closely ordered vertical window clefts recalling Klarwein's church designs in Germany. Neither design was realised.

HAIFA, BEIT GOTTESMANN 1940

4 Nordau St.
→ Article Dafna Berger; Source: CZA A455/7; Haifa City Archive
Condition: extant without substantial changes

The three-storey commercial and residential building with a tower-like exit to the roof terrace and a flagstaff stands out of its surroundings due to the rounded, generously extended balconies complete with roofing against the sun. The facade itself, however, remains strangely undetailed.

HEBREW UNIVERSITY, MASTERPLAN MOUNT SCOPUS AROUND 1940

Source: AJHS

First design before 1940. The Mendelsohn buildings are marked with No.s 1, 2, 3

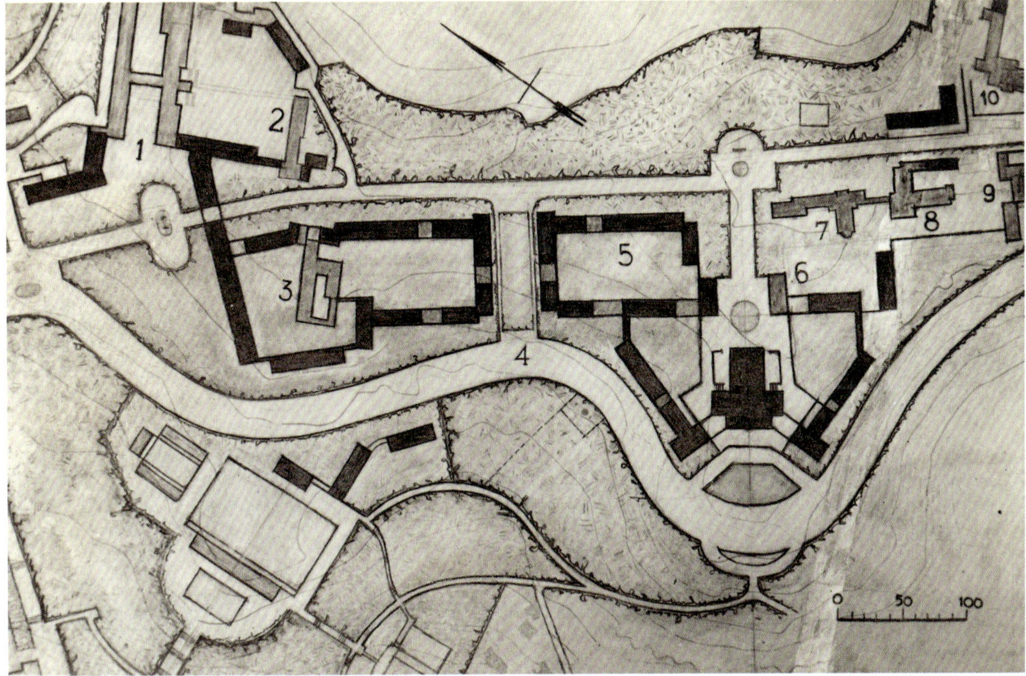

The Hebrew University Campus on Mount Scopus was opened on 1 April 1925. In a first phase, the Hadassah Medical Center was completed in 1939. Well before 1945 Richard Kaufmann and Joseph Klarwein developed an extensive masterplan for the development of the site. This was abruptly stopped after the Mount Scopus massacre in 1948 and the evacuation of the exclave. It was only in 1967 that renewed development commenced with a completely different conception.

Elevated view of the Mendelsohn buildings around 1939 / Model of the entire complex around 1940

TEL AVIV, NACHALAT YITZHAK, "MILITARY CEMETERIES" 1942–53

→ Article Doron Bar; Source: CZA A455/24; Maoz 2012
Condition: extant

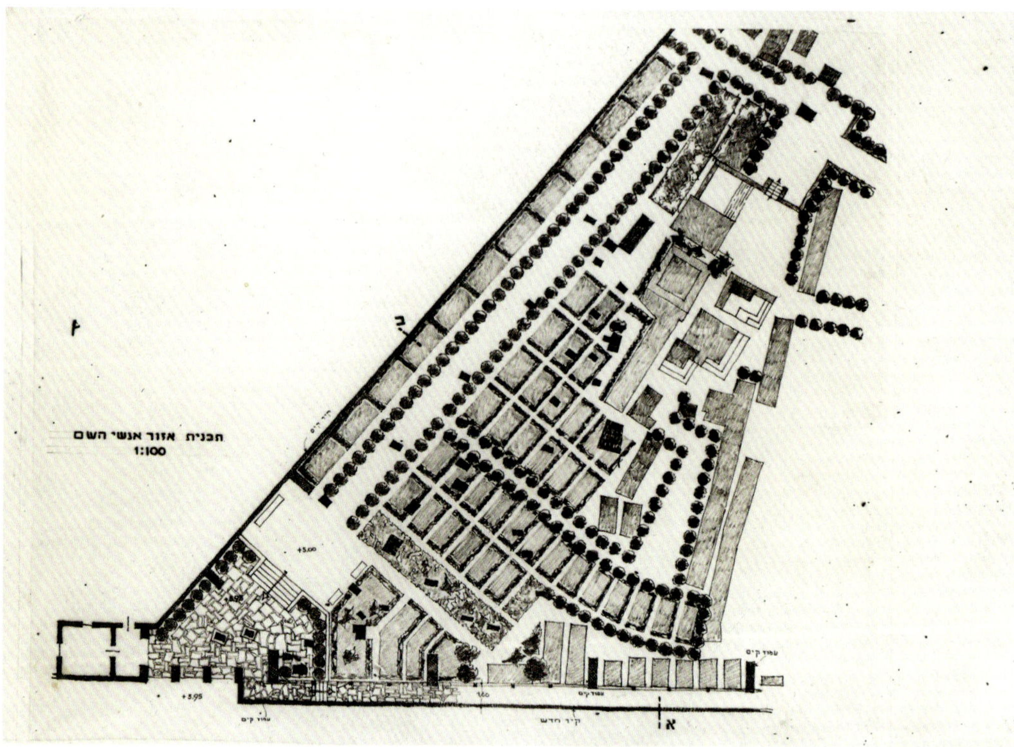

Field of graves in Nachalat Yitzhak cemetery in Tel Aviv

Apart from gravesites, Klarwein also designed three cemeteries for the victims of armed conflicts. ❙ In 1942, a competition was held for the design of a memorial site for the victims of Arab attacks in 1936-1939 – initially without a result. The subsequent expert assessment of the proposals submitted by the three studios Asher Hiram, Otto Hofmann & Benjamin Eckstein and Klarwein was won by Klarwein. ❙ Another draft design for civilian victims in 1942 was not built. In 1949, Klarwein was appointed juror for a competition to formulate general guidelines for the design of such cemeteries and in particular, their gravestones. The Palestine Post reported on 12 April 1950 that Klarwein had received a commission following a competition for a war memorial in Haifa. In 1953, he designed a memorial site for civilian victims of the bombardments of Tel Aviv for the national military cemetery Nachalat Yitzhak in Tel Aviv. ❙ It is unclear whether some drawings that have so far not been categorized are associated with this project.

Design for a cemetery with the grave of Rabbi Akiba in Tiberias

TEGART POLICE STATIONS 1939–42

Source: Cahill 2023; Kroizer 2004
Condition: extant, some with alteration

The forts in Jenin and Nablus

After the end of the Arab Uprisings (1936-39), British police commander Sir Charles Tegart ordered a total of 69 police forts to be built so that further uprisings could be quickly suppressed. Responsibility for the "Police Building Program" was given to the Public Works Department, where Klarwein was working at the time. He took charge of the forts in Latrun (010 – today a museum), Jiftlik (011), Nablus (029 and 030) and Jenin (030). ❙ Apart from two main configurations there were numerous special adaptations. Most often, a castle-like layout was constructed with towers at two opposing corners and a sparsity of windows at ground level, making attacks more difficult. Jiftlik was the only one retaining some reference to local building traditions while the other structures are in International Style with clear cubic masses and elongated bands of windows in the upper floors.

TEL AVIV, TRUMPELDOR CEMETERY – GRAVE SITE FOR JOSEPH AND FANNY ZAIDNER 1942

Source: private
Condition: extant

Joseph Zaidner (1860-1942) was a native of Ukraine, a close associate of Herzl and helped organize the first Zionist World Congress. In 1920, he immigrated to Palestine. He built a silicate factory in Tel Aviv, implemented numerous projects for the Jewish National Fund Keren Kayemeth and was made an honorary citizen of the city. ❙ The gravestones for Zaidner and his wife consist of two plain rectangular stone blocks with a hammered surface and embossed inscriptions.

TEL AVIV, TRUMPELDOR CEMETERY; MEMORIAL FOR SHAUL TSCHERNICHOVSKY. 1943

→ Article Doron Bar; Source: CZA A455/24
Condition: extant

Shaul Tschernichovsky (1875-1943) was a native of Ukraine, a doctor as well as a prominent poet and Zionist. He immigrated to Palestine in 1931. His poetry regularly deals with the Jewish state. | The drawings for his gravestone as well as perspective treatments are preserved in Klarwein's estate. A smooth cube has been assembled from large blocks. Against this, a slightly inclined, smooth stone tablet has been set on which the name appears in embossed letters.

JERUSALEM, MESHI SACKS OFFICE BUILDING, 1944

Source: CZA A455/22-16
Project

The design of a cubic office building is of a conventional kind. Above the open ground floor are situated uniform office floors topped by a prestigious penthouse floor. The prominent vertical facade elements recall numerous designs by Klarwein for office buildings but also churches in Germany. Further details about client, place or date are not known.

NAHARIYA, CASINO 1944

→ Article Sigal Davidi
Condition: demolished

With coastal tourism booming, the town of Nahariya in 1944 commissioned an open restaurant (Casino), covered by a sunroof, built on the beach. For Klarwein it was the first public commission after a long time.

JERUSALEM, MOUNT SCOPUS, HEBREW UNIVERSITY, HADASSAH MEDICAL SCHOOL, BIOLOGY BUILDING 1946

Source: CZA A 455/56; PP 30.07.1947
Condition: Incomplete, demolished

Klarwein with the sample facade in 1947 / Perspective drawing of the building, dated 1948 / Model of the building

After winning a competition with 36 participants, Klarwein began constructing the biology building at the northeastern border of the site in 1946. On 30 April 1947, the Palestine Post reported on the presentation of a sample facade. In the course of the war in 1947-48 and the founding of the State of Israel a massacre took place in 1948 among the staff of the hospital that had been built there in 1939. Subsequently, the site was abandoned. Klarwein's half-built school building was left incomplete. The ruin was demolished during the course of renewed construction in 1967.

NAHARIYA, SWIMMING POOL 1946

→ Article Sigal Davidi; Source: Lehmann 1960, 87-96; Jerusalem Post 1966, 2
Condition: demolished

Since the thirties, Nahariya had been a popular beach resort which was further developed from 1941 onwards by the "Galei-Galil" cooperative. In the forties, it grew into a substantial establishment as a result of booming tourism. Klarwein designed the infrastructure for the Olympic size pool, including change rooms, showers and a shop.

INITIAL STUDIES FOR YAD VASHEM? 1946?

Source: CZA A455/41; Brog 2002; Kirsch 2021; Bar 2023
Project

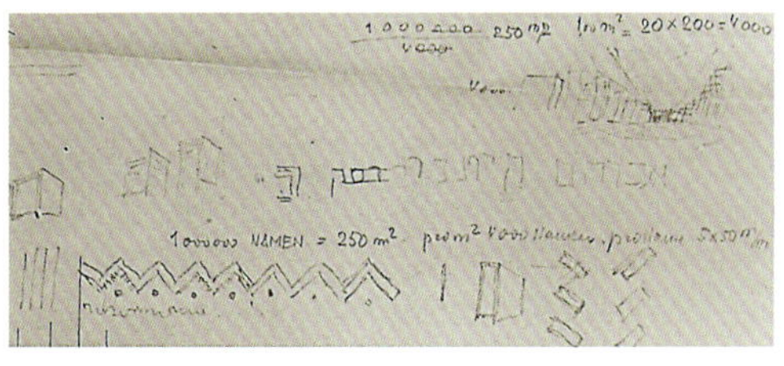

Two slightly different calculations: 1,000,000 NAMES = 250 m2 per m2 4'000 names – per name 5x50mm / Sketch of the entire proposed complex

In Klarwein's estate, a large number of sketches can be found of a sizeable, multi-storey complex set into a steep hillside with arcades arranged in a parabolic arch. An altar-like arrangement in the center as well as the trees arranged around the building give rise to speculation that it could have involved a ceremonial "cemetery" or solemn memorial (Hebrew: "Yad"). One of the sketches contains calculations of the space needed for 1'000'000 names (Hebrew: "Shem"). This could be an indication that Klarwein – unsuccessfully – tried to participate in the design of the memorial site of Yad Vashem, which had been discussed since the early forties and had been substantiated in a law passed in 1953. The plans were realized in the fifties based on other designs.

JERUSALEM, SULTAN'S POOL 1947

→ Article Noah Hysler Rubin; Source: CZA A 455/17
Project

"Sultan's Pool" refers to a large, ancient water reservoir directly outside the south-western corner of the city wall, to which a public fountain was added in Ottoman times (in 1905 still called Berket es-Sultan). Klarwein wanted to reconfigure the site, which today is often used for concerts, on behalf of a project developer. The scheme was never realized.

Kaiser Wilhelm II. and retinue in 1898 in front of the dam of Sultan's Pool with the Ottoman fountain; in the background the Jerusalem city walls / Elevated design of the site by Klarwein

ISRAEL 1948–1970

Buildings and Projects in Jerusalem

1 Hadassah Medical Center, Ein Karem, Masterplan (1961)
2 Hadassah Medical Center, Ein Karem, School of Pharmacy (1965-70)
3 Gravesite Gershon Agron (1959)
4 Mount Herzl, canopy over the grave of Theodor Herzl (1949)
5 Mount Herzl, Herzl Memorial (1951-61)
6 Mount Herzl, arch over the grave of Theodor Herzl (1954)
7 Mount Herzl, gravesite Ze'ev Jabotinsky (1964)
8 Egged bus station (1965)
9 Hebrew University, Givat Ram, Masterplan (1952)
10 Hebrew University, Givat Ram, Law Faculty – today Ross Building (1959)
11 Givat Ram, Maison de France (1952?)
12 Hebrew University, Givat Ram, Biology Laboratory (1955)
13 Givat Ram, National Stadium (1958)
14 Government Compound, Givat Ram, Masterplan (1952)
15 Government Compound, Givat Ram, three ministry buildings (1953-56)
16 Government Compound, Givat Ram, Ministry of Education (1964)
17 Jewish Theological Seminary of America (1959)
18 Knesset, House of Parliament (1957-66)
19 Beit Schocken, Rubin Academy of Music, conversion (1957)
20 Urban renewal for East-Jerusalem (1965)
21 Office building Lischkat HaMas (1954)
22 Nahalat Shiva quarter, rehabilitation (1958-60)
23 Office building Beit Joel, Jaffa Street (1960-63)
24 Alice L Seligsberg School, school building (1965)
25 Alice L Seligsberg School, school building (1966)
26 Jaffa Gate, wholesale market (1949?)
27 Sultan's Pool, urban renewal (1947)
28 Hebrew University, Mount Scopus, Masterplan (1940)
29 Hebrew University, Mount Scopus, Biology Laboratory (1946)

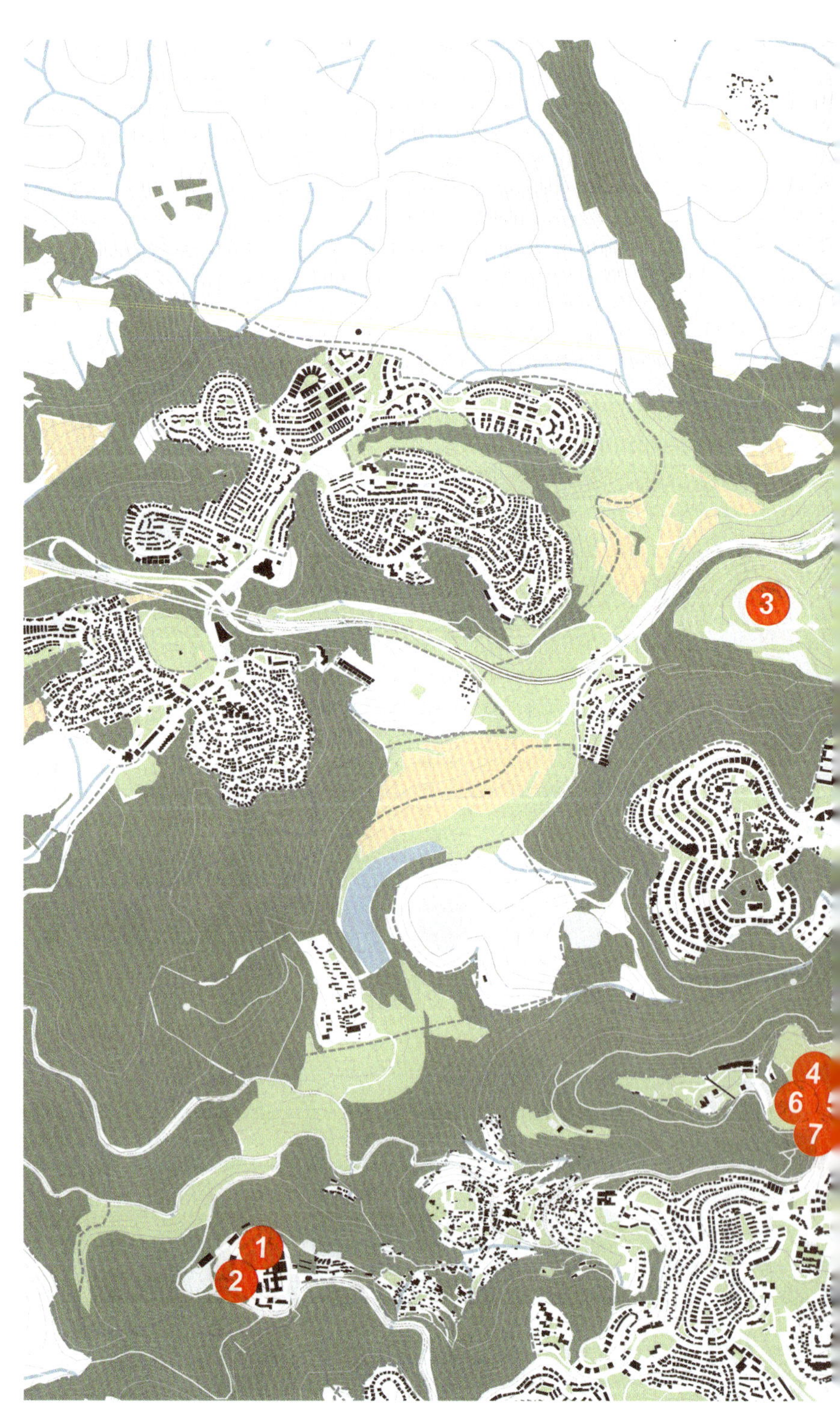

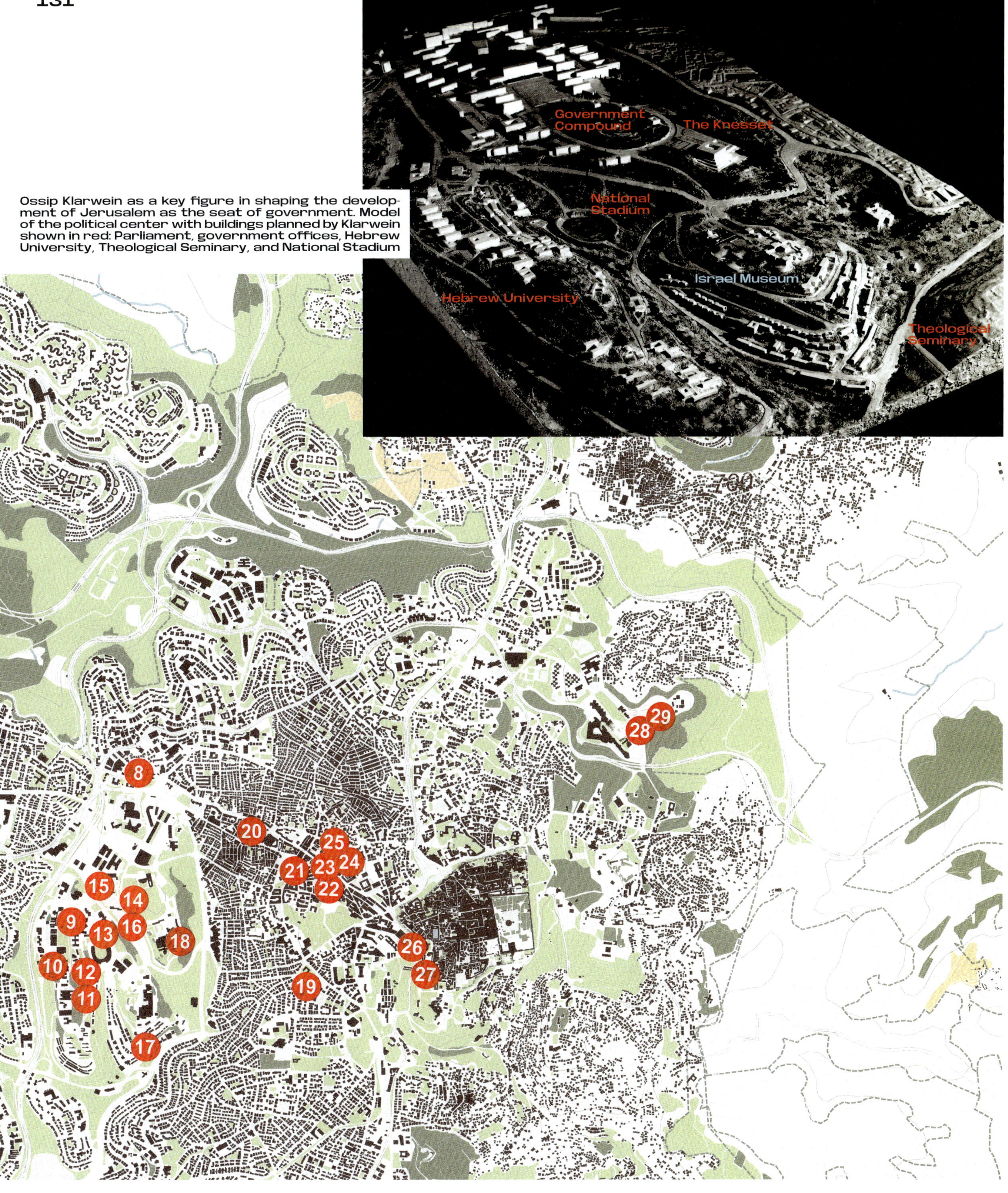

Ossip Klarwein as a key figure in shaping the development of Jerusalem as the seat of government. Model of the political center with buildings planned by Klarwein shown in red: Parliament, government offices, Hebrew University, Theological Seminary, and National Stadium

JERUSALEM, CANOPY ABOVE THE GRAVESITE OF THEODOR HERZL 1949 AND 1954

→ Article Doron Bar; Source: Bar 2020, 77; Condition: temporary installation

Presentation of the coffin on the way to Mount Herzl framed by Klarwein's ephemeral architecture

With his books "The Jewish State" ("Der Judenstaat" – 1896) and "Old New Land" ("Altneuland" – 1902) Theodor Herzl was the founder of Zionism. He died at the age of 44 in Vienna. In his testament he stipulated that he wanted to be buried in the State of Israel after its founding – which at the time lay in an indeterminable future. His mortal remains were transferred to Jerusalem on 17 August 1949 and solemnly interred on Mount Herzl. Klarwein designed the temporary installations along the waypoints and at the burial site, which was covered by a canopy in the Israeli colors and surrounded in a wide semicircle by flags of Israel. Beyond that, the gravesite was left until 1960 marked by a nondescript, provisional gravestone set in a circular field of white pebbles. On the occasion of the 50th anniversary of Herzl's death in 1954, Klarwein designed another ephemeral structure reflecting the outlines of a dome still envisioned at the time.

JERUSALEM, WHOLESALE MARKET NEAR JAFFA GATE 1950?

→ Article Noah Hysler Rubin; Source: CZA A455/20 Project

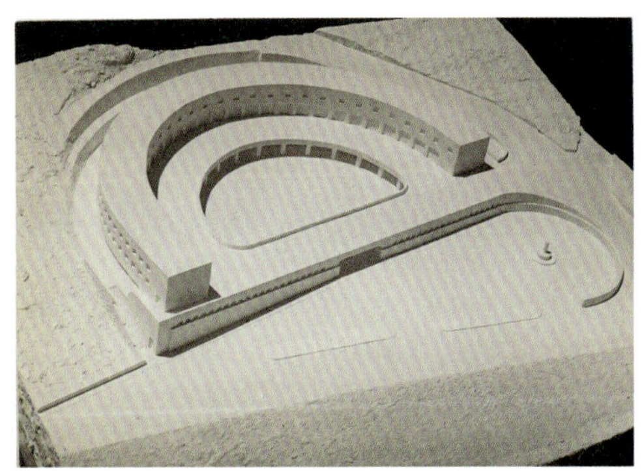

Model / Elevated view signed OK

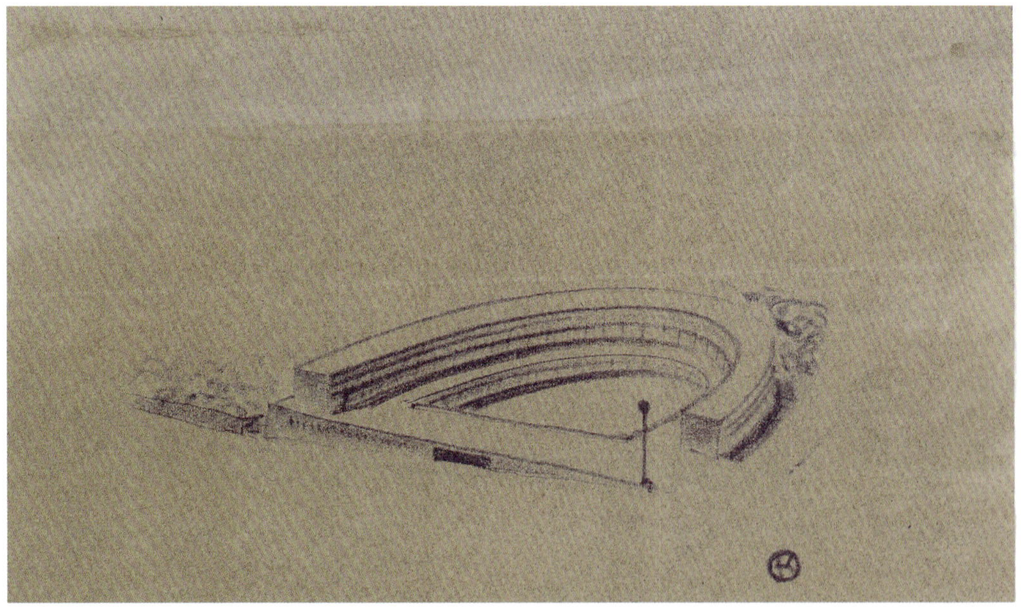

The Jaffa Gate to the northwest of the Old City is an important urban intersection. For this area, Klarwein designed a well-organized central market with excellent traffic access. The semicircular complex set into a hillside provides space on several levels for delivery, distribution and offices. The three-storey building with regularly set windows is of an unobtrusive design.

TEL AVIV, ZIONIST ORGANIZATION OF AMERICA (ZOA) 1949 COMPETITION

Source: CZA A455/21; Mozes 1952
Project

Klarwein's competition entry, 1949

The ZOA was an influential organization since the first days of the newly founded State of Israel. As a result, its seat in Israel was of special significance. A competition was held in 1949 for the new building in Tel Aviv, location of almost all foreign embassies. The concept envisioned a building with a club, a restaurant, a hall for events as well as offices. According to a letter to the Jewish Chronicle in 1966, Klarwein won first prize. However, the building was erected based on plans by Ibn Gabirol, Rosenblum, Dubnow architects.

RAMAT GAN, BEIT ZVI – TODAY: SCHOOL FOR THE PERFORMING ARTS 1950

Source: Media office, Beit Zvi
Condition: disfiguring additions and extensions

Construction site in 1950 / Condition after refurbishment in 1962 / Condition in 2007 after additions and extensions

In 1950, the "best architect" Klarwein was commissioned by the Klier family to construct a residence named after their son on this site. The building composed of two cubic blocks offset from each other is of a strictness in design bordering on bluntness. Large uninterrupted surfaces with sparse narrow windows contrast with a ground floor partly left open, partly given large panoramic windows. ❙ In 1962, the School of Theater commenced operations there after refurbishment probably superwised by Klarwein. The building was given an additional floor and minor extensions. Later, the height of the main building was once again increased, turning it into a tower with a projecting roof. The ground floor, originally left open, was almost totally enclosed. It is unclear whether Klarwein also planned these changes.

JERUSALEM, MOUNT HERZL; THEODOR HERZL MEMORIAL 1951–60 COMPETITION, FIRST PRIZE

→ Article Doron Bar; Source: CZA A455/25; Bar 2016; Bar 2020
Condition: modified execution, extant

The remains of Theodor Herzl (1860-1904) were transferred to Jerusalem on 17 August 1949 and solemnly interred on Mount Herzl, but in a provisional grave. The final design was to be determined by an international competition in 1951, in which 63 architects and sculptors from 11 countries participated. Many submissions envisioned a monumental structure on the summit of Mount Herzl. This included the design by Klarwein with its low concrete dome. His submission recalled almost exactly an idea for a competition in 1932 for an "Imperial Memorial" for the fallen Soldiers of the (first) World War in the town of Bad Berka (Thuringia) in Germany. Herzl's almost altar-like gravestone was

Sketch by Klarwein for the competition "Reichsehrenmal" (1932) in the Höger studio / Design for a monumental complex, possibly an alternative to the domed proposal? / Cutaway model of Klarwein's entry to the competition (1951)

National Memorial Hall for Israel's Fallen (Kimmel Eshkolot Architects 2017)

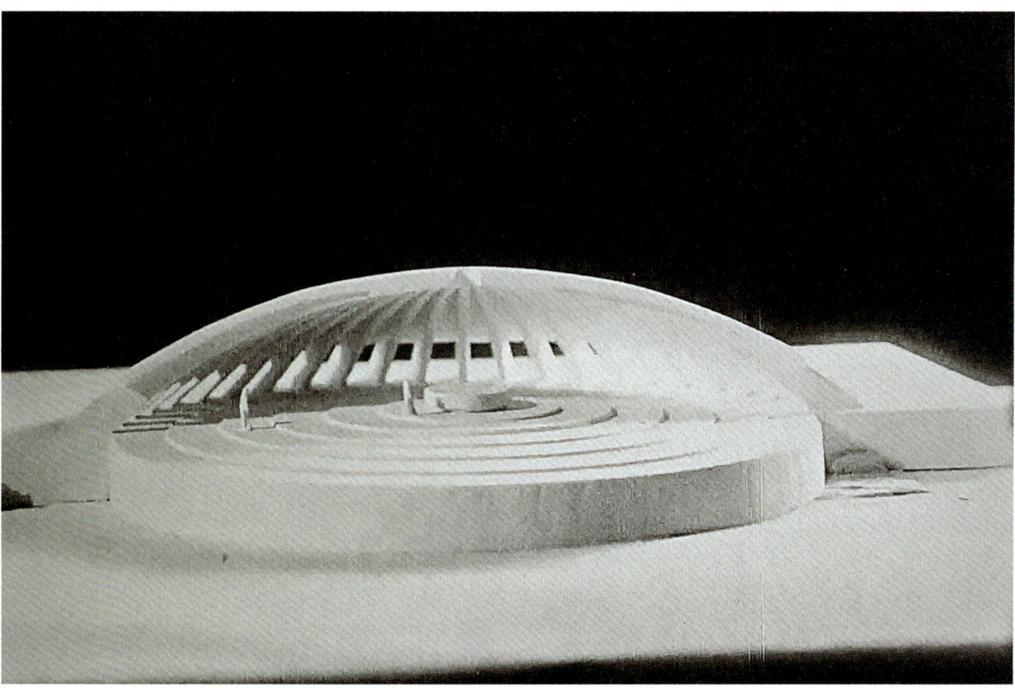

to be placed under a wide opaion within the dome, which itself was open on its lower rim. ❙ The size and pretension of this design soon gave rise to criticism. After extensive and controversial discussions, first the dome, then the stepped approach were dropped. What remained was a square, dark black stone block bearing Herzl's name, set on a slightly raised pedestal. It was inaugurated in 1960. Form and material subsequently became iconographic norms for the graves of prominent politicians (e.g. Levi Eshkol, Ze'ev Jabotinsky, Golda Meir, Yitzhak Rabin, Teddy Kollek and Shimon Peres). The dome found an echo in the "Memorial Hall of Israel's Fallen", realized in 2017. ❙ The original landscaping of the surroundings was dropped and replaced by a strict symmetry, in the interest of allowing larger events. ❙ It is unclear whether a monumental design in the form of a Magen David had been considered as an alternative.

JERUSALEM, KIRYAT HAMEMSHALA, GOVERNMENT COMPOUND 1950

→ Article Diana Dolev; Source: CZA A 455/49 and 50; Minta 2008
Condition: altered

After the founding of the state, the construction of the government compound was advanced speedily under the direction of Richard Kauffmann by a group of architects of which Klarwein and Rau were part. Ministries were given unspectacular office buildings stepped across the inclined site. Only three of four blocks originally planned were built. The resulting lack of space was overcome in the mid-sixties by adding additional floors to the buildings, changing their previously handsome silhouette. The almost purely white limestone facades have yellowed over time. In the early sixties, further building took place in which Klarwein was also involved.

Government buildings shortly before completion / Israeli Ministry of the Interior after vertical extension

HAIFA, DAGON SILOS 1952–55/1960/1962/1971

→ Article Dafna Berger; Source: CZA A455/12
Condition: extant, with minor modifications

Starting in 1952, the young industrialist Reuben Hecht had the silos built for grain imports in several phases and commissioned Klarwein to design an artistically sophisticated facade. The complex was technically advanced with almost complete automation including conveyor belts, elevators and pneumatic tubes. The Silos were enclosed by a concrete facade with a decoration reminiscent of the Sprinkenhof building in Hamburg. The vertical transport shafts are situated on the narrow sides. Klarwein worked until his death on the expressionist designs crowning the narrow building and the towers.

The decorative facade under construction with climbing formwork (circa 1953) / Postcard of the Dagon Silo following the completion of the first construction phase (1955) / Postcard of the Dagon Silo after the third construction phase, featuring the loading bridge and redesigned tower crown (1962)

JERUSALEM, GIVAT RAM, HEBREW UNIVERSITY 1951–53

today Edmond J. Safra Campus
→ Article Diana Dolev; Source: CZA A455/13
Condition: extant, changed as a result of additions

Panorama of the university buildings in 1965, with the national stadium on the far left, the faculty buildings evenly spaced along the ridge, and the library at the center

After the forced abandonment of the university site on Mount Scopus, Kauffmann, Klarwein and Rau were commissioned to design a masterplan for a new university on a new site on the crest of Givat Ram close to the government compound. The characteristic comb structure visible in all variations of the faculty buildings is strongly reminiscent of Klarwein's designs while in the Höger studio for the administration building of I.G. Farben in Frankfurt am Main in 1928.

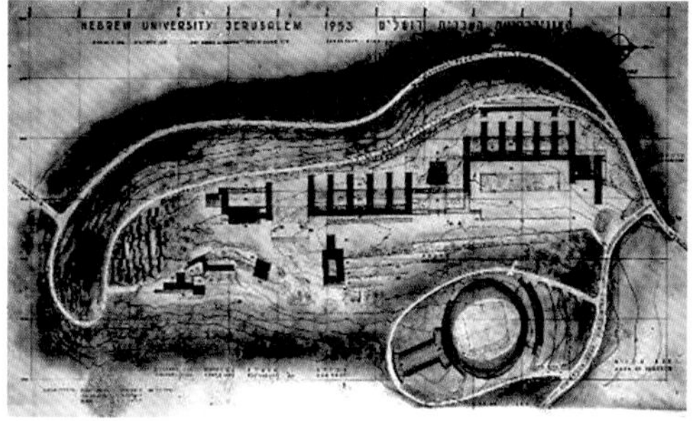

Different variations of the layout for the university and the national stadium, plan and models

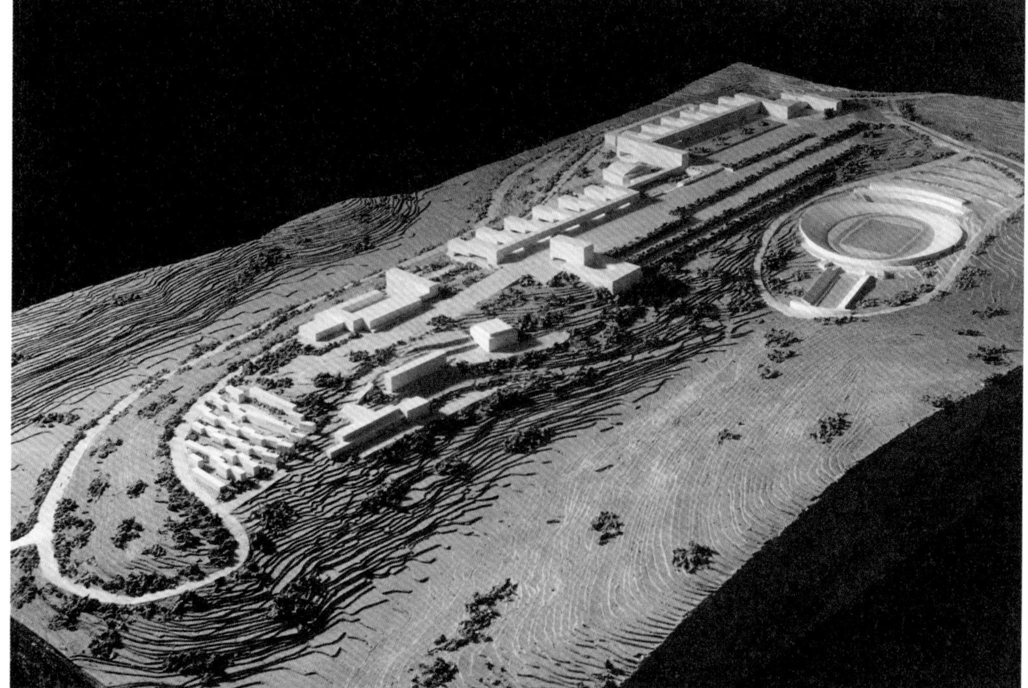

JERUSALEM, "BEIT FRANCE" / HÔTEL ET MAISON DE FRANCE 1952?

Source: CZA A 455/61
Project

A drawing entitled «Avant-Projet pour la Construction de l'Hôtel et la Maison de France» shows a massive cube, windowless on its narrow sides, crowned with flagstaffs. It is fronted by an elaborate facade with regularly spaced windows and corner balconies on the upper floors set above an arcade. The building is massive and graceful at the same time. Neither the exact date of this proposal is known nor whether it was meant for the current position of the Maison de France on the Edmond J. Safra Campus of the Hebrew University.

NEVE ILAN, HOTEL 1952

Source: CZA A 455/16
Project

Neve Ilan is situated in harsh surroundings, but with a generous view of the Jordan valley west of Jerusalem. The location was only developed by Jewish settlers in 1946 in order to control an important road to Tel Aviv. After the independence wars, Neve Ilan grew rapidly. That may have given rise to considerations for a hotel complex which Klarwein designed in 1952. However, the project was not realized. ❙ The complex was set in a craggy landscape and consisted of a compact main building and three terraced wings fronted by gardens.

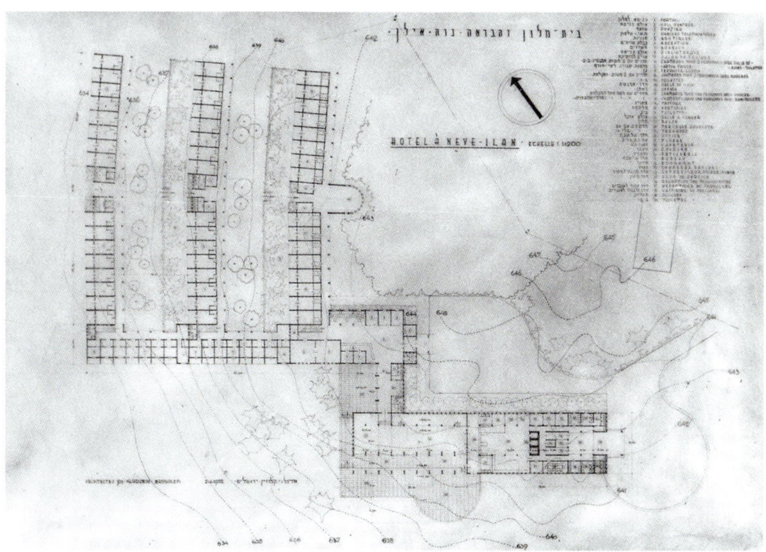

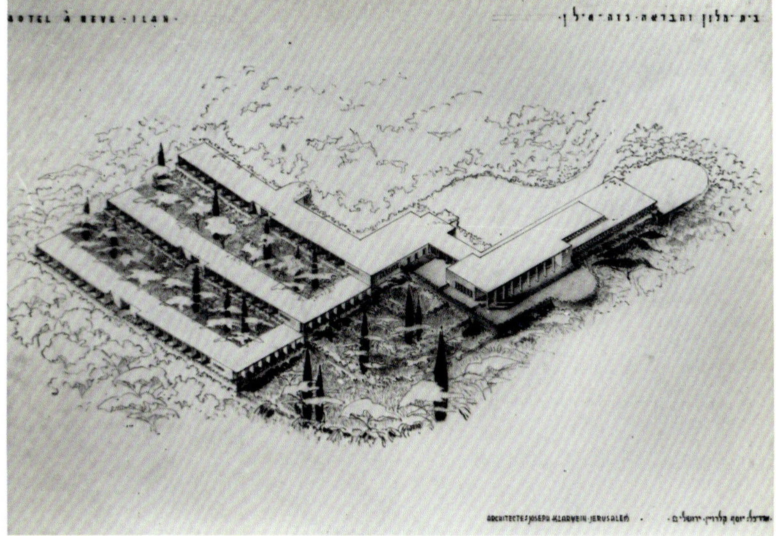

Floor plan and isometric drawing

JERUSALEM, LISCHKAT HAMAS OFFICE BUILDING (TRADE UNION) 1954

26 Ben Yehuda Street
Source: Private archive
Condition: extant without major changes

Photo soon after completion in 1954

The building with four floors is situated on a narrow-fronted site between Ben Yehuda and King George Street in a prime position in the center of Jerusalem. The structure is ordered horizontally by cornices while at the same time emphasizing the vertical through tall narrow rectangular windows. The deeply recessed windows are joined into bands by clearly defined frames. The long wing on King George Street takes a graceful turn into Ben Yehuda Street to continue slightly set back from the road. **I** The facade of the flat roofed building is characterized by rough-hewn blocks set in regular bands in a traditional Palestinian style. The prominent window pillars add a marked dimensionality.

TEL AVIV CENTRAL / TEL AVIV SAVIDOR MERKAZ 1954

Source : CZA A 455/7 and 26
Condition: extant

Condition around 2010 / Photo soon after completion 1954

Tel Aviv Central Station was originally designed in the fifties as a terminus for the normal gauge trains from the north (Nahriya, Haifa). The site east of Hamedina Square was far away from the southern suburbs. In 1993, the tracks were rerouted and Tel Aviv Central restructured as a through station. The station building, however, was retained. **I** Klarwein's design is simple. The single-storey building with a prominent flying roof has a tall, airy hall which gave access to two tracks covered by roofing supported by concrete pillars as well as a third track in the middle. These were removed during the reconfiguration.

TEL AVIV, POLICE HEADQUARTERS 1954

Source: Private; Jerusalem Post August 30,1966; Jewish Chronicle 1966,2, Project

A competition was held for the Tel Aviv police headquarters in 1954, which Klarwein won. For unknown reasons the project was not realized. Klarwein's design has not been preserved.

NAHARIYA, CITY CENTER MASTERPLAN 1956

→ Article Sigal Davidi; Source: CZA A455/53; private archive
Condition: changed

As a framework for orderly growth of the quickly growing town Klarwein designed a new town center with water fountains which, apart from shops, also comprised the town hall as well as a cinema. It formed a contrast to the surroundings characterized by rural settlement patterns. In 1964, Klarwein extended the plans further.

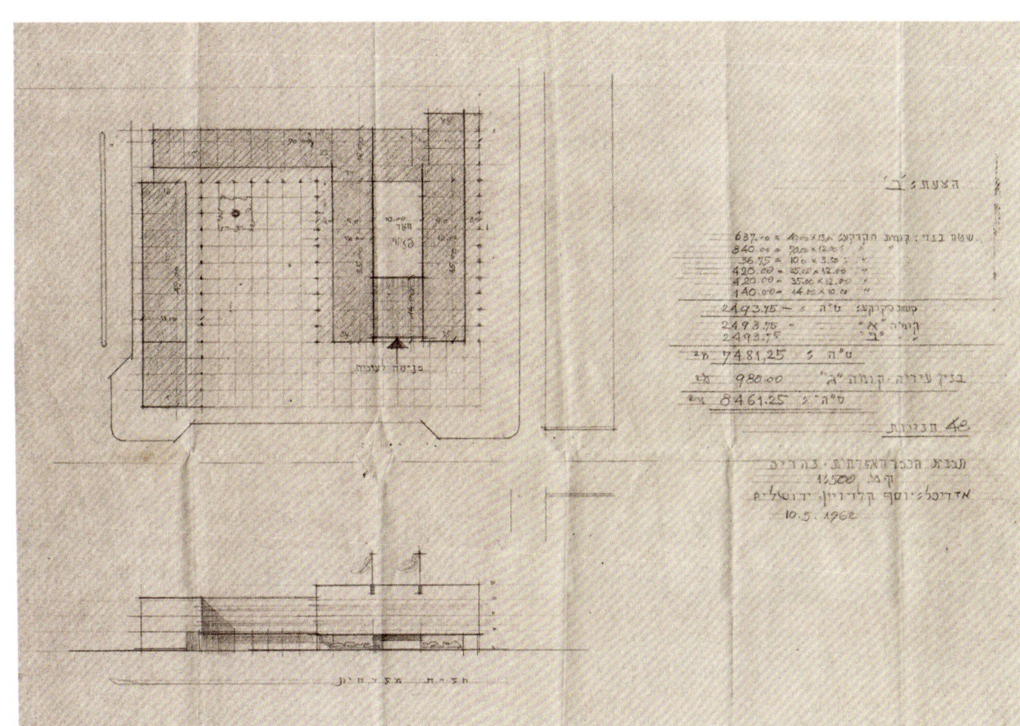

1962 city map with the swimming pool area and the city center / Design for the town hall 1962

ARCHITECTURE OF THE KNESSET 1957–66

→ Article Talia Margalit; Source: CZA A455/9; Roleff 2000; Singer 2022
Condition: extant, extended

Competition model for the Knesset by Klarwein (1957)

The open national competition for the building of the Knesset was announced on 25 July 1956. Only 35 architectural firms participated. On 24 July 1957 the jury[1] awarded first prize to the Klarwein entry. Second prize was not awarded, while third and fourth place were given jointly and without further differentiation[2] to the studios Aba Elhanani/M. Ben-Horin/

Ankara, Mausoleum for Atatürk by Onat/Arda (1953) as embodiment of the traditional / Brasilia, Congress Palace by Oskar Niemeyer (1960), praised by critics as a counterproposal.

Hanna Elhanani as well as Lothan/Yitzhak Moore/Otto Toren. ❙ Klarwein's rectangular building is a closed block surrounded on all sides by an arcade set with tall pillars, 20 on the longer, 15 on the narrower sides. On two sides, the block is placed on the edge of the hill while the second longer side faces a large internal courtyard lined by lower building elements. The trapezoid parliamentary hall is situated in the middle of the rectangle, flanked by two inner courtyards. Offices and smaller meeting rooms face towards the outside. The entire appearance is one of monumentality and dignity radiating far into the city. ❙ In contrast, those participants in the competition that are known – hardly a dozen – do not take the character of the site into account at all and assign various parliamentary functions (plenary hall, meeting rooms, offices, functional spaces) as if on a single level, in accordance with the International Style. They appear to have been influenced by capital cities being discussed and built elsewhere somewhat earlier or later such as Chandigarh (India/Le Corbusier) or Brasilia (Brazil/Oscar Niemeyer) as well as the United Nations headquarters in New York. ❙ To bridge the gap between these two positions, Klarwein in collaboration with Shimon Pows-

Second redesign (model) with terraced office floors and recessed columns, around 1961

ner (1919-99) presented a redesign in 1959. The parliamentary hall was now to be clearly marked by a gently domed roof and the functional spaces were to be grouped around an inner courtyard. The colonnades were retained on the longer sides only, with twelve rounded columns. There are clear similarities in massing and grouping between this design and the competition entries no. 1, 4 and 7[3]. ❙ Eventually, Dov and Ram Karmi together with Bill Gillit were added to the team. The joint design in 1960 reverted to one of the major structural features of Klarwein's competition entry: A building surrounded by pillars on all sides. The monumentality of the building, which had been criticized, was reduced by positioning the pillars closer to the facade, adding a projecting shade roof and especially by terracing the site to make space for further offices beneath the building. ❙ The parliamentary section, which is now square, gives the impression of crowning a much more extensive building complex – similar to the New National Gallery by Mies van der Rohe in Berlin soon afterwards – and no longer has the brooding aspect of a fortress above the city. The austere impression given by Klarwein's competition entry is much reduced by placing the rectangular concrete supports – ten per side[4] – much closer to the outer wall. After large scale models had been built, they were given almost figurative capital-like upper endings without structural function. They are placed in isolation, almost as decoration, in front of a facade clad in reddish rock and with narrow, slit-like windows. ❙ The interior design was assigned in 1963 to architect Dora Gad – against Klarwein's will.

Berlin, New National Gallery by Mies van der Rohe (planned 1962-68) – square building / Athens, American Embassy by Walter Gropius (planned 1956-61) – square building, ten pillars in the front

Inauguration 30 August 1966

The Knesset by Joseph Klarwein, ten pillars in the front

Klarwein's contribution Publications on the architectural history of the Knesset give the impression that Klarwein's success in the 1957 competition was, above all, due to the initial lack of interest in the project by leading architects of the time. His "old-fashioned" plan, it is said, had not been acceptable and eventually intrigues had led to his being pushed out of the project. The real architects behind the Knesset are said to be Karmi/Gillit[5] together with Dora Gad. In fact, however, the building that was constructed is, despite all the controversy and some marked changes, a design clearly based in large part on Klarwein's proposal of 1957, somewhat reduced in its monumentality. **|** The building continues to stand out as "crown of the city". The facade ordered by strong supporting pillars gives the seat of parliament an air of dignity. The projecting roof combined with the playfully figurative "capitals" of the raw concrete pillars avoids the severity that gave rise to criticism of the original complex. Moving the functional spaces into the terraced lower floors reduces the distance between the public and parliament. Contemporary authors as well as the opening ceremony for the Knesset on 30. August 1966 acknowledge Klarwein's authorship without qualification. Newspapers name Klarwein (and not Karmi/Gillit) as architect and for the celebratory dinner, Klarwein was seated at the head table. The inscription on the building itself names both Klarwein and Karmi. **|** Clearly, assessments in recent years have been distorted.

1 Uriel Schiller was chairman, expert jurors were the architects David Anatol Brutzkus, Nahum Saalkind, Max Loeb and Chanan Pavel together with Shlomo Arazi and Genia Averbuch as engineers. **2** The plans of 13 additional firms were purchased: two submissions by Schulamith/Michael Nadler/Bikson; by Rechter/Sarchi/Rechter; by Eithan Kaufmann/Amnon Gelbmann; by Schaag; by Ortner/Posner; by Levy Meir; by Menachem Cohen; by Adina und Nissan Kna'an; by Almoznino/Shapiro; by Rubin/Friedmann; by Werner W. Witkower/A. Baumann and by Noy/Pardo. The prize money amounted to IL 30,000, of which Klarwein received IL 7,500. **3** The authors of 1 and 4 are unknown, No.7 is by Menachem Cohen. **4** The American Embassy in Athens by Walter Gropius (completed 1961) also has ten recessed pillars in its facade. **5** Ram Karmi took this position in later years: "The truth is that we felt sorry for Klarwein. We chopped up his building... So I said to my dad, that even though we had prepared the new plan, if we wished to create a good atmosphere, so that the plan would go through as smoothly as possible, we ought to forego mention of our name, and leave Klarwein's name" (Roleff 2000).

BEIT SCHOCKEN, CONVERSION TO RUBIN ACADEMY OF MUSIC 1957

Source: CZA A 455/7
Condition: Changes and additions dominate

Villa Schocken after completion in 1936 / Rubin Academy of Music after extensions in 1957 / Supplementary wing by Klarwein 1957 / Situation around 2010

Salaman Schocken (1877-1959), a businessman, publisher and founder of a department store, had to leave Germany in 1934 and initially emigrated to Palestine. Here, he commissioned Erich Mendelsohn to construct a comfortable villa of limestone blocks in various hues influenced by the Bauhaus, which was completed in 1936 in the Jerusalem suburb of Rechavia. When Schocken moved to New York in 1940, the building was used by the Mandate government. In 1957, the complex was adapted and extended by Klarwein to house the Rubin Academy of Music, later called the Jerusalem (Rubin) Music and Dance Academy. The delicately composed existing building with an unusual variety of windows was given a complete third floor which significantly reduced its original sculptural quality. In addition, there were various supplementary buildings. Today, the appearance is dominated by the later additions.

JERUSALEM, NAHALAT SHIVA REHABILITATION 1958–60

→ Article Noah Hysler Rubin; Source: CZA A455/19; Levine 2021
Condition: partly completed

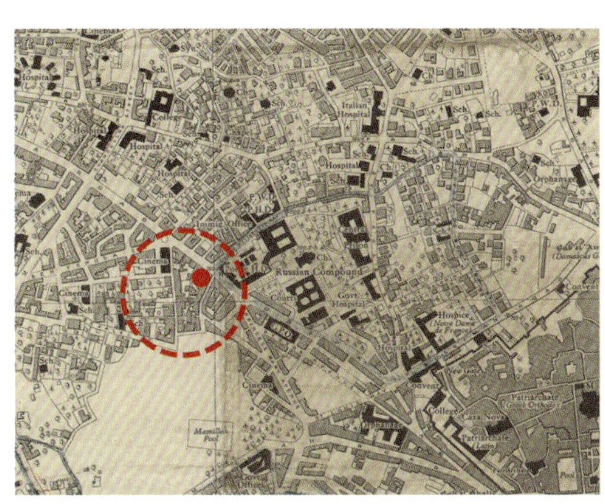

The Nahalat Shiva quarter was founded in 1869 to the north-west of the Old City. Based on the masterplan for Jerusalem by Michael Shaviv from 1955-59, the entire area was to be demolished and rebuilt according to plans by Klarwein in 1958. After eleven houses had been razed, the continuation of the project was stopped by resistance from residents. Klarwein constructed Beit Joel in two phases 1960-63.

JERUSALEM, HEBREW UNIVERSITY, SPORT CENTER AND STADIUM / NATIONAL STADIUM 1958

Source: Handassa We-Adrikhalut 4,1958, 125
Condition: substantial modernisation

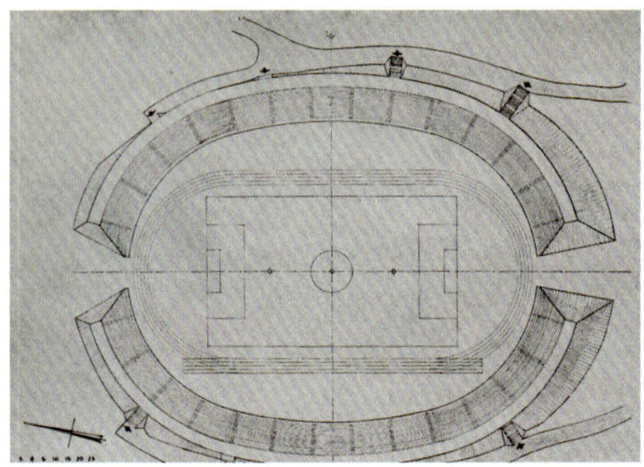

Plan of the stadium from 1958 / Construction site around 1957

The stadium was a central part of the masterplan for the university. Probably due to a lack of funds, Klarwein made no plans for specially constructed stands and instead placed the stadium within the valley floor so that seating could be built into the hillside reminiscent of similar stadiums in antiquity. This resulted in a generous complex which could also be used for representative state events. The fact that spectators were seated at some distance away was a disadvantage which later led to substantial changes being made to the original complex.

DEIÀ (MALLORCA), BEIT MATI KLARWEIN 1959

Source: Private archive
Condition: largely unchanged

Klarwein's son Mati (1932-2002) had studied art in France from 1948 at the École des Beaux-Arts. He later lived part-time in Mallorca and moved there permanently in 1984. For his son, Joseph Klarwein constructed a simple house situated on a steep hillside with a view of the Mediterranean near Deià. There is a terrace facing the sea covered by a roof supported by pillars built of natural rock. The living room positioned diagonally divides the space into two halves. Towards the hillside, the building nestles against the rock-face. Many old photographs show Klarwein in this house.

JERUSALEM, HAR HAMENUCHOT CEMETERY; GRAVE SITE FOR GERSHON AND ETHEL AGRON 1959

Condition: extant

Gershon Harry Agronsky (1893-1959) was born in Ukraine. In 1906, his family emigrated to Philadelphia (USA), where Agron became an early supporter of Zionism. In 1932 he founded the newspaper "Palestine Post", which in 1950 was renamed "Jerusalem Post". From 1955 to his death in 1959 Gershon Agron was mayor of Jerusalem. | The graveside consists of two limestone blocks reminiscent of sarcophagi. Apart from the tops and their edges, they have been left roughly hewn. The lettering has been incised into the carefully smoothed upper surfaces.

JERUSALEM, HEBREW UNIVERSITY, GIVAT RAM, LAW FACULTY (TODAY ROSS BUILDING) 1959

→ Article Diana Dolev; Source: CZA A455/56
Condition: extant with minor changes

Situation after completion 1959

The building for the Law Faculty (later: Ross Building) was part of the first phase. The uncompromisingly cubic, three-storey building is placed on oversized pillars and has upright, regularly spaced window openings. The ground floor was originally left almost completely open. The facade is notable for the vertically arranged stone slabs from local quarries.

JERUSALEM, JEWISH THEOLOGICAL SEMINARY 1959–61

4 Avraham Granot Street
Source: CZA A 455/19; Schechter Institute
Condition: Modernized

The first construction phase during the recently completed restoration

The Jewish Theological Seminary of America in New York City commissioned Klarwein in 1959 with the design of its branch in Jerusalem in a prominent position close to the government and university quarter. In three phases, accommodation for 150 students was to be constructed first, followed by a second residential wing, a synagogue seating 750 and finally a specialist library housing 100'000 volumes together with a lecture building. According to correspondence and his fee income, Klarwein was actively involved in the first construction phase until 1961, which initially encompassed all the aforementioned functions. The further development of the area at the foot of the Israel Museum was then continued by others.

NAHARIYA, CITY CENTER, MEXICO HOUSE 1959

→ Article Sigal Davidi; Source: Lehmann 1960, 9
Condition: demolished

“Mexico House” was financed by the “Mexico-Nahariya Development Company“ and designed by Klarwein to comprise shops on the ground and offices of the local administration on the upper floor. The simple rectangular building with a smooth facade and regularly spaced windows was part of the city center which had been growing slowly since the end of the fifties.

JERUSALEM, BEIT JOEL, 33 JAFFA ROAD, OFFICE AND COMMERCIAL BUILDING 1960–63

33 Jaffa Road
→ Article Noah Hysler Rubin; Source: CZA A 455/55
Condition: extant

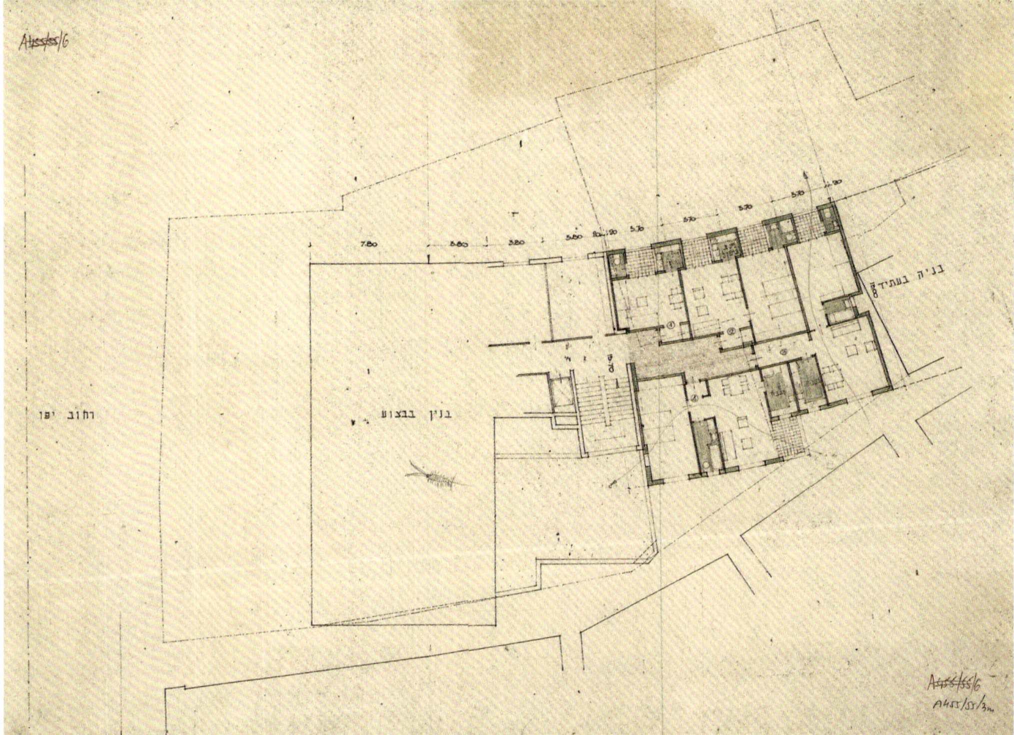

Current situation with additional wing / Plan for a standard floor; the wing on the left is completed, that on the right being built.

The flat-roofed seven-storey building from 1960 is situated on Jaffa Road in the center of Jerusalem within the reconstruction quarter of Nahalat Shiva. The cleanly ordered facade with great plasticity makes for a lively appearance given additional impact by the slight curve of the road and the use of different materials. The contemporary media praised the unique design. In 1963, Klarwein extended the complex to the south with a wing of mostly small apartments. The stairwell is shared by both wings. The facade has trapezoid balconies which clearly reference the design of the ground floor of Beit Joel.

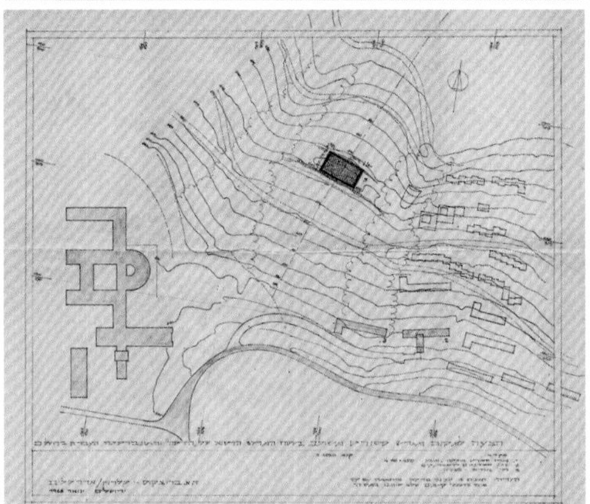

Study on the development of the western flank of Ein Karem (hospital outlined on the right) / Plan for the development of the eastern flank with sports fields and residential buildings from 1966; the hospital on the left / Model of the complex from 1961

JERUSALEM, EIN KAREM, HADASSAH MEDICAL CENTER, MASTERPLAN 1961

Source: AJHS; Israel Film Institute
Condition: extant; several expansions

To replace the buildings of the Medical Faculty on Mount Scopus, which could no longer be used after 1948, a new campus was founded on Ein Karem hill west of the Old City in the late fifties and expanded several times. Klarwein and Brutzkus were commissioned to design a masterplan of the campus. The cylindrical main building housing operating theatres is adjoined by multi-storey wings of patient accommodation. Building design is by Joseph Neufeld.

NAHARIYA, CINEMA HOD 1962

→ Article Sigal Davidi; Source: CZA A455/53
Condition: major refurbishment

Part of the upgrade of the city center was cinema "Hod" which was used not only to show movies but also for other events. Today, this use has been abandoned, and the building has been significantly altered.

BASLE, JEWISH CEMETERY; GRAVE SITE FOR JACOB AND ELLE HECHT 1963

Source: private
Condition: Project? / extant

Jacob Hecht (1879-1963) was an influential German businessman who emigrated to Switzerland at an early stage. He was the father of the Zionist Reuben Hecht (1909-1993), who commissioned Klarwein in 1951 to design the Dagon Silos in Haifa. ❙ Against this background Klarwein made a proposal to the widow, Elle Hecht-Mohr (1887-1972) after the death of Jacob in 1963 for the design of a grave site for the couple consisting of two adjacent gravestones with recessed lettering. As is evidenced by correspondence, this design was extensively discussed with the participation of Reuben Hecht. ❙ The rather conventional gravestone (from 1972?) records the couple not next to but above each other and makes use of embossed lettering, as is the case with almost all other gravestones of this cemetery. It therefore seems possible that Klarwein's project was never realized.

JERUSALEM, MOUNT HERZL, MEMORIAL FOR WLADIMIR ZE'EV AND JOHANNA JABOTINSKY 1964

→ Article Doron Bar
Condition: extant

Wladimir Ze'ev Jabotinsky (1880-1940) was born in Odessa. He was one of the earliest Zionists and an internationally active, multilingual activist. His remains were reinterred on Mount Herzl in 1964. The memorial has been fashioned of polished, hard black rock, as is the case with the Herzl Memorial.

JERUSALEM, KIRYAT HAMEMSHALA, MINISTRY OF EDUCATION 1964

Source: CZA A 455/55, private archive
Project

In the early sixties, Klarwein designed an office building for the Ministry of Education which was to be built up in the government quarter. Four slightly angled wings were to be grouped around a central access building. The wings were joined together by lower buildings, forming a closed complex. The plans comprise a complete set for the eight-floor building in the scale of 1:200. It is not known why construction did not take place.

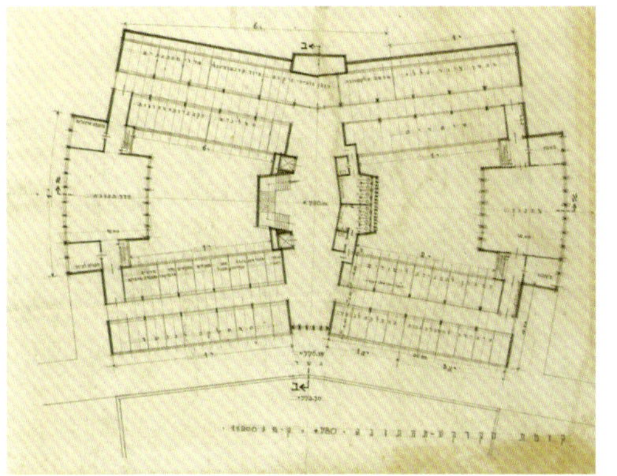

Floor plan / Isometric drawing of the complex / Elevation

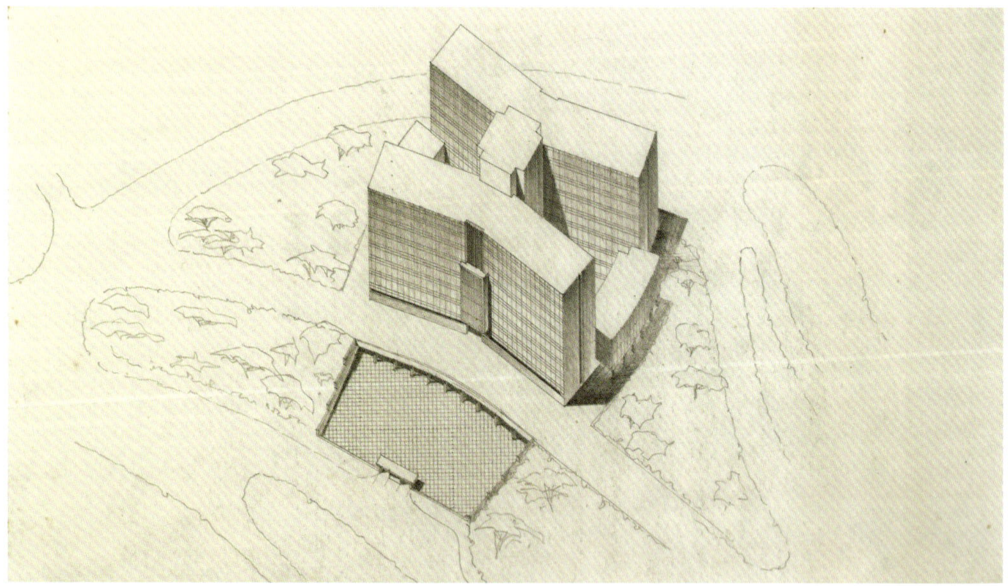

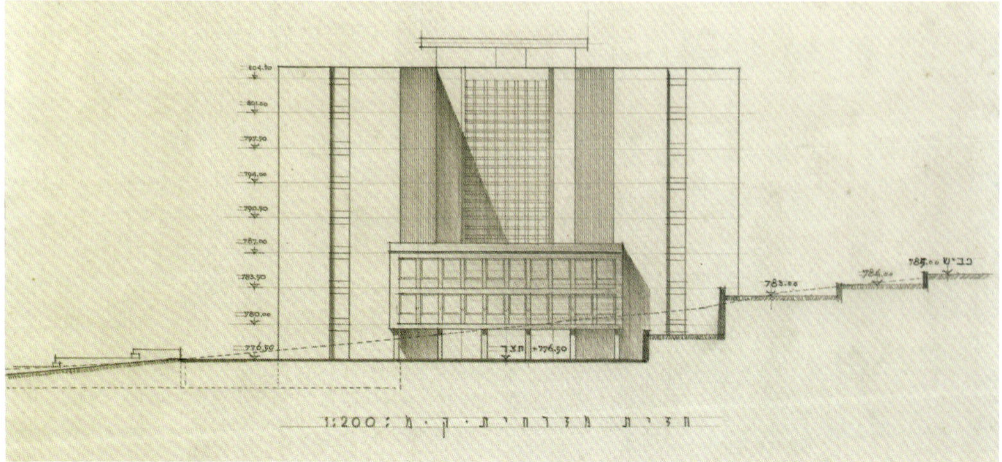

HAIFA, DAGON SILOS, ADMINISTRATION BUILDING ON PLUMER SQUARE 1965

With S. Mandel
→ Article Dafna Berger
Condition: largely unchanged

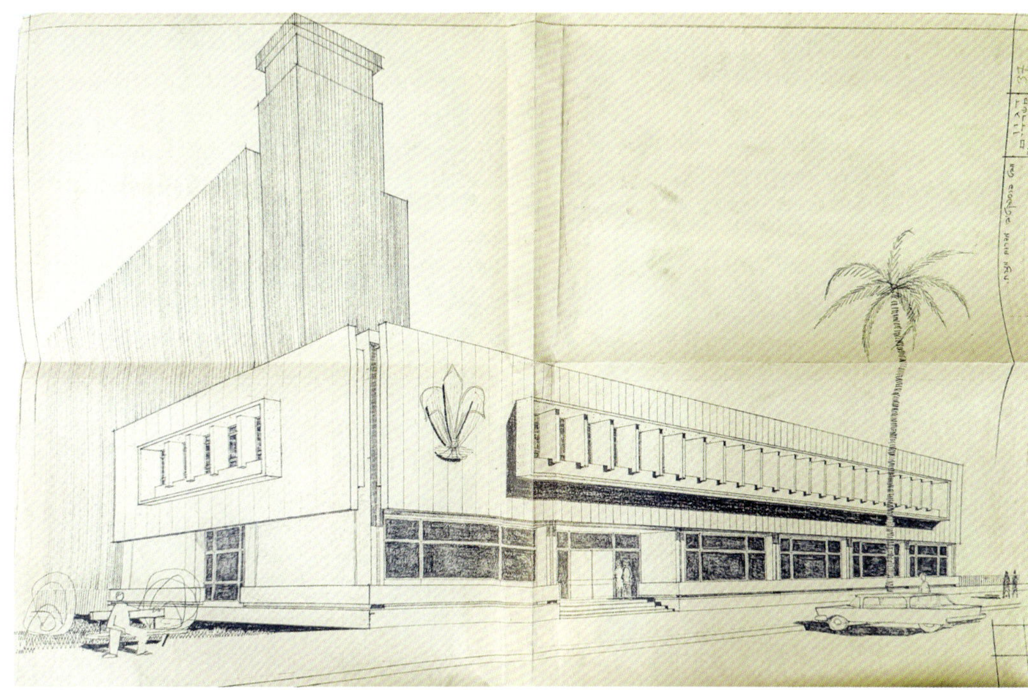

Perspective drawing of the whole complex

The distinguishing feature of double storey flat roofed building are prominent sun shades projecting from the row of windows. The owner, Reuben Hecht, put great emphasis on the representative nature of the building. Klarwein developed numerous design alternatives which, following the wishes of the client, were to be enhanced with artistic features. The result was an elaborate concrete construction filled with colored glass reminiscent of church windows. Today, the building houses the "Dagon Grain Museum".

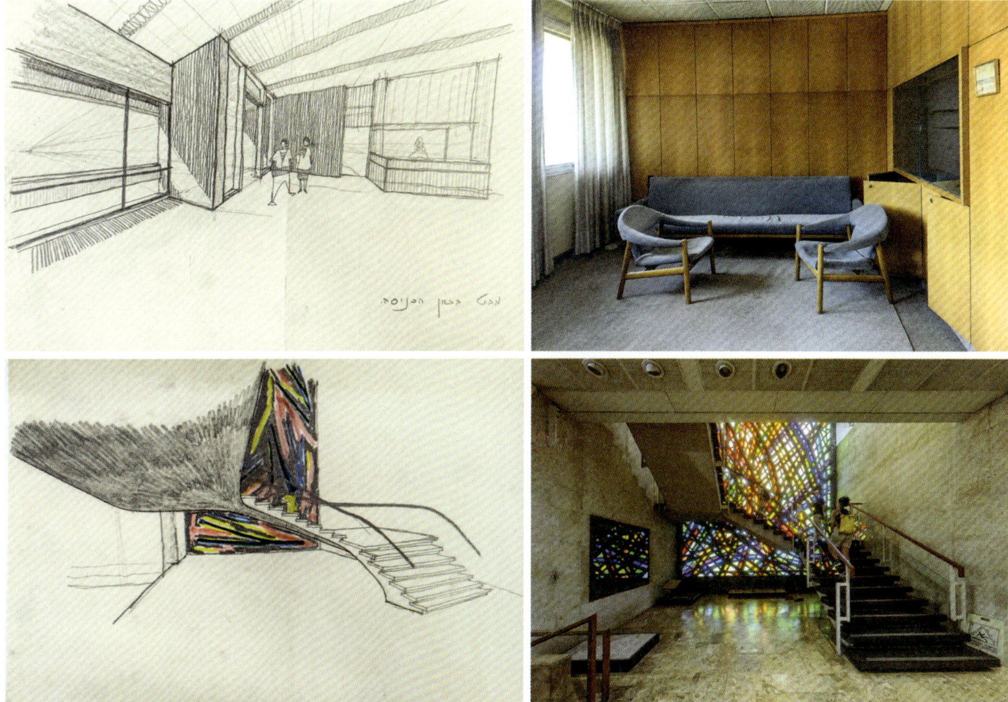

Sketch for the interior with wood paneling by Klarwein / Interior with wood paneling and contemporary furniture / Sketch of the stairwell by Klarwein / The stairwell with colored glass set in concrete frames by Naomi Henrik

URBAN RENEWAL EAST JERUSALEM 1965 COMPETITION

→ Article Noah Hysler Rubin; Source: CZA A455/57
Project

Until 1967, "East Jerusalem" was the designation given to an area of small-scale housing dating from the 19th century along Jaffa, Agrippa and Prophets Roads, which at the time formed the eastern limit of the Israeli-controlled part of the city. Five years after the controversial discussions about the almost complete razing planned for Nahalat Shiva, the Jerusalem city administration initiated a competition for the modernization of the area west of King George Street. Klarwein's proposal envisioned the widening of main roads, the creation of generous squares, new access openings in the interest of a motorized city and large blocks of buildings. Nothing is known about the architecture of the buildings. The result of the process also remains unclear. Substantial areas were later cleared in accordance with Klarwein's planning, but then reconfigured with solitary buildings rather than with building blocks along the perimeter.

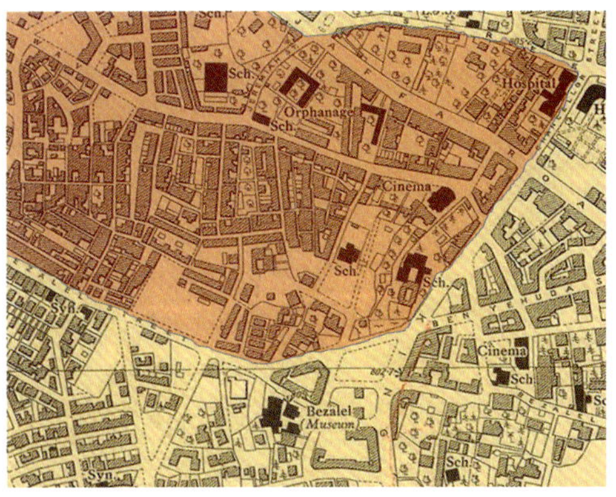

1945 city plan with the development area marked, and a 1965 plan by Klarwein

JERUSALEM, EGGED BUS TERMINAL 1965

Source: CZA A455/52; EGGED history department
Condition: demolished

Interior and general view around 1965

The long-distance bus service always was and remains an important transport system for Israel. The first bus terminal in 1932 was already situated on Jaffa Road near the intersection with King George Street. In 1965, it was moved further to the west to the beginning of Jaffa Road and enlarged. Klarwein designed the new complex for the EGGED Company, the largest operator at the time. ❙ Klarwein's construction makes do with a building that is only partly double-storey and has arcades that open up to the surroundings. On the inside, some walls are covered with natural stone. The complex was demolished in 2001 to be replaced by a new building.

Current situation of the buildings of 1965 (top) and 1966 (bottom)

JERUSALEM, HAHAVATSELET ST., ALICE L. SELIGSBERG VOCATIONAL HIGH SCHOOL FOR GIRLS 1965/1966

HaHavetselet St. und HaNeviim St..
Source: CZA A455/51; AJHS
Condition: unchanged, today Hadassah Academic College

In 1888, Jacob Baron Rothschild founded a hospital named after his father, Mayer Rothschild, to care for the needy population in the rapidly growing area west of the Old City. In 1918, the running of the hospital was taken over by the Hadassah Woman's Zionist Organization of America, which had been founded in 1912. In 1939, operations moved to a new hospital building on Mount Scopus which had been built by Erich Mendelsohn. In the older building, a vocational college for girls was established in 1942, which was named after a previous president of the Hadassah Movement, Alice L. Selisberg, who had died in 1940. The school expanded steadily and in 1965, Klarwein was commissioned to design an additional college building. In 1966, plans for a second building followed. The unencumbered design is characterized by a smooth limestone facade, impressive volumes and regularly spaced windows.

JERUSALEM, EIN KAREM, PHARMACY SCHOOL 1965–72

With David Anatol Brutzkus
Source: CZA A455/7
Condition: largely unchanged

Current situation

During the course of extending the Ein Karem campus, David Anatol Brutzkus and Klarwein designed the School of Pharmacy at the foot of Mount Ein Karem – clearly one of his last projects. The six-storey building with a strongly contoured calcite facade is characterized by its deeply set niche windows. Klarwein did not live to see the completion of the building.

MUNICH, MEMORIAL SITE FOR THE FORMER MAIN SYNAGOGUE 1967 COMPETITION

Source: CZA A455/35; Klei 2017, 302-10
Project

After extensive preparations, the city of Munich in 1967 launched a sculpture competition for a memorial at the site of the Main Synagogue which was forced to be demolished in 1938. Klarwein participated with a design consisting of joined metal plates. His written comments state: "The two walls joined at an angle symbolize the former synagogue. The hands symbolize the blessing given by the priests." | His submission was unsuccessful when the jury took its decision on 27. August 1968. This design was probably the last project Klarwein worked on.

Photograph of the model. Between two metal walls two hands touching

UNIDENTIFIED OFFICE BUILDINGS IN GERMANY AND ISRAEL

In the Klarwein estate there are numerous sketches for large office buildings. Only a few can be identified as part of particular projects. Almost always Klarwein is looking for an interplay of larger and smaller building volumes.

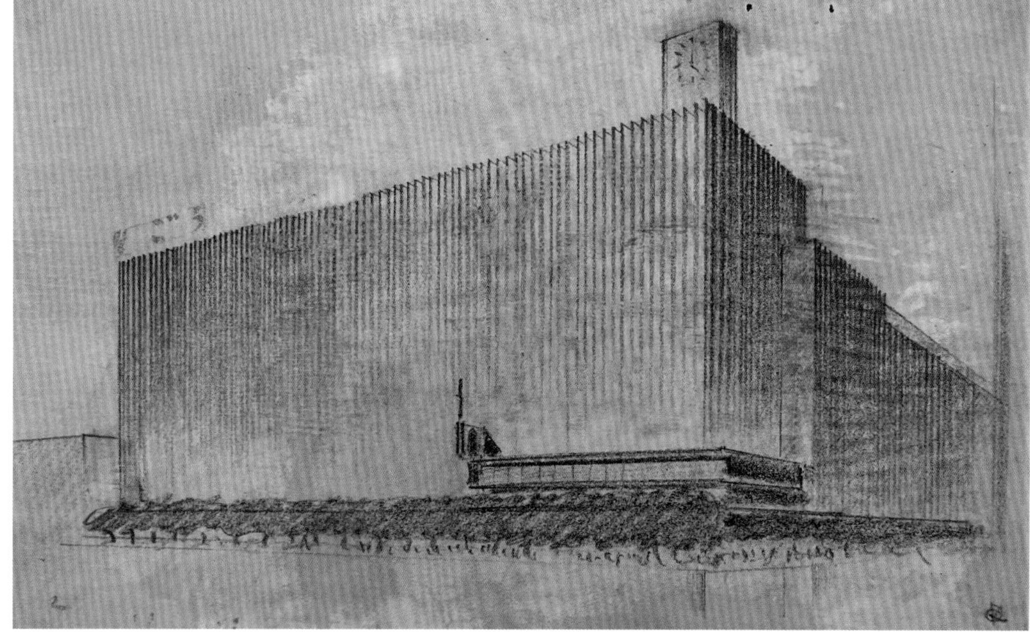

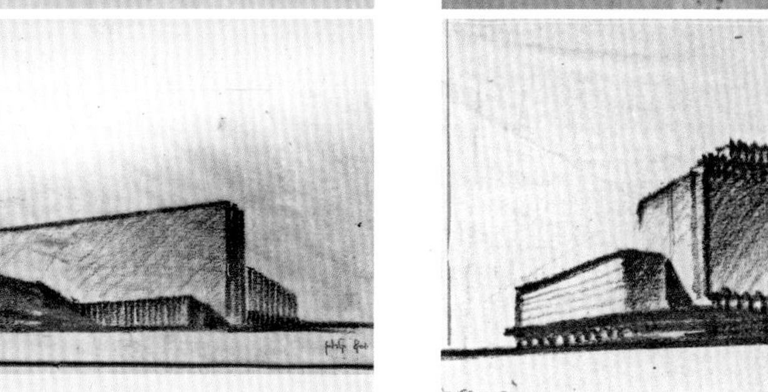

Abbreviations

AJHS	American Jewish Historical Society, New York City
BG	Berlinische Galerie, Berlin
CJH	Center of Jewish History, New York City
CZA	Central Zionist Archives, Jerusalem
ISA	Israel State Archive, Jerusalem
JP	Jerusalem Post
KuBi	Staatliche Museen zu Berlin, Kunstbibliothek, Berlin
PP	Palestine Post
StHH	Staatsarchiv Hamburg
YBZ	Haim Heller's collection, Yad Ben-Zvi photo archives
ZB	Zentralblatt der Bauverwaltung

Joseph Klarwein's files at the Central Zionist Archives

Guy Jamo

The archive of Joseph Klarwein (1893-1970) remained with his family in Israel after his death. For many years, the artist and painter Dan Hoffner (1921-2000), Klarwein's stepson from his second marriage to Elsa Loewy (born Oestreicher), kept it. Hoffner was also the director of the Bezalel Academy of Art and Design in Jerusalem.

Initially, Hoffner transferred the collection to the Israeli Architecture History Archive, a non-profit organization founded in 1987 to collect documentation on the history of architecture in Israel. This was done in collaboration with historians of Israeli architecture, including Michael Levin and Uriel Adiv. Shortly afterward, in the mid-1990s, the organization faced difficulties. Due to a lack of funding and suitable storage for the collected materials, it chose to deposit them at the Central Zionist Archives (CZA). This occurred only a few years after the CZA moved to their permanent location, where the storage and preservation conditions were highly advanced for that time. At the same time, the CZA established a dedicated department for maps and plans, assembling a professional team, adopting methods for registration, handling, and optimal storage, and began absorbing archival materials from various institutions and individuals. In June 1995, the non-profit organization transferred the Klarwein collection, along with collections from other architects to the CZA.

The Klarwein collection (A455) was organized and cataloged at the CZA with the assistance of Uriel Adiv. The collection is divided into three main sections: The first section (Files 1-7) contains correspondence, documents, and personal and family records; the second section (Files 8-48) includes photographs of plans, models, and buildings he designed; the third section (Files 49-61) contains architectural plans of projects Klarwein designed or was involved in.

Also deposited along with the collection was a small-scale model of the Department of Law building at the Hebrew University. The organization also provided a portfolio of Klarwein's works, which includes sketches and original drawings Klarwein made for buildings in Germany. Before being deposited in the archive, the items were restored in Germany with the help of Dan Hoffner and the deputy director of Deutsches Architekturmuseum Frankfurt, Wolfgang Voigt.

The CZA produced a catalog with a list of files in the Klarwein collection. Over the years, most of the graphic items in the collection (photographs and plans) were digitized and entered the archive's computerized system. All the graphic materials, as well as the catalog, are available for public viewing on the archive's website.

In the CZA's collections, one can also find supplementary documentation regarding Klarwein's role in public institution projects, including the Mount Herzl complex in Jerusalem, Beit HaKranot in Haifa, and the Hebrew University campus in Givat Ram.

Bibliography

Aharonowitz, Haim, ץיבונרהא, סייח (1958): למרכה רדה : למרכה רדה דעו .סינובו סידסימ רוד לש הריציו למע תכסמ

Aleksandrowicz, Or (2019): הירוטסיה :רחמ ןיא וליאכ לארשיב תואובת ילדגמ לש תיגולונכט [As if tomorrow would never come: A technological history of rural silos in Israel]. רפסה ןותמ :ולים ילארשי (יסוי ןמדירפ ןוחצי אוסטרובסקי).

Azaryahu, Maoz (2012): Soldatenfriedhöfe – die ersten Jahre (Verteidigungsministerium Hrsg.); Jerusalem

Azaryahu, Maoz (1996): Mount Herzl – The Creation of Israel's National Cemetery (=Israel Studies Vol. 1, No. 2; 1996), pp. 46-74

Bar, Doron (2016): Landscape and Ideology: Reinterrment of Renowned Jews in the Land of Israel, 1904-1967, Berlin

Bar, Doron (2020): Zionist Pantheons? The Design and Development of the Tombs of Herzl, Weizmann and Rothschild During the Early Years of the State of Israel (=Israel Studies, Volume 25,2, 2020), pp72-94

Bar, Doron (2021): From Vienna to Jerusalem: Herzl's Final Journey, Jerusalem: Schechter Institute of Jewish Studies; Jerusalem

Bar, Doron (2023): Yad Vashem, The Challenge of Shaping a Holocaust Remembrance Site, 1942-1976 (= Jahrbuch des Dokumentationsarchivs des österreichischen Widerstandes); Berlin

Ben-Artzy, Yossi, ןב יצרא, יסוי. (2004): "למרכל רבדמ ןופהל" תאצוה .1948-1918 ,תברועמ ריעב לדבנ בחרמכ למרכה תווהתה תירבעה הטיסרבינואה ,סנגאמ ל"י ש"ע סירפס

Ben-Sira (1958): Y. Ben-Sira, „The University Compound, Jerusalem"; in: Handasah veadrichalut (Engineering and Architecture Magazine), Tel-Aviv (English version) pp131ff

Boness, Stefan (2012): Tel Aviv – The White City; Berlin

Brog, Mooli (2002): In Blessed Memory of a Dream: Mordechai Shenhavi and Initial Holocaust Commemoration Ideas in Palestine, 1942–1945; in: Yad Vashem Studies, XXX, Jerusalem 2002, pp. 297-336

Bucciarelli, Piergiacomo (1992): Fritz Höger – Hanseatischer Baumeister 1877-1949; Berlin

Buckton, E. J. (1936): The Construction of Haifa Harbour; Institution of Civil Engineers' Journal, V239

Cahill, Richard (2023): The Tegart Police Fortresses in British Mandate Palestine; in: Jerusalem Quarterly 75/2023

Carmel, Alex (1969): The History of Haifa under Turkish Rule, Jerusalem

Dean, Macabee (1966): Joseph Klarwein. The competitive architect; Sonderbeilage der Jerusalem Post vom 30. August 1966

Dolev, Diana (2000): Architecture and Nationalist Identity, the Case of the Architectural Master Plans for the Hebrew University in Jerusalem (1919-1974) and their Connections with Nationalist Ideology (PhD-thesis); Jerusalem

Dolev, Diana: An Ivory Tower in the National Precinct: The Architecture Plan for the University campus in Giva'at Ram; in: Zmanim 96 (2006), 86-93 (in Hebrew)

Fröhlich, Anja (2008): Sonne, Luft und Haus für Alle – das wachsende Haus; ein Versuch zur Lösung der Wohnungsfrage unter besonderer Berücksichtigung der Rolle Martin Wagners; Dissertation Weimar

Fuhrmann, Christine (2019): Eine Stadtkrone für Halle a.d.Saale von Walter Gropius; Weimar

The Settlement House Movement Revisited: A Transnational History (John Gal, Stefan Köngeter and Sarah Vicary Ed.), Bristol 2020

Herbert, Gilbert und Sosnovsky, Sylvina (1993): Bauhaus on the Carmel and the Crossroad of Empire; Jerusalem

Hilbig, Henrik (2006): Das Reichsehrenmal bei Bad Berka: Entstehung und Entwicklung eines Denkmalprojekts der Weimarer Republik. (Schriftenreihe Architekturtheorie und empirische Wohnforschung).; Aachen

Kirsch, Jutta (2021): Religion and Memory, The Importance of Monuments in Preserving Historical Identity (= Missionsgeschichtliches Archiv, Band 32); Regensburg

Klei, Alexandra (2017): Jüdisches Bauen in Nachkriegsdeutschland, Der Architekt Hermann Zvi Guttmann; Berlin

Kreppel, Klaus (2010): Nahariyya und die deutsche Einwanderung nach Eretz Israel – Die Geschichte seiner Einwohner von 1935 bis 1941; Tefen

Kroizer, Gad (2004): Back to Station Control: Planning the ›Tegart‹ Police Fortresses in Palestine; in: Kathedra, January 2004

Kroyanker, David et al. (1975): Developing Jerusalem, 1967-1975: The planning process and its problems as reflected in some major projects; Jerusalem

Kroyanker, David (1982): Jerusalem Planning and Development, 1979-1982; Jerusalem

Kroyanker, David (2001): The Rothschild Compound Story – Jerusalem Hanevi'im Street; Jerusalem

Lehmann, Erich (1960): Nahariya, Selbstverlag

Levin, Nicole: The Historic Neighborhood: Nahalat Shiv'a – Jerusalem; Slated for demolition by city planners, this architectural gem was saved by the public; May 2021

Minta, Anna (2004): Israel bauen. Architektur, Städtebau und Denkmalpolitik nach der Staatsgründung 1948; Berlin

Minta, Anna (2013): Städtebau und architektonische Kultur als Faktoren der israelischen Identitätspolitik nach 1948; in: Neue Städte für einen neuen Staat: Die städtebauliche Erfindung des modernen Israel und der Wiederaufbau in der BRD. Eine Annäherung (Karin Wilhelm und Kerstin Gust Hrsg.), Bielefeld, pp. 141-154. https://doi.org/10.1515/transcript.9783839422045.141

Minta, Anna (2008): Government Quarter, West Jerusalem, 1950; in: Munio Weinraub Amos Gitai, Architektur und Film in Israel (Winfried Nerdinger Hrsg.); München, 112-17

More than Bauhaus, the Architecture of the White City Tel Aviv (Regina Stephan Hrsg.); Baunach 2019

Mozes, Samuel R. (1952): Contemporary Design in Israel, Planning and Architecture; in: Architectural Record (New York) 11/1952, 154-157

Rolef, Susan Hattis (2000): The Knesset Building in Giv'at Ram: Planning and Construction; in: Cathedra Magazine, 96th Edition, July

Singer, Saul J. (2022): www.jewishpress.com/sections/features/features-on-jewish-world/wandering-jews-israels-knesset-finds-a-permanent-home/2022/09/14/

Stern, Shimon (1974): The Development of the Urban Layout of Haifa 1918-1947. PhD-thesis Hebrew University, Jerusalem

Taut, Bruno (1919): Die Stadtkrone; Jena

Turtenwald, Claudia (Hrsg.) 2003: Fritz Höger (1877-1949), Moderne Monumente (=Schriftenreihe des Hamburgischen Architekturarchivs, Band 20; Hrsg. Hartmut Frank und Ullrich Schwarz); München

Vermittlungswege der Moderne – Neues Bauen in Palästina 1923-1948. The Transfer of Modernity, Architectural Modernism in Palestine 1923-1948 (Stabenow, Jörg / Schüler, Ronny Hrsg.); Berlin 2018

Wagner, Martin (1932a): Das wachsende Haus; Berlin

Wagner, Martin (1932b): Das wachsende Haus; in: Deutsche Bauzeitung 3, 41-44 und 53-60; Beitrag Klarwein/Höger 58

Warhaftig, Myra (1996): Sie legten den Grundstein – Leben und Wirken deutschsprachiger Architekten in Palästina 1918–1948; Berlin

Warhaftig, Myra (2005): Deutsche jüdische Architekten vor und nach 1933 – das Lexikon. Berlin

Warhaftig, Myra (2007): They laid the foundation: Lives and Works of German-speaking Jewish Architects in Palestine 1918-1948; Jerusalem

Wiernik, Michal Naor and Doron Bar (2012): The Competition for the Design and Development of Herzl's Tomb and Mount Herzl, 1949-1960; in: Cathedra 144 (2012) 107-136 [Hebräisch]

Wilderotter, Hans (Hrsg.) 2000: Das Haus am Werderschen Markt – Von der Reichsbank zum Auswärtigen Amt / The History of the New Premises of the Federal Foreign Office; Berlin

Yazbak, Mahmud (1998): הפיח האמב השתע-עשרה :תודלות יברע ידוהיה זכרמה .(ןוכיתה חרזמה רקחב סינויע) .הרבחהו ריעה ,הפיח תטיסרבינוא.

Acknowledgments

The Klarwein Project has grown over three years into an extensive collaborative work with many contributors. The order in which their names are listed here is more chronological than hierarchical. Every contribution, no matter how specific, has enriched the whole.

First and foremost, I would like to express my gratitude to the descendants of Ossip Klarwein: Eléonore, Sérafine, Balthazar and Salvador Klarwein, Anat Raccah-Hoffner and Yigal Hoffner. With great openness and warm hospitality, they have supported the project from the very beginning—whether in France, Barcelona, Mallorca, or Israel. They granted unrestricted access to their private archives, including unpublished documents, writings, photographs, photo albums, and drawings by Klarwein. Without hesitation, they entrusted me with originals from their collection so that they could be further analyzed and processed in Berlin.

In Israel, architectural historian Sigal Davidi from Tel Aviv University took on the time-intensive role of academic advisor. When we first met in September 2023, it was impossible to foresee how deeply she would become involved in the practical aspects of the project. Her in-depth knowledge, valuable recommendations, and generous access to her networks have significantly contributed to the project's success. For this, I extend my heartfelt thanks.

I would also like to thank Jörg Gleiter, Professor of Architectural Theory at TU Berlin, who showed early interest in the project and facilitated contact with Sigal Davidi. Together with Gyöngyvér Győrffy, his research associate at the Chair of Architectural Theory, and Israeli documentary filmmaker Ran Tal, they inspired 27 students from Berlin and Tel Aviv to participate in a joint research project on Ossip Klarwein's work during the 2024/25 academic year. The students' work has been incorporated into the exhibition in the form of short film contributions. Many thanks to you all.

Guy Jamo, Head of the Maps and Graphic Collections Department at the Central Zionist Archives (CZA), made an invaluable contribution to the project. When flights to Israel were disrupted following October 7, 2023, he arranged for Klarwein's collection at CZA to be photographed on site. Special thanks to Michal Minsky, who undertook this task and made repeated trips from Tel Aviv to Jerusalem during uncertain times. In later stages, Guy Jamo consistently facilitated access to the original documents for the catalog's authors. Ultimately, CZA scanned Klarwein's entire archive in high quality and provided the materials free of charge for both the catalog and the Berlin exhibition. What began as an initial contact—made possible by Hungarian lawyer Agnes Peresztégi—has developed into a valuable partnership. For this, my sincere thanks go to Guy Jamo and his colleagues.

The core exhibition team came together thanks to Hans Gerhard Hannesen, my first collaborator and invaluable advisor. Through discussions with many contacts in Berlin's cultural scene, we were able to enlist exhibition architect Rainer Lendler and graphic designer Matthias Wittig for the project. Our collaboration was a fantastic experience. Also of great help was the support of exhibition organizer Monika Hingst, who brought the project to life with enthusiasm and precision. Ursula Bongaerts shared her extensive experience in cultural projects with us, Kai Roloff provided advice on all digital aspects, and Manuela Strehober professionally developed the website. Following a recommendation by Dorothea Hauser, we found an ideal partner in the

Aktives Museum Berlin e.V., whose experienced and pragmatic director Kaspar Nürnberg deserves our deep gratitude.

I would like to thank all the authors for their dedication: Doron Bar, Dafna Berger Shperling, Sigal Davidi, Diana Dolev, Noah Hysler Rubin, and Talia Margalit conducted pioneering research in Israeli archives, shedding light on Klarwein's contributions to architecture between 1933 and 1970. Sue McRae and Hans Brandt not only translated texts between languages but also resolved ambiguities and inconsistencies in our writings with great care. I would also like to acknowledge the contribution of architectural photographer Eli Singalovski, whose remarkable photographic series on Klarwein's architecture in Israel today plays a key role in the exhibition.

In Berlin, architect, building researcher, and architectural historian Johannes Cramer played a crucial role in the project's success. For both the catalog and exhibition, he not only investigated the history of the Church at Hohenzollernplatz, but also took on the lion's share of work on the first annotated catalog of Klarwein's works. I am grateful for his dedication, meticulous support, and, above all, the unexpected friendship that developed through our collaboration.

I am also deeply grateful to our funders and sponsors, who have supported us not just as institutions but as individuals: Sebastian Giesen, Managing Director of the Hermann Reemtsma Foundation, who has supported the project with great personal commitment, and thanks to his introduction, Karsten Müller, Director of the Ernst Barlach House in Hamburg, took an interest in Klarwein and will present parts of the exhibition during the Jüdische Kulturtage Hamburg 16 November 2025. Martin Hoernes, Secretary General of the Ernst von Siemens Art Foundation, provided quick and clear funding decisions for the catalog. Manuel Hartung and Christine Neuhaus, Chairman and Head of Funding at the ZEIT STIFTUNG BUCERIUS, generously supported the project. Ansgar Wimmer, Chairman of the Alfred Toepfer Foundation F.V.S., and Hermann Simon, former Director of the New Synagogue Berlin – Centrum Judaicum, were valuable discussion partners.

Without the openness of the Church Congregation at Hohenzollernplatz, this project would never have come to fruition. Since 2008, the church has hosted the NoonSong concert series, where I first became aware of Ossip Klarwein. Special thanks to Pastor Marita Lersner for her early willingness to dedicate the regular summer exhibition to Klarwein and for her constructive support throughout its development. The church's building association, led by Pastor Claudia Wüstenhagen, and particularly Uwe Meybohm, provided invaluable assistance. A special mention goes to Geri Chust, the longtime church secretary, who not only knew the church's archive inside out but also created the first lovingly designed panels on Klarwein.

In Israel, I extend my gratitude to: architect Vittorio Corinaldi for his personal memories of Klarwein, Haifa's longtime city architect Robert Karpel, architectural researchers Edina Meyer-Maril and Alexandra Klei, art historian Galit Noga-Banai, my colleague Gisela Dachs, historians Moshe Zimmermann and Gad Kroizer, Noga Kunda, friends Marion and Dan Freudenthal,-curators Kobi ben-Meir (Haifa Museum of Art) and Sharon Soffer (Knesset Collection),Knesset archivists Inda Novominsky and Tahel Yishai, David Weil from United Studio Archives in Herzliya.

On the German side, I thank: Claudia Quiring (Turtenwald), Ines Sonder, Anna Minta, Ruth Leiserowitz, Roland Jaeger, Monika Sommerer, Dorothea Hauser, Ute Joksch, Christa Finkenwirth, and Michael Mönninger for their guidance, Bernd Finkenwirth for intensive discussions on cultural-historical contexts, Günther Schlusche, Gabriele Minz, Ingeborg Becker, Wolfgang Voigt, and Chana Schütz for stimulating discussions, Florentine Baumann, who introduced the Nelson Mandela School's art students to the exhibition's themes, Volkwin Marg in Hamburg for his consistent support. My sincere thanks to Sybille Blomeyer, Immo Boyken, Harald Braun, Shula Donnebaum, Thomas Ernst, Daniela Franz, Horst Hamann, Cord-Georg Hasselmann, Caroline und Christoph Hollenders, Josefina Lacouture, Helen Müller, Roland Metzler, Heike Schmoll und Susanne Wasum Rainer for their warm and supportive friendship.

Lastly, I extend my deepest appreciation to the many librarians and archivists who provided invaluable assistance across institutions in Berlin, Hamburg, Warsaw, and New York.

Thank you all!

Authors

Doron Bar Professor of Historical-Cultural Geography, Former President and Dean of the Schechter Institute of Jewish Studies. Research focus: Popular and National Holy Sites

Dafna Berger Shperling Architect and architectural history researcher, Haifa

Johannes Cramer Architect, Architectural Historian and Building Archaeologist. Professor Emeritus of Building and Urban History at the Technical University of Berlin

Diana Dolev Historian of Architecture, former Lecturer at the Holon Institute for Technology, Holon

Sigal Davidi Architect Architectural Historian, and Lecturer at the Azrieli School of Architecture, Tel Aviv University

Jacqueline Hénard Historian and Journalist. Author of several books on cultural history topics

Noah Hysler Rubin Urban Planner and Cultural Geographer, Senior Lecturer at the Bezalel Academy for Arts and Design, Jerusalem, School of Architecture

Guy Jamo Geographer. Head of the Maps and Graphic Collections Department at the Central Zionist Archives, Jerusalem

Talia Margalit Head of the Azrieli School of Architecture, Tel Aviv University, Architect, Urban Planner, and Researcher

Translators

Sue McRae German-English Translator, Teacher and Editor

Hans Brandt Journalist, English-German Translator and Editor

Colophon

This book is published on the occasion of the exhibition "Ossip Klarwein – From the 'Power Plant of God' to the Knesset."

Project Host Institution

AKTIVESMUSEUM
Faschismus und Widerstand in Berlin e.V.

Concept and Curatorship
Jacqueline Hénard

Academic Advisors
Johannes Cramer
Sigal Davidi

Exhibition Architecture
Rainer Lendler

Architectural Model and Video Production
Studio Wookol

Graphic Design
Fernkopie, Matthias Wittig

Lithographs
Peter Hansen

Catalog Production
Druckerei Kettler

Published by
Verlag Kettler
Robert-Bosch-Str. 14
59199 Bönen
www.verlag-kettler.de
info@verlag-kettler.de

1st edition
ISBN: 978-3-98741-198-4

Illustration credits

Ajepbah: 108
Alamy Stock Photo: 80-Hanan Isachar-AWC1YA, 101+142-Danita Delimont-CEDAKK, 140-ITPhoto-E84G85, 141-GreekStock-ARB615
Architekturmuseum der TU Berlin: 10-3332
Berger, Dafna: 36, 40, 62, 70, 73, 149
Beit Zvi, History department: 133
Berliner Adressbücher: 11
Berlinische Galerie, Berlin: 28
Bezirksamt Charlottenburg-Wilmersdorf von Berlin: 26, 27, 30, 31
Biedacha, Piotr: 135
Bitmuna Collections: 44-Schwartz, 44: Batya and Moshe Levin Album
Central Zionist Archives (CZA), Inventory A 455 (Klarwein), *folder*, page
8: 94, 95, 99, 100, 140, 141; *12:* 65, 66, 67, 69, 135
13: 77, 78, 79, 123, 127, 136; *15:* 36; *16:* 137; *17:* 86, 129
18: 143; *19:* 89, 90, 91; *20:* 87, 132; *21:* 133;
22: 126, 137; *23:* 33, 40, 42, 135; *24:* 54, 124, 134;
25: 114, 115, 134; *28:* 153; *29:* 86, 115; *30:* 33, 34, 42
34: 105, 106; *35:* 152; *38:* 22, 107, 109, 112, 113;
41: 53, 126, 128; *42:* 11; *47:* 11, 12, 15, 17, 18, 127;
52: 151; *55:* 146; *57:* 150; *61:* Cover, 22, 23, 76, 104, 105, 107, 108, 109, 110, 111, 112, 113, 114, 117, 118, 119, 122, 153
S113M-2752_2: 50
S5-10434-5: 55
ChristinaHZ: 114
Egged History Department: 151
Evangelische Kirchengemeinde Am Hohenzollernplatz: 29
Getty Images: 74-David Rubinger
Haifa City Engineers building files: 33, 36, 38, 62, 63, 64, 71, 72, 120
Hénard, Jacqueline: 34, 38, 40, 52, 120, 125, 134, 144
Köhler, Tom: 108
Lumu: 113
Nahariya City Administration: 49
Preker, Israel: 58
Schoelzel, Andreas: 24
Schröder, Christian A.: 111
Staatliche Museen zu Berlin, Kunstbibliothek: Cover inside front, 22-3731480, 25-3731479, 26-Hdz.12977, 26-12974, 27-12808, 28-12976, 28-Hdz.07369, 110-Hdz.12985, 116-3731481, 116-Hdz.12805
Staatsarchiv Hamburg: 14, 15
The Government Press Office: 44-Cohen Fritz
YBZ photo archives: 119-0651_089, 123-0651_080, 127-0651_044, 131-0651_085, 136-0651_083
Yeshiva University Museum, New York: 147
Ynhockey: 138